A CENTURY OF MEMORIES

Stephen Pedrick

Steve Pedrick.
12/2009.

Acknowledgements

~ Salcombe Maritime and Local History Museum, Harry Fulcher, and Ann Lidstone -
for starting me off on this project and for the loan of recording equipment.

~ Dave Wade - for audio-technical support throughout.

~ Reg and Betty Sampson - for their unstinting work and support,
in typing the script from my hand-written notes.

Published by Stephen Pedrick.   ISBN 978-0-956-3966-0-0

Layout by Nicola Fox

Printed by Nick Walker Printing, Kingsbridge 852812

Front cover photograph: Rhymes Builders, West Alvington, c. 1900.

Introduction

For five and a half years, up to October 2008, I have been talking to, and recording, a hundred people living locally here in the South Hams of Devon. Their memories, and their accounts of their own and their families' lives and experiences, form the basis of this book. These fifty men and fifty women, born between 1900 and 1940, have lived through a time that has encompassed significant changes in the way that people live and work, and have all experienced, to a greater or lesser degree, the effects of war. It will be difficult, in another generation's time, to find people who have memories the likes of which are preserved here.

The oldest person, at time of recording, was 103, and 38 of the 100 were aged 90 or over.

They have all lived in the towns of Kingsbridge, Salcombe, Modbury, Totnes and Dartmouth, and surrounding villages and hamlets. Most of these people have had several, and in some cases many, generations of ancestors living in the South Hams area; just five of them came to the area to live and work having no previous connections here: one from Plymouth, two from North Devon, and the other two from Cornwall.

Covering a broad range of subject matter these peoples' accounts give an insight into aspects of life in the early twentieth century and before. Of interest is the fact that 88 of the 100 could remember a time when they did not have at least two of three amenities that are now taken for granted in all households:

1.   cold water from a tap inside the home,
2.   a toilet inside the home,
3.   electricity in the home.

Also of interest are the facts that 64 of the 100 learnt to drive some form of motorised vehicle, 59 of the 100 had travelled in some form of air-borne craft or transport, all 100 had a telephone and television, but only 1 of the 100 had learnt to use a computer.

As well as recording and capturing the memories, it was also my intention to record and preserve the local dialect, which I have attempted to reproduce, as heard, into written form as well as is possible; accent cannot be reproduced easily, but a reader who knows, or knew, any of the persons represented here may have a distinct advantage in being able to hear that person's voice speaking the words as they are read.

Some recordings were made with more than one person, and some people were recorded more than once; thus some accounts are more lengthy, and more detailed, than others.

Permission has been granted from every person included in this book, or a close relative of a person pre-deceased, to reproduce their spoken words. Some sentences and paragraphs have been compiled from more than one part of a recording, or from parts of more than one recording made with any particular person, in order to make easier reading. It should be noted that there is the possibility of minor error in the detail.

It has been a privilege and a pleasure to have met, talked with, and recorded all of these interesting characters, all of whom appeared to be as enthusiastic in recounting their stories to me as I was in listening to them, and I hope that the reader will enjoy this book as much as I have enjoyed compiling and producing it.

Steve Pedrick
2009

CONTENTS

Bill Blank

Born 12th March 1913

Died 14th June 2009

Recorded on 6th May 2003
& 11th June 2004

Bill. I was five years old when my father died in Devonport hospital; that was in 1918, just at the end of the War. He died of the 'flu with double pneumonia setting in … 'twas terrible, it killed off any amount of people, thousands… right after the War. I'd have loved to have known me father.

I've lived in Kingsbridge for ninety years - I came up from Devonport when I was just a toddler. Where I lived as a boy, in Brunswick Place, there was an old sink and an outside tap away from the house, and you had to share it with two or three others. There was washhouses next to it, one for one cottage, and one for another: you had to get out there and wash of a morning - well, you think…a freezing cold morning!

You had no sanitation in the house, you had to walk to the bottom of the passage, and I think there was five toilets down there, wooden toilets, where you had a tap outside and you'd take a bucket with you and flush down what you left behind; there was no hygiene hardly at all in those days.

There were about twelve cottages down there, and George Kennard next over, which is part of the car park now. He was a blacksmith but he kept his horses down there as well in stables, and you'd hear them kicking at night, you know; it was all lath and plaster, and it was rat-ridden; we'd hear the rats moving around inside the partition, and it could happen that they'd nibble their way through sometimes.

Kingsbridge was very quiet then; no traffic about, just horses and carts. Fishmongers used to bring in their fish; a lot of people used to buy fish, salted cod-fish that came over from Newfoundland. They'd have some of that in stock in case they ran out, you know. You'd get a fair-sized fish, a couple of pound for a bob: you know, bloaters and herrings and stuff like that, that was already smoked when the fishmonger had it. It made a decent little meal for a family.

That was one of the industries; of course there were other small industries - the Foundry was one, in Duke Street. There were several hands there and they used to turn out some really good stuff, you know, lengths of iron; today they get it from a dealer up-country, but then it was all made locally. Cooking stoves was one of their prime objects - nearly every cottage had a Lidstone range. Lidstones had a little side shop in the corner beside the Foundry, which sold saucepans and kettles, and…you name it. Yes, it was quite industrious.

There was the 'Town Mill', the Trant brothers were the principals. They used to turn out a good bag of flour; nearly all the bakers around would buy Trant's flour. They had three shifts going at the Mill at one time, three eight-hour shifts, so it was going twenty-four hours a day…and there was William Pitts, he ran a corn store on the Quay.

Steve. Can you describe what the Quay was like when you first remember it ?

Bill. Oh yes, well the water came up to about thirty, forty feet in front of what is now 'Boots'. That used to be Balkwill's Stores then, a general hardware store. There was a stone wall at the top of the Quay about two, three foot high, and the two leats, one from Eastern Backway and the other from Western Backway, they used to flow out through; there'd be no mud there then.

The left-hand side was used as an unloading bay, more or less, for the boats coming up, and just at the top of that area was a weighbridge; so when

1

the boats used to come up, coal boats especially, they'd come up to 'Crabshell' and Holman's Quay, and they'd bring up their horses and carts full of coal and weigh them on that weighbridge …'course as a boy, and Mother a widow, she used to send me down onto the Quay when the boats were in to get any coal that had come off the carts!

There'd be sand boats, and brick boats and manure boats; when the tide came in these boats would come up there and off-load.

There on the right-hand side was a sawmill; there was a rugged old path leading over there and the horses and drays used to bring in forestry wood, big trunks of wood. Two horses would drag that in: they had to come *down* Fore Street and they had to put on what they called the 'drug', underneath the back wheel, so as to stop that back wheel going around; and it would gradually slide down the hill… mind, it was hard work for the horses to keep that sort of weight back; in fact I've seen some horses go down with it, you know. It was quite an industry.

They used to employ several men down there in the sawmills, and further down was Burgoynes, big engineering people in those days, and also 'Bandy' Ryder used to be the rope-maker down there. They reckon he was absolutely flawless, none of his ropes would fail, you know.

It was all orchards down behind there then, Boons had an orchard right down through there; there was no bungalows up on the side.

I learnt to swim down at Square's Quay, where the car park is now. Burgoynes used to have a lot of threshing-machines down there, they used to lend them out to farms to thresh their corn.

We boys used to go down there evenings when we came out of school, or left work; there were no swimming pools. You'd dive in at Square's Quay, over to Promenade steps, then you'd see a steamer coming up, the 'Ilton' or the 'Kenwith Castle', and of course he would be throwing out a lot of waves so you'd dive out and get in the throes of the waves. It was great to be able to swim.

You'd see plenty of 'Admiral Brown' floating down the estuary because they had no 'up-to-date' sewage scheme then, you see.

Steve. *You survived all that and lived until you're ninety.*

Bill. Well you didn't swim with your mouth open! When they laid the new sewage scheme then that took it right down to Gerston.

The drinking trough was in front of what was Ryeford garage, next to Balkwill's hardware store. It was a commemoration to Queen Victoria. It was a lovely-looking thing, right in the middle of the road. I think the top of it was destroyed, but they've still got the actual drinking troughs. The horses could drink one end or the other, and there was a little trough down by the side for the dogs to drink out of.

You can't help valuing what it was like really… 'course it used to tower up, and there was faces to it, looking four ways… and it had a pinnacle on it. Yes, lovely: because the inscription on it was in memory of Queen Victoria, for her Golden Jubilee, I think it was.

In Mill Street there was a chandlery. They used to supply the old boats that came up here years ago with foodstuffs: coffee, tea, and candles - in fact I think they had a place out the back and used to make their own candles years ago; and on from Hannafords, before you come to the 'Seven Stars' was Pain's Dairy. The Pains originally had a farm at Bowcombe and they used to sell their milk and cream in there. They called it 'High House Dairy'. Then, next to 'Seven Stars' was a house attached to a small shop, 'Elliott's Grocer's Shop'… it became Frank Trezona's fish and chip shop after.

After that it was a sort of a vegetable garden; a walled garden all the way up through which took you up to the corner where Mill Street met Ilbert Road; it was a hairpin bend, and on your right was 'Bowringsleigh Lodge'.

Up Fore Street years ago it was gas lighting. You'd get the lighterman going around just before dark, he used to come along with a little 'flicker', on a pole, flick the light on…then he'd walk around again in the morning with a little tool and flick them out.

The Police constabulary was then under the Town Hall, and there used to be a couple of shops in Duncombe Street, up the top end. There was a small Garage there, and Stumbles' electrical shop where he used to make up his crystal sets for radios.

The Fire Station was at the top of Duncombe Street facing the Methodist church, and up over the

Fire Station was the Public Library. To summon the Fire Service you had to go to the Town Hall, get hold of the fire horn and pump him - all the way around the town and back around, so as to call the firemen; mind, if you got that job you'd get seven and sixpence for that... anyone could do it - first one there! In the end they appointed somebody to do it: 'Tiddly' Brown, he had a saddler's shop down the town.

Steve. At the bottom of Duncombe Street was Welle House; that was a lovely old house wasn't it.

Bill. They reckon there was a vault that led you from one part of Welle House right up to Dodbrooke church.

At the top of Church Street, on the bank, was Mrs. Ford's sweet shop, and then there was the old School. I went there as a kid, three years old. There were two teachers, Miss Hannaford and Mrs. Treeby, that was all.

When I first left school I had an old trolley, and we had two 'clients', two dear old ladies who used to like us to get them firewood from down the sawmills, where the car park is now.

So we went down one day, a packet of woodbines in our pocket, and said to the chap in the office, "Nine penn'orth of wood please". "Oh no" he said, "nothing less than a shilling". I said, "Gidout, don't be so daft, here y'are have a fag". We baited him with a fag for a shilling's worth of wood for ninepence; so we made thruppence on that deal ... and they would give you thruppence for bringing it up, so that's sixpence you'd win on that one, and a nice ride down through Fore Street on the old trolley !

There were no cars in those days - take 'Brittons' corner on two wheels and possibly bend your back wheel into the bargain! Then we'd do it again, second trip; you had to be shrewd in those days to get by.

Steve. You told me once about the first cars owned in Kingsbridge.

Bill. Leslie Oke had an 'H E' - that was similar to a Bentley, open top. Dick Blackler had a car, and I've got an idea Roland Britton owned one ... they were the only ones that owned cars in the town. Brittons had the shop on the corner; I came home from school one day and Mother said to me, "Go on down Brittons, a car have careered down Fore Street and broke the plate-glass window; there's school caps going free!"

I used to go ferreting: rabbiting with nets. I didn't have a dog when I first started but afterwards I bought a little fox terrier. An old fella was moving away from one farm to another and couldn't take the dog with him. I said, "How much do 'e want for 'en?" "Give us 'ounce of baccy" he said. "What?" I said, "he's worth more 'n ounce of baccy!" So I gave him a five- pound note. I said, "That's a sin to sell 'n for 'ounce of baccy"... and he was a little beauty. He'd tell you exactly where there was a rabbit in a sett.

I remember going up Blackridge Cross one afternoon and the old dog made a bit of a fuss of it, so I 'tealed up', and put the ferret away in the sett, and I waited there for two hours. I said to 'Spot' on the field side, "Where is it then Spot?" and she started clawing away, so I put me hand in and there was the ferret on the backside of the rabbit, the rabbit wouldn't bolt. I thought, 'Well, I can't go home with one rabbit' so I went down the valley and 'tealed up' again, and put the ferret away, and cor, they scat out of there 'bang, bang, bang'! I picked up seven rabbits out of there; as fast as I was knocking 'em over the head another one was

coming out. Half an hour later I was going down the road with eight rabbits in me bag !

Steve. What did you do with the rabbits then?

Bill. Well, anyone would give you two bob for a rabbit then, and if I had any surplus I took them over to 'Tonkins', rabbit and egg dealers.

Old lady Noyce had a shop there with two entrances, one in Bridge Street and the other in Duke Street, and she used to hang the skins up outside on a hook. A notice said 'We buy rabbit skins'. So I nicked a skin off the hook, went around to the other entrance and she paid me tuppence for it!

Talking of the pubs in the town, you didn't have the 'Creek's End' on the Quay, you see that was just a private house there, but over here you had the 'Spit and Chow'… sorry, 'Ship and Plough': we always used to call it 'Spit and Chow'! The old boat-men, years ago, used to rendezvous outside there, you'd see 'em lined up waiting for a boat to come up… a brick boat or a sand boat…they used to park up then at the top end of the Quay, which is now the 'Town Walk'; all that used to be open, so barges and boats would come up and off-load there… and they'd line up there for a couple of days work. Of course, down at the 'Crabshell' you'd have coal boats coming up there… and then you had the 'George Inn', what is now 'King of Prussia'.

They were hard times, but they were also enjoyable times, that's the most remarkable thing about it. They say about the youngsters today, they're bored…they've got too much; I mean, Sundays we'd roam the countryside, go for country walks, out as far as Stokenham, or somewhere like that… or up the old railway line, picking wild strawberries on the way. There was no trains on a Sunday and we'd go up just inside the tunnel and play cards.

Harold Widger

Born 6th August 1913

Died 5th August 2005

Recorded on 6th May 2003
& 13th May 2005

Harold. Us used to go to Harleston church from Lower Norton Farm - Auntie Bessie used to take us in the pony and trap; I think it was once a month they used to have a service out there.

Steve. That was the little corrugated-iron chapel?

Harold. Yes, 'tidn very big…well it's a ruin now, just falling down. There was a 'mission room' up Cole's Cross too, we used to go there sometimes and a vicar used to come there. A lot of places would have these 'mission rooms' for a small congregation; but with the large families then, there was quite a few people there; it was really a nice atmosphere.

Steve. How many of you would go in the trap?

Harold. Oh, four of us, it was a trap you got in at the back… open the door at the back.

Father used to repair our hob-nailed boots with scoots and nails: a toe scoot and a heel scoot put in the bottom with nails, to save them from wearing out. We handed the boots down from one boy to the next, or from boy to girl even.

The first bike I bought was in Balkwill's... four pounds, nineteen shillings and sixpence. That was when I was first going to Coombe to work, and I had sixpence left then. Then I got out 'Allaton' and Efford's used to do bikes, so I had a posh bike then, a 'Rudge Whitworth'; I had three-speed then!

Steve. What food did you like when you were a boy?

Harold. Rabbits...and pork. I mean, up Nuckwell we had a big sow pig that had one litter of piglets, and we couldn't get her in pig again. I can see 'en now, hanged up in the cart linhay; twenty-five score he was, and we ate the lot! When you come to think of it, fat bacon nearly four inches thick, fried for breakfast. The taste was wonderful, really; I mean, fresh pork - I know it wasn't always fresh because 'twas salted in, but it was fresh to start off with... and harvest time we used to catch the rabbits, and Mother would do us a rabbit each for dinner, roast rabbit; or in a pie, it was beautiful! Oh and hogs pudding, and Mother used to make lovely yeast buns and 'teddy cake'.

Steve. What would you use to clean your teeth when you were a boy?

Harold. Well - carbolic soap! It tasted terrible...or salt was a very good thing too.

I left school and went to work at Higher Coombe Farm, East Allington. I took on driving the horses then, when I was fifteen. You'd get up about six and do the milking first. On Sunday mornings Aunt Rose would bring out half a tuff cake with cream on it, out in the separator house. Then go up and see to the cattle: there was Wallaton barn up 'cross the fields - well summer time they was out, but winter time we used to feed 'em up there; hay and straw.... and bruised corn. They had a Lister engine and a mill and I used to bruise the corn for the cattle and grind some meal for the pigs.

We always ploughed one grass field in the winter, well, when the hedges had been done up all the way round; 'course rabbits used to dig them down then. That was the worse time, going out after dinner and go hedging until milking-time. Three hours up there digging and heaving with a shovel - I used to hate it, but it had to be done! They have a fore-loader now on a tractor and pick it up, build it up; they don't do no digger and shovel now.

When I was at Pitt farming I ploughed three and a half acres in two days, on me own with a single-

furrow plough, what we'd call a 'balance' plough. You turned the handles and pulled down the plough; the horses, you didn't have to drive them very much, they knew what to do, but you had to be pretty quick at turning the plough round at the end.

Star was the youngest one, in the middle... and Prince... and Nora was the mare; oh, they was three lovely horses. Prince and Star was the main pair. I drilled fourteen acres in one day with they two, and as soon as you filled up the drill and put the cover down they was gone! You didn't have to say, "Get on", as soon as the cover went down they knew... it's amazing; and that Prince, for scuffling turnips, I'd turn him round out the end and put him in the line, and he would go right 'cross the field. I would just hold the scuffle and he would keep in that line, he wouldn't go out of line. We used to thatch the corn ricks and the hay ricks...used to grow wheat for making reed, take it into the barn when 'twas dry, and then if it was raining you'd go in the barn making reed with the reed-comber; 'twould thresh it out and comb it, tie it into bundles, and that was used for thatching the ricks.

Pulling mangold: that was alright if 'twas dry...but cor, if they was wet they wouldn't twist, and wouldn't it try your hands! You weren't allowed to have a hook to cut 'em because it would spoil the top. The mangold used to be put in a 'cave' up against the hedge, and covered in with a bit of straw and all the broil: that's the parings from the hedges - that would keep them, or the frost would spoil them and they'd rot in no time.

Steve. Did you have to cut them up for the cattle?

Harold. Not very often. They could usually bite the mangold but some of the turnips had to be cut up. We used to grow 'flatpole' cabbages then too, huge great cabbages they were - to feed to the cattle.

Steve. Did the fields all have names?

Harold. Well, yes, you see they took down all the hedges and that was the end of the names of the fields : 'Ten Acres', he run right out against Pasture Cross, then there was 'Varney Field'... you see they'm all tillage now, they used to be all 'ferns' and 'brimbles'.

Steve. Why did farmers start to tear down the hedges?

Harold. Well, that was to do with the tractors coming in on the farms.

Steve. I suppose those fields had been called the same names for centuries?

Harold. Oh, of course; there was 'Lower Crooks', 'Middle Crooks' and 'Higher Crooks', then 'Bikken'; eleven acres right on top of the brow. 'Bikken', that means 'Beacon'... and adjoining that was 'Straw field', a narrow field, only two acres. Next up it was the 'Brakes', the first brake was twelve acres, level as a penny, and it was just 'fuzzes' and 'brimbles'!

I farmed Pitt Farm for twenty-three year, then I went in Rectory Farm for ten and a half year before I retired from there.

Farming was so bad in the late twenties and early thirties, before the War, and I had a chance to go to Newton Abbot in a pork butcher's shop. I thought, 'Well, farming is no good to me at all now'.

We used to collect all farm produce round the South Hams. Pigs was killed on the farms but when the War came everything was rationed and that was stopped and I said, "I can go back on the land again". Me brother-in-law over Blackawton wanted somebody to help milk the cows, half past three in the morning. I thought, 'That's just the job, I can do

that alright'. He used to take the milk to Paignton in a Austin 10 car, twice a day - that was before any churns or anything, see.

Steve. That was quite a change going from working on the land into a shop- you didn't mind that change?

Harold. Oh no, I liked it; skinning rabbits, drawing poultry and cutting up pigs. You know, I skinned ninety rabbits before breakfast one morning. Yes, I used to go to work early.

I told you about the French boy who came with us in the War... they asked us from the Rectory, would we have this French boy? Oh yes, we would have 'en. He was sent off from London, all on his own, not knowing a bit where he was going or who he was going with. I can see him now on Totnes station, eight year old, with a great big case. Anyhow he was wonderful, and ever after that, if he had chance for a holiday he was going to Pitt Farm, he didn't want to go anywhere else... from eight year old until fifteen. Then when he was fifteen his mother was gone back to Paris and he had to go back there. His father was deported to Germany and they never knew nothing of him after; they was Jews, you see...

– ❖ –

Ethel Ellis & Harold Widger
Ethel

Born 2nd October 1917

Died 4th June 2008

Recorded on 19th August 2003

Ethel. We were both born at Coles Cross, East Allington, I remember my brother Bill saying that when I was born they were threshing, like with the old fashioned threshing-machine, and he was 'heaving back douse'. They used to call it 'draishin' in they days.

Harold. When I was ten year old we lived at Aveton Gifford then, and goin' school. I used to walk up from Aveton Gifford school to Offields Farm to milk the cows - that was a proper job!

Ethel. When I used to go to school I used to take cocoa, sugar and milk… and the kettle was boiled on the 'Ideal' fire, which they used to put coke in, and we'd make ourselves a cup of cocoa mid-mornings. There were no school dinners and we used to run all the way home for dinner, and all the way back.

At Chillaton Moor we used to have to go down across two fields to fetch water for Mother's washing. We had two large buckets and we used a 'square', so you didn't feel the full weight of those buckets: it's as easy as pat to pick up those two buckets using a 'square'.

Work! Oh crikey! … I remember when I was nine year old my mother went into hospital to have an operation and I was left at home to look after them. I'd make a big potato cake and the blighters would come in and eat it, and I'd have to turn round and make another one. I'll tell you this much, Harold and brother Charlie, they was supposed to help me with the washing… but they was off somewhere… I had to do the blimmin' lot!

Steve. You said that when you were at school you did cookery lessons at Kingsbridge!

Ethel. That's right, I used to walk from Staunton to Loddiswell Butts, that's two miles, and then down to catch the train at Loddiswell station, which was another mile, so you can guess what time I had to

start away in the morning. Of course, we'd come back on the train in the afternoon and then I'd have to walk all the way back to Staunton Farm. Sometimes it would be pitch dark, and there wad'n nobody else to go with me, I was on me own.

Mother used to make yeast buns, and very often she used to ask me to bring home 'couple ounces of yeast. I'd get about three parts way home and forgot it. I had to turn round and go all the way back again.

Once I went to Dawlish to stay for a week, on the train… wondered where I was going… on me own. Of course you didn't have cases in those days, you had these straw baskets like… there's a proper name for 'em, and they used to have a buckle strap round 'em, to tie 'em up. It was all straw raffia…Moses baskets! That's what you packed your clothes in.

We used to go across the fields to Wizaller from Staunton… we used to go over there for an evening and play cards, or play games with Mrs. Maddick… cor couldn't she play the piano!… 'singing polly-wally-doodle all the day'!… cor! she could rattle out that tune - and us'd be singing at the top of our voices.

I can remember you and Charlie used to sleep together in a good old feather-tie bed.

Harold … and not always in there, us very often would sleep out in the cart, in under the cart linhay… summertime like; 'course without the horse in 'en the shafts was down on the ground and the cart was a slope…. and there was a walnut tree and me and Harry put up two hammocks.

Ethel. I used to sleep with my sister, and Fred and Frank were in another bed in our room.

Steve. When you were children do you remember people in their eighties?

Harold. I remember Grandfather dying at Nuckwell. I remember seeing him in his coffin.

Ethel. They were old, yes, definitely, well Grandfer was eighty, wasn't he, and Gran was eighty-seven. She died later at Pullyblanks; and I remember at

Grandfer's funeral you and Charlie was left home to look after the sandwiches.

I can remember shifting from Nuckwell down to Pullyblanks: Father with his horse and wagon, and sitting up in the back of the wagon in one of these leather chairs was Gran, I can see her as if 'twas yesterday.

Harold. I remember going from West Alvington to Nuckwell on top of a wagonload of furniture, sitting in a chair. I was seven year old then. I expect it was Father driving the 'oss in the spring wagon, cor that was the thing!

Ethel. When we went out to Bantham with the Sunday school it was on the spring wagon… out to Bantham, bathing. Mother used to make meat pasties and apple pasties - yes they went down well, they did.

My first school was Aveton Gifford and I used to hate it there… and another thing I hated was cars. I'd be on my own and hear a car… I'd start running, or else jump in the hedge because I was scared stiff of them. Brother Charlie, next one up, he didn't like school either, he couldn't bear it. Anyway there was a hen-house up in one of the fields and we used to go up there during the day… we had our sandwiches you see… we knew when to go home from school because we could see the school kids coming over Aveton Gifford bridge. That went on for a while, until the Attendance Officer came to ask why we weren't at school… 'course, then look out!

I left school at Christmas 1931 and started into the Big House service on the first of January, at Curtisknowle for Mr. and Mrs. Welch-Thornton. They used to have seven servants indoors: there was the cook and the kitchen maid, the housemaid and under housemaid, and what was called a 'betweeny maid', who helped both in the kitchen and in the house. There was a butler and a footman; they used to do the silver, in the butler's pantry. See, the silver didn't used to come out into the kitchen, only the china stuff, and I used to do that out in the scullery. Then a chauffeur for her, chauffeur for him … head gardener, under gardener, head gamekeeper and under gamekeeper. I was the kitchen maid, did all the dirty work!; got out at six o'clock in the morning to scrub the kitchen floor, light the black Lidstone range, ready to get hot enough to make scones and girdle scones, for they to have their breakfast at nine o'clock.

Oh yes, hard work it was, you didn't finish until about eleven o'clock at night, seven days a week. You might have a half day off, yes, that used to be a laugh, because I'd never leave there 'til two o'clock or more, times you'd washed up all your dishes after cooking, perhaps there was a luncheon party; washing up all they dishes, and the saucepans; and I used to walk home, which was two miles. Of course you were supposed to be in again by nine o'clock, but we said, "We're not coming in 'til ten", otherwise by the time you got home 'twas almost time to turn 'round and come back again.

Steve. Did the Thorntons have a car each?

Ethel. Yes, back then the chauffeurs lived near the garage 'cause they had to look after the cars.

They used to have shooting parties… you'd have to go and do a lot of cooking and send it out to where the shoot was…and of course it had to be warm… hot you know, they wouldn't have cold sandwiches, it would be hot pork pies. They'd find a place in a hay field…take picnic table and chairs, and of course knives and forks; they wouldn't be eating it with their hands.

Daughter Sandra. What about when you took the tea in?

Ethel. You mean when there wad'n no tea in the teapot? She had visitors for tea, you know… and of course the bell goes and I thought, 'Oh crikey, what do 'er want now?' … of course, I opened the door, and she said, "Well we would like a little tea in the teapot, Ethel!"

Steve. They had a bell system there?

Ethel. Oh yes, you'd see 'em all up on the wall, you know… somebody presses the bell and you'd know which room it was in, perhaps the Gentleman's bedroom, or the Lady's boudoir.

Steve. Were you appreciated?

Ethel. Gidout, no! tid'n for what anybody used to earn… used to be a pound a month - from the first of the month to the first of the next month… you'd get hardly five bob a week. You'd get a day off once a month; I would tell my two brothers, Fred and Frank, "If you help Mother and do some work, come down Gara Bridge and us'll get on the train and I'll take you to the pictures".

It was a hard life although we used to make our fun, 'course there was always a green baize door to keep the noise from the kitchen and the servants' hall from the gentry inside. Many a time they've sent the butler out and said, "Ethel be quieter, don't laugh so loud", 'course that would start me off again!

I remember once we put bicarbonate of soda in the footman's chamber pot …'course it frothed up and he had to go across the bedroom and stick it out the window ! Well you had to have a bit of fun.

I was three and a half years in that place and then I went across to Hazelwood, a big house across the valley, and I was there for another three and a half years… and oh! I did some terrible things there! They had this big mirror, and you'd got to have a stepladder to get up and dust everywhere. Anyhow, I got one of these stepladders at the end of the settee, pushed the settee and the stepladder crashed right into this great big mirror… crash! 'course I had to go in 'on the carpet' then - but she was very good about it I must admit. Another time I was carrying a tray all laid up for breakfast, and I tripped… 'way went the tray… I broke every blimmin' bit… teapot, marmalade, sugar, jam… I had to clear it all up.

Then I went to Dawlish and was what they called a cook-general for an old lady up there. I was with her for eighteen months, until my brother Fred said, "I'm leaving the bakery at 'Allaton', see if you can get my job". So I came to East Allington and they took me on like a shot. I loved that job, baking bread: one pound fourteen and a half ounces you had to cut off the dough for a loaf of bread; that was real bread, you can't get it now.

I used to hump around a half sack of flour to make the dough… tip it in the bin. Then you'd have a bucket and a half of warm water with yeast mixed in … about two pound of salt. The machine had a crooked arm and he'd work around in the bin mixing up the dough. Then I'd go around the village with what they called a 'skip': a wheel in front with handles and legs, and this hamper. I used to push it around the village to deliver the bread; a loaf was fourpence ha'penny then.

Steve. Ethel, you must have been evacuated from East Allington?

Ethel. Yes, and that was another turmoil. We had to be out about five days before Christmas, and every-

thing…everything had to go out of that village: cats, dogs, animals, corn, turnips, hay…and gates…you just imagine packing all that up.

Harold. … and, oh wad'n it wet that Autumn, us had Land Girls there topping the turnips and pulling the mangold, because us took all they out Soar, t'other side of Malborough.

Ethel. I wanted to go on baking; Fox's in Modbury would have took me, but the Officer wouldn't let me go. I was sent to Salisbury in a piston factory, 'Wellworthys'. I used to start seven o'clock in the morning, 'til seven o'clock at night. The next fortnight was from seven at night 'til seven o'clock in the morning.

I was up at 'Wellworthys' when it was 'D-Day'. I heard the planes going over because I was on night duty…drone after drone…but there wasn't so many came back. That was a sad night that was, to think of all they boys… terrible!

Mother, see, had three in the Forces and they all came through it. Brother Charlie was in the Navy, they had to go up to Russia; their guns would be blazing and their barrels would be red hot, and still the ice would form on them. We had a cousin in the Merchant Navy, on H.M.S. *Dunoon*, and he was killed, first time going up there, their ship was torpedoed and sunk… he was a lovely boy too.

Another cousin, Bill, was in the Air Force. He did his thirty flights out and back, and then he was grounded for a certain amount of time. When he went out again he was shot down…. he was only a young man!

We never lost any brothers, but we lost two cousins.

I was married at East Allington church, July 17th 1946… I baked bread in the morning; I had about twenty minutes to go upstairs and get dressed to go to the wedding… 'course 'twad'n paint and powder in they days!

We had the whole family and practically all the village coming into the Reading Room for the reception.

When we were first married my husband had a motorbike, and I remember brother Charlie used to come and pick me up on his motorbike as well - it was beautiful, just like flying!

Harold. We went to London to see the World Speedway Championship, when I had a Standard 9 car…cor, wad'n I excited, going to London to see these motorbikes going round, and I was driving like hell!

Harry and Edna Jervis

Harry Born 17th April 1913
Died 26th October 2004

Edna Born 2nd December 1917
Died 17th January 2006

Recorded on 11th June 2003

Harry. My grandparents lived at Bickerton at Hallsands, and every week we used to walk from Salcombe, go across the ferry and then walk all the way from the ferry to Bickerton. We'd have lunch and tea, then walk all the way back again… never think nothing of it; it must have been five or six miles each way.

Ella and Patience Trout were the two fisherwomen in Hallsands then, 'used to know them very well, 'used to go out in their boat fishing with them. Me uncle used to run the crabs from Hallsand to Kingsbridge twice a week; he used to go down with a horse and cart, the old hay cart. I often used to go with him, we'd leave Hallsands about seven o'clock in the morning… it would take about four hours to get there… unload the crabs at the Station, give the horse a break, then come down on the Quay, and if any of the tradesmen had any parcels for Hallsands they'd bring them down and put them in the cart. Then we'd go out to where the 'Crabshell' is now, that was a coal yard, load up with coal to fill up the cart, which made the journey worthwhile…. take the coal back to Hallsands and he used to deliver it to the fishermen's cottages before he went home… that was his day's work!

There was no traffic whatsoever in them days. I remember the first motorcar to come to Salcombe, old Russell, the greengrocer in Salcombe, he had the first car, one of those old 'Trojans'. It had this great chain drive, and he used to walk up Church hill alongside the car, because it wouldn't take the weight going up there.

We had no running water in those days, we had to go right up through the willow orchard to get to the toilet, where running water was the stream coming out of the wall… take your bucket out and get it from there… and during the War they put the Air Raid siren on the wall, right on top of the toilet! You'd be sitting on the toilet and …!

We never had water in the house and no electricity, only oil lamps and candles… until during the War when Dad had the electricity put in… but we never had the water put in. We had a bath up in the washhouse and Mother used to boil up the copper, put the hot and cold water in, in bucketfuls, and all the family used to go in the bath: youngest to eldest…or cleanest to dirtiest!

Steve. *When you left school at fourteen had you travelled far?*

Edna. Plymouth, I think, probably! My old Gran Best never went outside of Salcombe, so they say.

Harry. Well, in those days there were no buses, no nothing. When I was a youngster old Russell had his charabanc, he used to take on coach tours, and coming up Aveton Gifford hill you'd always have to get out and walk up the hill, the bus would never take you up there. He'd stop at the top and you'd all get back in.

When my sister was born my dad was stationed at Dartmouth; he was a blacksmith in the Navy and he was on the 'Britannia' there, on the 'old wooden walls': they didn't have the College up on the hill then, there used to be all wooden ships there. He used to walk from Dartmouth to Hallsands, that was about six miles on the cliff paths… there was no other means of transport; when 'twas dark you had to be careful, you never had any torches in them days.

I remember the blizzard in 1927; I remember trying to walk to Hallsands with Dad to take some bread to my grandparents. We went across the ferry and went about four hundred yards along the bottom road, and we had to turn back; you couldn't see the hedges let alone walk on the roads.

Everything was cut off then: Salcombe, Hope Cove, Kingsbridge, everything.

They took bread to Hope Cove and Hallsands by boat in the end. That was real blizzard, worse blizzard ever seen I think, down here in Salcombe.

My dad came out of the Navy and he took the blacksmith's shop in 1920, down Church hill. He carried on here until during the War when the trade simply petered out… no horses, and the boats all became machine-made and so the blacksmith's shop wound up.

You see, all the ironwork for the boats was all made by hand then. After the War all the horses in Salcombe had finished, all the farmers had got tractors and everything like that, that's when the blacksmiths finished. My grandad was the blacksmith at Bickerton, near Hallsands, and once the horses went out they were all finished.

When I joined the Navy in 1928 there was no means of transport from Salcombe to Kingsbridge. A Dockyard bus left Kingsbridge at half past five in the morning, so if I wanted to stay the night in Salcombe I had to get up at three o'clock in the morning and walk the old road to Kingsbridge, up through Batson… pitch dark… you can imagine in wintertime, along that old country road.

Steve. *What do you remember about the railway in Kingsbridge?*

Edna. I can tell you one story: Grandad had been to Plymouth by train and when he got back to Kingsbridge he got out, went over and patted the engine and said, "Well done old 'oss, you did well coming up that hill din'e!"

It was a lovely old line that 'Primrose Line'; it was a beautiful ride, through the bluebell woods.

Harry. But it was touch and go, you'd never make the connections - you'd get to Kingsbridge and just miss the bus to Salcombe!

Steve. *Was there a cinema in Salcombe?*

Edna. Yes, down Church hill, on the corner there.

Harry. You were lucky if it ran the full programme; you used to have to fight to get your seat and sit down… on hard forms, you used to have to sit on

these hard forms. You'd be watching the film and the damn thing would break down, and he used to say, "Very sorry, can't get the thing to go. I'll give you all tickets to come again next week".

Miss Provis used to play the piano, and whatever film came on she used to try and play the piano like the film, see.

Edna. We used to go in the front seats, the tuppenny seats, and when it was dark we used to crawl back under to the best ones.

Harry. I joined the Navy in 1928. I was working in the blacksmiths shop as a young apprentice and I used to see the sailors come home on leave. I used to think, 'That's a better life than I've got here', so I decided to join the Navy. I did about twenty-five years, because I had to do extra time for the War: I should have come home during the War but I had to do the extra time. I was Chief Coxswain - on destroyers all the time. It was a hard life on destroyers during the War, you were out in all weathers. I got the DSM and the BEM during the War. Look, there's a photo of the ship I was on when I won the DSM, the H.M.S. *Rockwood*, out in the Aegean. We got hit off Crete by a glider bomb, went right through the ship. She lost one engine

and they said it wasn't worth repairing. We were in Alexandria and they said the ship was too damaged so she was ditched. I was on her from the time she was built in Barrow until the time she was broken up, about two and a half years.

Steve. What was your job when you left the Navy?

Harry. I joined the Air Force then! They were out at Bolt Head in nissen huts; they had the fighter squadron out there during the War and they carried on. They had a radar station out there and I did five years there. Radar stations were dotted all around the country, for security.

Frances Goodman

Born 27th November 1907

Died 4th March 2007

Recorded on 7th July 2003
& 14th June 2004

Frances. My Grandfather Furneaux lived at Lower Poole, East Allington, but I was brought up in Sampford Brett in Somerset and we could see the Quantock hills from where I lived. We were three girls and three boys, and we, the children, were the main thing in the family. We weren't spoilt by any means, my mother would chastise us girls, but Father dealt with the boys. My father was a disciplinarian, very strict he was…what you were told you did then, you know, "Hands off the table", "Walk up straight", the boys: "Hands out of your pocket"… things like that, old-fashioned now I suppose, but *his* father was very strict, much more than my father, I think.

We were all musical and Sunday evenings, after Sunday school in the afternoon, Mother would play the organ and we would sing hymns. My father had a concertina he would play… Sunday was kept Sunday… my mother would never sew

on a button on a Sunday, and my father wouldn't even sharpen the knife to cut the Sunday joint. It would be done on Saturday… and the 'cut-throat' razor, he had a strop on the wall to sharpen them, and that had to be done on Saturday.

We had the simple things, but we were contented; we were never spoilt and we had to behave ourselves, but it was a happy atmosphere. I always remember I had a lovely doll. We used to make things out of the black stockings that we used to wear years ago - oh I daren't mention it now… 'golliwogs'; stuff them, have wool for the hair and put buttons in for eyes, and we loved our old golliwog!

We had two shops in the village, one was a general shop and the other was the tailors. I remember when we went to school we liked to look in the window because there were two of them, the master and his helper, I suppose. He'd be sat on a big table with his legs crossed, sewing. They made my mother's costume for her nephew's wedding… and if the boys wanted trousers or anything, they would make them. I remember, when my mother got a bit older, we'd go behind her and pull in the corset at the back and tie it; it was laced in, it must have been very uncomfortable. There were no bras in those days, because you had the corset up to here, you see.

I remember I caught ringworm from the calves, and I had to have all my hair shaved off because it was so difficult to put a dressing on with hair you see; so Mother cut off all those beautiful curls, and they said, "Oh, it'll grow back double thick afterwards"- and it did. I would have been about seven then probably.

When I was young I used to come down by train to my aunt and uncle at Fallapit Farm. My father would put me in the guard's care at Woolaton station and I think it was half a crown, which in those days was a lot of money, because I had to change at Taunton and again at Exeter, so he would always pay the guard, and he'd say to me, "Now you sit there and don't you move". I would have been about eight.

I can only remember one grandmother, Granny Mitchelmore. I didn't know her very well because I was only about eight when she died. I never saw Granny walking, she was always sat down, with black skirts all around her, little black hat tied right around the top, and she was always sat up prim and proper... if your boots weren't laced or buttoned up properly you had to go over to her and she would do it for you... if something wasn't right, you know, that had to be put right... and she seemed so old to me, but I don't think she was in her eighties.

Fallapit was a big estate because it involved not only the village, but the farms around Fallapit House. Oh, that was a lovely house, it was Lord Ashcombe's 'country seat' then, he used to come to stay there. The butter and cream used to be sent from Fallapit Home Farm, my uncle's farm, up to Lord Ashcombe every fortnight. He lived in Dorking, Surrey, and it went through the post in a biscuit tin; there'd be the big tin of cream and I think two pounds of butter, farm-made.

There are more animals kept on a farm today than years ago. There would have been about fifteen milking cows, and, in my grandfather's time, they used to keep a lot of fat cattle, because, being a butcher, they used to kill their own bullocks, sheep and whatnot. They had the butcher's shop up there at number one, Dartmouth Road, East Allington, but also went to Dartmouth

market with their meat, with a horse and van, the meat all hung around the sides. In those days there'd be so many cows, so many sheep... horses of course. My grandfather used to ride the pony around to see the cattle each day, and sometimes the pony would drive in the jingle. There was a lighter horse you could ride if you wanted to, then there were three other working horses. One was called Madam and she used to have a foal every other year ; when they were old enough they were sold. Then there was Prince, Violet and Blossom... and all the cows had names. There was Buttercup, Primrose the first and Primrose the second, yes, they all had names. We had fowls, geese, and turkeys all running about on the farm.

We always had a goat because they always said that a goat would ward off abortion in cows, yes, and pigs in the houses out there.

Steve. I imagine there was a lot of noise with all those animals!

Frances. Well, you see you grew up amongst them, you didn't take any notice. There was more noise with animals then than there is with machinery today, it's a natural noise. Now all you hear is the tractors and the mowers and whatnot.

There was more labour on the farm in those days; we had four or five labourers, you see you'd hand-cut the hedges, and you'd need somebody for the horses. There was always two to do that, harness them up, and they'd all be gone from the yard by eight o'clock in the morning, out in the fields.

I came from Somerset to Fallapit Farm, East Allington in 1922, to help my aunt as she'd just had a baby, and in 1927 I married Tom Bond and moved to Lower Poole Farm, where my father had grown up.

During the Second World War we had bombs dropped here. There were soldiers billeted at Fallapit House, and the Parish Hall, which was called the Reading Room at that time, was open every night for the soldiers to come up and have coffee and biscuits. Well, I was there until ten o'clock and when I came home I said to my husband, "I'll make a hot drink before bed", so I made it and with the same I heard like a rushing wind and then this terrific bang... four bombs had dropped: one up in the football field, one in behind the bend in the lane here: that one, the blast came across the field and killed four of our cows... and the next one, if it had come straight down would have been on the house, but it didn't, it veered and dropped up in the field just above the pond… lucky it was. It felt as if it had dropped in the dining room… I went in and the window was gone and, of course, it did a lot of damage. The children were really frightened because it was so close, and so sudden.

I remember my sister in Somerset saying, "Well, you are alright down there, they'll never find you"… but they came across here when they bombed Plymouth. Anyrate we were thankful we weren't hurt ourselves, I hadn't been home long, and I'd come down that lane.

Steve. Did you have any evacuees here?

Frances. Oh yes, we had some from the East End of London and they were billeted on us, these two girls… and the habits of them! I used to go to Totnes market with the butter and eggs and when my husband met me from the bus at Stanborough he said, "You'll have the fright of your life when you come home, the whole family's here"; mother, daughter, another baby; there was five of them had landed! They did it on their own, not through the Government or anything… oh, goodness me! Well, what could I say, I thought, 'I suppose it's my bit to help the War'. I got to put them up. I had to get all the beds ready, they occupied the two spare rooms, the five of them… but oh, the language! - and their habits weren't ours. I was very cross with them, they used the curtains instead of toilet paper! Yes! but they hadn't got any money to give me so I had to keep them. Then the Billeting Officer, who was the Rector's wife, found them a cottage: and they used the bath to put wood in.

Steve. You had to leave here during the evacuation in the South Hams!

Frances. Yes, to Englebourne, a big house near Totnes, and we were allotted what used to be the servants' hall. When I stood on the table I couldn't reach the ceiling with a sweeping brush, it was a massive place. We had two large bedrooms, a bathroom and toilet, and downstairs we had a huge room, four times as big as this kitchen, what used to be the butler's pantry. They said that the Bowes-Lyons used to live in that house years ago.

We had a sale in Kingsbridge and all the cattle were sold up and neighbouring farmers took the horses. We took one cow with us to get our own milk… 'course your living was lost. We had six weeks to get out; get rid of all the cattle, furniture, everything, just before Christmas. It was an upheaval, and when we came back the place was absolutely filthy…filthy! I can remember in the sitting room, having a broom and water to broom out the mess. The auctioneer came if you had a claim, you see. We stood in the sitting room and I said, "How much do I get for cleaning this room?" … a shilling!!

We went out a week before Christmas and came back the following September. Then there was a lot of work to be done in the fields, but you thought, well, that was our bit towards the War.

Bill Hurrell

Born 25th June 1908
Died 23rd May 2006

Recorded on 9th September 2003
& 19th November 2003

Bill. I was born in Rosecote, Inner Hope and a lot of the beams in the cottage were from wrecks; there were holes in some, where the ropes had been pulled through. It was about 1760 or something like that, when the 'Ramillies' ran ashore; 'course in they days there wouldn't be no line sheaves, or anything like that, it would be just holes in the mast, and they used to go up the rope ladders and put grease in them to pull the ropes through.... and Rosecote had the beams with the holes in.

I remember at Christmas, when I hanged up my stocking on Father's bedpost. I was sleeping in a camp bed in the same room, my sisters were in another room. He used to have leather waders, came nearly up to his thighs, and big stockings inside. They used to put a lump of coal in the bottom, and an orange and.... and hang it up on the rail at the bottom of the bed.

We used to go gulls-nesting a lot of the time; we went places where we shouldn't have gone, collecting the seagulls' eggs. They'm lovely eggs you know, they're richer: the yolks are mostly red, and very, very tasty.

Yes, me and the other boys used to go in the cliffs getting 'em. Two boys got killed, coastguard boys they were. They slipped down the cliff and all they found was the hairs off their heads.

A postman used to bring the mail from Malborough on a pushbike and deliver round about: ol' Lethbridge - quite a character! he used to have a proper uniform, peak cap. He liked cider: Father used to say to him, "You can have some of that cider", and the old beggar would help he'self - besides having a drink he'd put a bottle of cider in his postbag.

Steve. Did people have birds outside their cottages in cages, I've seen it in old photographs?

Bill. Yes, now, a lot of them birds they got from a liner that was wrecked; it was coming back from Africa in thick fog and it missed the Eddystone and ran into the cliffs at Bolt Tail; they call the place 'Jebba' now, after it. It come right into the cliff and couldn't turn and got wrecked; and she had a lot of these songbirds on board. People caught these birds and had them in their cottages.

I was about one of the last pupils at Galmpton school, before it was joined to Malborough.

Steve. Did you like school ?

Bill. No, I didn't. I wanted to be on the water all the time. The old boy that used to look after the schoolroom and made up the fires and that, he used to urinate over the coke in the cellar. We had an old 'tortoise' stove in the schoolroom and when it was burning it would stink! You can imagine!

My grandfather, Tom Bailey, used to work for a firm in Plymouth that took the stage-coaches as far as Exeter... in they days there was no cars. There was a stage-coach running from Plymouth to Exeter and there they joined another team to go on to Taunton and that. I think they were called 'four-in-hand', two horses in front and two behind them. I remember the old boy, he used to have an old top hat on.

Dear old Grandfather Hurrell, he was an ol' seaman on the sailing ships.... dear old boy! I can picture him now, sitting in the corner of the Reading room. I used to squat and listen to them telling yarns: where they'd been, what they'd seen and what they'd done. I've got an old cane he used to rest on... his little old hat; he used to wear a little old flat panama thing. He used to smoke a pipe, and I've seen him have a big claw of a crab, break off the point of the big toe and have it for a pipe.

Father used to go to sea; he worked for an old gentleman called Sir Thomas Freake, at Outer Hope. He came from Warfleet, in Dartmouth and he had a Cornish lugger. Father made up the crew with Ike Jarvis, the two of them used to man this Cornish fishing boat.

Father was born in Hope Cove... he was a great, strong man, he was a tough old nut!

I was fishing all of my life, for forty years. Me and Father worked together, we had some experiences. Very often we would leave home about half past two in the morning and go up and

down from the Ham Stone to Burgh Island fishing for crabs, lobsters…anything.

We had nets for everything we could catch: rays, turbot, conger eels. We used to catch squid for bait for conger; we had a pilchard net, caught pilchards and little mackerel and that in it…all means of fishing, it didn't matter what it was.

The first year I started I was fourteen. I slipped up and and lost me fingers and I've been without them ever since. I was switching off the engine when I slipped on an old conger tail… in goes me hand, and when I pulled it out there was two fingers missing. There was a lot of blood and we were, I suppose, about three miles off shore at the time. Father tied his handkerchief around there tight, twisted a piece of wood around to stop the blood, and made for the shore. When we got to Salcombe Dr. Twining was seeing to a baby being born in Prawle, so Dr. Moore was there, and he dipped my hand in what must have been iodine, for I nearly jumped through the ceiling!

We had to wait for Dr. Twining to come before he'd do anything, and when he came he put a thing over me head and put me to sleep.

Steve. *That was a nasty accident!*

Bill. Yes, but I got over it and I went back to sea again the next year, after they'd healed up. The season started around April but we were busy in the winter making crab pots and mending them. We cut our own willows; in the orchard we had a willow plot and used to cut them to make our crab pots.

I went out on my own after Father retired. I've been sometimes trawling three o'clock in the morning, down the other side of Challaborough, on me own in the dark, the other side of Burgh Island. I've been a stalwart old fisherman, in me way.

There was a 'smack' come down from Southampton and she had a well in her, to collect fish. She'd call on different villages on the way down - Hallsands, Beesands, Salcombe, then came round to Hope Cove. She'd take it all back live to Southampton in this built-in well.

There was five double-handed boats in Inner Hope, that's where the Lifeboat House is, and there was four boats at Outer Hope when I started with Father. That's two men in an eighteen-foot fishing boat.

Steve. *Was it a good little community?*

Bill. Yes, They had to work together you see, to help each other pull up their boats, so Outer Hope men helped Inner Hope, and Inner Hope helped Outer. The families had been there in those cottages for generations, smugglers some of 'em, I expect!

Smuggling was the thing in Hope Cove years before; they used to smuggle from France - the coastguards had covers in Hope Cove, on the look out for smuggling, but the smugglers had their own ideas of what to do. They were notified by a keg of tar, set on fire in a cave somewhere, not to come in. Smuggling was a way of life, and the brandy was brought in for the parson and the farmers, people of notoriety.

I'm the last of the lifeboatmen, all the rest have long, long gone. There were some of 'em twenty year younger than me, now there's only me to tell the tale. I reckon I was eighteen when I joined the Lifeboat, and I had a job, really, to hold the oar.

Father used to come and take my place; he was the Second Coxswain, and he would relieve me. The two villages made up the crew: there was sixteen of us in the crew, all our oars was painted blue and white. The starboard side was blue and the oars on the port side were white, and we all had our positions on the boat.

Steve. *How was the alarm sounded, if there was trouble?*

Bill. We had a team on shore who fired the rockets to get the crew together, and people brought horses and that, if we had to take the lifeboat away.

Steve. *Tell us about some of the rescues.*

Bill. There was the 'Liberta' that got aground at the Mew Stone at Salcombe harbour: that was an Italian ship, and when we got there the lights was on the ship, but as the tide rose the dynamos went 'phut' !

We had a job to launch the lifeboat, the great heavy wheels sunk into the sand, but we managed to put her on wooden skids and take her down the rest of the way. We were up to our shoulders in water before we could get the boat afloat, and jump aboard.

We were out there for about eleven hours, wet through - oh, it was cold! Some of 'em had to be given whisky to revive them. There were four of us that wasn't sick; me and Father, Edwin Partridge and Ike Jarvis; all the rest was urging their hearts up! Poor old George Legassick was sick, he was numb with cold - he had to be given whisky to revive him.

They were eventually taken off by the coastguards with rocket-line and breeches buoy, to the top of the cliffs.

Steve. *Could you swim?*

Bill. No. I was never a good swimmer.

Steve. *I bet a lot of your mates on the lifeboat couldn't swim, could they?*

Bill. No they didn't think of it like that.

Steve. *Tell me about some of the wrecks around Hope Cove.*

Bill. Oh well, there've been several there, long before my day. The first was an Armada ship that came ashore, he was wrecked there at Woolaman Point, close to Outer Hope Cove. He'd been trying to escape Drake in Bigbury Bay and was getting closer to the land every time he tacked. The last tack was at Woolaman Cove and he came to grief there.

I think he was called the 'St Peter'. The crew were taken to Fallapit House at East Allington…years afterwards they found money there, that was on him.

Steve. *Tell us about the 'Herzogin Cecilie'.*

Bill. Oh yes, well it was 1936, and there was a lot of commotion in the village, and the Rocket brigade, they were getting ready to go to a wreck. I had a Wolseley 10 car, a lovely car, and my cousin, my brother, Norman Thornton and Jack Jarvis, I took them all up to Bolberry Down and we could see the 'Herzogin' ashore along-side of the Ham Stone there off Soar Mill Cove… all sails set. We were the first to get there and the only person who could talk English was the Captain's wife, Captain Ericksson's wife. He wanted a tug immediately so we went up the valley and we were able to 'phone Torpoint for a tug boat to come up. It was some time later that the lifeboat came from Salcombe, and from Brixham and up from Plymouth; 'course the Hope Cove lifeboat wasn't in existence at that time, that had been done away with years before. That lifeboat finished around 1930 , the 'Alexandra', it was a rowing lifeboat and she was no longer needed as a rowing boat. I heard that they turned her into a yacht.

We were the first to contact the 'Herzogin' to know what they wanted, before the Salcombe lifeboat got down there and took off the Cadets running the ship.

Steve. *Do you remember anything of the First World War?*

Bill. Yes, airships in they days, more than aeroplanes. I can remember the first seaplane that left Plymouth with some important Navy person on board. It got into difficulties over Hope Cove and landed on Thurlestone beach. They had to take the man then by another seaplane to Portsmouth. Yes, we all went and saw this seaplane at Thurlestone.

I was about seven when my Uncle Steve was killed … late 1915: dear old Steve. I remember the trousers he wore when he left us, there was a red seam down the outside, and his uniform was very dark blue. They was taking 'em by bus to the railway at Brent and he ran up the hill to go to catch the train.

– ❖ –

Gladys Williams

Born 9th December 1904

Died 14th June 2004

Recorded on 9th October 2003

Gladys. I was born in Plymouth but we moved up to Batson because I was delicate, and they said the air would be better for me, and oh, it was lovely growing up in Batson; peaceful, quiet, all the people were friendly, nice. You'd never come to any harm in those days, there was always somebody looking out for you.

Steve. It must have been very quiet years ago - I can only imagine.

Gladys. Oh there was nothing, it was different altogether. You could hear something coming down the hill from a mile away: 'clip - clop, clip - clop'!

If I stood outside and you were talking down on the Quay I could hear what you were saying, it was so quiet. Of course there was no traffic, no noise.

Steve. What toys did you have?

Gladys. I had one little black doll, that one was rubber, and a little wooden one... a hoop and a

stick. The boys had metal ones, the girls wooden ones. Oh yes, whips and tops ... lovely, we never had a dull moment.

Daughter Ann. What about when Grandad brought the phonograph home?

Gladys. Oh yes, the phonograph! It was about that round: a tube, and a handle. We used to put it on a wooden chair outside the door and all the village used to be down on the Quay to hear it.

Mrs. Friend, she used to take in all the washing, do all the washing outside her door there on the flat, and my mother used to help with the wringing and hanging it out to dry, then take it all in and iron it all.

Daughter Elizabeth. You also used to put it on the hedges and bushes to dry!

Steve. Did everyone wear big hats then?

Gladys. Oh yes, massive great hats: hats with feathers, hats with bows, hats with streamers hanging down. Oh, my, you never knew what you were going to see with a hat! We kept them under the bed and before you put the lid on you had to make sure that the edge was flat: poke it all down, otherwise when you got it out the edge was all curled up. Oh, dear… those were the days, my dear!

Steve. *Do you remember when the first cars came in?*

Gladys. Oh yes! They had hard wheels first going off, we thought it was ridiculous, fancy having that… like that… we thought they'd never last, we all thought it was a load of old rummage.

Daughter Ann. *You used to come up from Plymouth sometimes, didn't you, in a horse-drawn wagon?*

Gladys. Oh yes, it was a wagon with seats on the sides, and the children used to sit on the floor. We'd moved back to Plymouth by then, see, and we had to get out and walk up the hills, 'cause it was too much for the horses. Oh, nobody was in a rush in those days.

My grandmother, Gran Ball, of Dartmouth, she had fifteen children of her own, and everyone called her 'Mother of Dartmouth'; she was out, this one, that one, there was no other nurse; she was the only one to do anything for anybody.

Daughter Elizabeth. *If anybody wanted a nurse or a midwife…*

Gladys. By the side of her bed was a great big bell, like you have in a church, and the rope went out the window down into the street… and at the bottom was a big knot at the end. No children ever pulled that, because that was for trouble that was, when the bell was pulled.

Father was a Chief Stoker, then a Chief Petty Officer, during the First World War. He was in one of these small boats…'picket' boats… in the North Sea, 'course it was dreadful because they'd fire at 'em and miss 'em by inches. That was the Battle of Jutland.

Gladys. I went to school in Salcombe, Courtenay Street, and we had to walk in all winds and weathers.

If she could afford it - Mother didn't always have it - but when she had a ha'penny to spend we'd give it to the baker that lived next door to the school, and then he'd write your name on a bag. At play time the teacher came out holding the corners of her apron with these little white bags with your name on, and you'd have a Chelsea bun, still warm and all sticky with sugar…lovely!

I wore button-up boots for Sundays, lace-up boots for in the week, and I had to wear a white apron. You always had a 'Sunday best' - you should have seen me on Sundays: white Chinese silk that was sent home from China where my father was. Mother used to get the dresses made up. I tell you… I was the 'cow's hind legs' I was on Sundays, and thought I was somebody too!

You should have seen me… silk dress, button boots up to me knees, and this hat with an ostrich feather sent by Uncle Jack from Cape Town.

After I left school I worked at 'Tinside', Plymouth Hoe bathing pool. I was about sixteen when I started there. If anyone went into the water and got into trouble, couldn't swim - which happened a lot - we had to go in and fetch 'em out. We had plenty of that, and one lot, three girls was in there larking about with three men who could swim. The men finally got out leaving these girls, they thought the girls could swim. They just went off and left them. Anyway, we had to go and fetch 'em in, so we each had a girl by the back of her costume and a lump of her hair… but anyrate we got 'em in.

Daughter Ann. *You had those bathing suits that went down to your toes. Somebody knitted you one once, didn't they?*

Gladys. Oh yes! I went in the water with this knitted bathing costume on… right up to here, lovely, posh! When I came out, the costume was right down here! Oh, dear!

We used to do flood-lit swimming in the evenings. The Hoe was packed with people sitting and standing just watching us swim. We did demonstrations and the one to go under water was always me!

Daughter Elizabeth. *Tell us about the people going out from Plymouth onto the Moor at night during the raids in the Second World War.*

Gladys. That was terrible, something that I shall never, ever forget. Round about four o'clock they would start coming out from Plymouth, some with prams with a few belongings on it, some carrying it, what ever way. Not speaking a word, just silent; and off they'd go, out to the Moors and get in around the banks… because the bombs were dropping everywhere. They used to get up there and get in under the hedges… in all winds and weathers. You had to go, or else… that was it… it was miserable.

One day we were standing at the end of Granby Street in Plymouth, waiting for a bus. Ann was small and they were making such a fuss of her. I was then told the bus would take off from the top of the road so we all moved and got up to the top of the road. I turned round and, right where we'd been standing, there was nothing left. It was a land mine and we'd been on that one… you see, you wouldn't know they were there.

Another time we were waiting for the bus and Ann was messing about, and then they called for us to get on the bus. As I was pulling her I thought, 'Come on, come on'. I turned round and she'd got her head stuck through the railings! The siren went for an Air Raid and we were there right through the blimmin' lot! Bombs were dropping down… bang, bang…. I was more concerned with getting her head out from the rails than the bombs coming down.

Oh dear, we've had some capers I can tell you… I wasn't never meant to die in the War!

Eileen Bartlett

Born 17th April 1905

Died 4th April 2004

Recorded on 12th December 2003

Eileen. I lived in Torquay and went to the Grammar school there, but I didn't want to become a teacher then: I was interested in doing telephone work, perhaps as an operator. I used to go on holiday to my grandmother's at Halwell and used to carry buckets of water from the pump down opposite the Rectory, all up to my grandmother's, up steps and all … and I was only a girl. You can pick up two large milking buckets full, quite easily with a 'square'.

We had to go to see the animals in the dark, the sheep and that so we took a farm lantern, an oil lantern - but you had to be careful with that one against your legs. Well, you see, you knew the way, and another thing, there wasn't all this crime about in those days. You were safe to walk on the roads and go anywhere. There used to be old tramps going around, they used to go around to the houses for a cup of tea, with their can; but they wouldn't hurt you.

Anyrate, some years later the vicar and one or two managers came to ask me if I would apply for the teaching post at Halwell, and between them and my grandmother they persuaded me… I was very fond of children.

Eileen is on the left with the spade

I went to Curledge Street in Paignton for a month, to do my training, which I didn't enjoy… waiting for the trams at Torquay seafront.

I taught at Halwell for twenty years, and I can tell you something interesting about school dinners: I think the actual person who started school dinners worked with me at Halwell, Mrs. Kerswell. The children used to have to walk to Halwell - there were no buses - and they used to get very wet. We used to dry all their clothes around the grate. Well, she felt sorry for them, and she had an idea… that every Wednesday the children could bring two potatoes each and a penny, so they could have a hot dinner… that was if a child walked to school; not those that lived in the village. She made arrangements with the butcher in Totnes and they would send her out a nice piece of beef.

She cut up the meat, and two of the bigger boys, different boys each day, skinned the potatoes as soon as they came in. Some farmers' boys would bring a turnip and carrots, and the stew was made every Wednesday. She bought a boiler to go on top of the old stove, and I think that was the beginning of school dinners!

From that one day a week it gradually increased to every day. The County supplied us with an oil stove then, which she put in the washhouse, and she used to make pies. Then they supplied a cook, Mrs. Penny - one of my Uncles' wives - and everything was set up in Halwell school… they used to enjoy it… and of course, the parents thought it was marvellous.

We had flush toilets at Halwell school and later on, when I went to East Allington school we didn't have any - the caretaker used to have to empty the buckets. I was disgusted, I really was; it shook me, because there at the cottage we had a flush toilet, yet up the hill at the school they hadn't.

Steve. *Do you remember when the first cars came in?*

Eileen. Yes, we thought they were awfully funny and used to laugh at them, but in the towns there were trams that ran along the main streets, we always caught them everywhere.

I had a Baby Austin 7, and used to drive myself. I had to learn to change the wheel and the plugs, and change the oil from underneath; that's a job I hated doing, lying on your tummy on a rag, and get in under and unscrew this thing; it was all greasy, I hated doing that. It was registered '7484' and all the handwork was on the steering wheel: the gear change was by little levers on the steering wheel. Some of you youngsters wouldn't be able to drive the car I drove then! Sometimes it wouldn't start, we'd have to push it down the road… the carburettor would sometimes overflow. Somebody in Dartmouth taught me how to drive and he used to say, "Take your duster with you"- well I did, I always had a duster and put it in the carburettor then wait a minute or two, and then it would start.

It was hard work when you had to use the starting-handle… you had to be careful with your thumb in case it backfired.

We were in Plymouth, going shopping, and as we were going in 'course there were Police there on duty, and he stopped the cars and of course my engine stopped. I knew I was going to have some trouble. The policeman came through and said; "You having trouble Missie? - let me have a go". He couldn't start it either… so I got me duster, pushed it in the carburettor… the carburettor was outside then, but of course now it's under the bonnet. I went to give it a turn and it turned beautifully! The Policeman said, "Well, I've learnt something today that I've never seen before, I've never seen anybody start a car with a duster"!

– ❖ –

William Stone

Born 23rd September 1900

Died 10th January 2009

Recorded in January 2004

William on his 106th birthday

As William was no longer living locally this interview was conducted by William's daughter, Mrs. Anne Davidson, using prompts and questions prepared by Stephen Pedrick.

William. I was one of fourteen children: George, Alice, Jack, Annie, Susan, Elsie, Carrie, Walter, Nellie, me, Laurie, Mabel, Flo, and Cecil.

I was born in a house called 'Pound House' in Ledstone. Pound house was where they pounded the apples... they crushed them down below the house where the horse used to go round in a circle working the crusher. The machinery was fixed on a rock to crush the apples... and then the pulp was put in a press... crushed apples and then layers of reed. They put the big press on it and the juice was put in barrels. Different farms used to bring their apples to be crushed and take the cider away.

There were three bedrooms, a living room and a large back kitchen... and a little pantry to keep all the small things. There were probably no more than four children living at home at any one time, because, as soon as the girls got of age they went to 'situations' - 'living-in service'... and the boys went on to farms to work.

Father's mother lived there, in one of the bedrooms, she was about eighty- odd, and she was confined to bed. Down under the rooms was a stable where we kept the pony... and his head used to bump the roof, up under the kitchen. Father used to say, "Tom's knocking his head again".

At the other end was fowls; we always used to keep about twelve fowls and it was very amusing in the morning, about five o'clock, when the cockerel crowed. Father used to say, "I'll cut his head off soon". In the distance from the house an extension was joined on and that was the pigs' house... and we kept a lot of wood and coal down there too. The lavatory was out in the corner of the garden; just slate to slide down, and in the back was a big pit, closed in with a door at the back where you cleaned it out. Mother used to paunch the rabbits, that all went in there as well... and when Father used to put it on the garden, oh, what a stink!

We didn't have any gas or electric in those days, just oil lamps and candles; in fact, we had a pony and trap with candles for lamps, big candles on each side of the trap.

People used to go to bed about half past eight, nine o'clock so they could get up early in the morning.

Anne. What jobs did the children do for Mother?

William. Once a week, on Saturday morning, 'cause we were home from school, we put the knives, forks and spoons out on the steps, and with a piece of wood with a piece of leather stuff on it... brick dust... we used to rub the knives up and down on there; principally to clean them, but it would sharpen them as well.

Anne. You said your father once lived at Stanborough Cross.

23

William. It was a Turnpike house years ago and my father's parents lived there; and across the road was a well where they used to get their water.

There's nothing there now at all, but years ago people had to pay to go along the turnpike.

Anne. How much did your father earn each week?

William. His wages as a farm labourer was about two pounds a week... but he used to slaughter pigs. He used to go all around the district, he used to ride a pony, and he charged a shilling a pig... then if he went the next morning to cut it up it was another sixpence.

We always kept two pigs. Father used to say you must have two... as one would try and eat faster and more than the other, and then they'd be fat quicker.

Sometimes we used to keep about half a pig and salt it in. Mother got the brine ready - put a peeled potato in the big container, and added salt until the potato floated; then that was good enough for salting in the pork.

Anne. In 1914 you were too young to join the Forces!

William. I went to join the Navy as a boy, but my father wouldn't sign the papers, he said I was too young. I had two brothers in the Navy... if he had signed my papers and I had joined I wouldn't be here today. That was the first year of the War, but in 1918 my father came to where I was working and said, "Your papers have arrived at home, for you to join the Army". That was two weeks before I was eighteen, so I caught the next train to Plymouth and joined the Navy! They sent me home, and the week before I was eighteen they called me up. I was doing my training in the Naval barracks while the end of the 1914 / 18 War was still on, and then I got the 'flu... the terrible 'flu.

I woke up in the gymnasium as the sick bay was full. Thousands of men died with the 'flu, more men than was killed in the War.

The Armistice was signed on the eleventh of November, 1918, and the gates was opened; we danced in the streets, singing and having a fine time.

After training in the Naval barracks I was drafted to 'H.M.S. *Tiger*', a battle cruiser being repaired at Rosyth Dockyard, after the beating up at the Battle of Jutland. After the refit we cruised to Scapa Flow and saw the German fleet that had

been scuttled, and we could still see some of the masts and funnels after they were on the seabed. Our cruiser had thirty-nine 'Babcock and Wilcox' boilers, and when we were coaling the ship we used to take in thousands of tons of coal. Everybody was in, all the Officers on deck, even the Band had their overalls on; in fact, we'd be nearly all day and all night coaling.

'Course we stokers were down in the bunkers, lit by our little oil lamps. Now, each boiler had four furnaces, and one was cleaned every twenty four hours... you used to rake out all the fire underneath, then put the hose on the ashes... all the steam would fly up in the air and then all the

ashes would be ejected; there'd be an ejector by the side of the ship that would blow it through.

Anne. When you'd been in those conditions with all that coal dust and yet you are so healthy and now a hundred and three!

William. It was hell, red hot, and when I came off watch I'd take off my flannel trousers - they were called 'fearnoughts' - and me vest, and hang 'em up on the rails... and when I went on watch again my trousers stood up on their own with the perspiration and the coal dust.

While I was based at Portland I bought a 'Swift' car, so I could drive to Kingsbridge where I lived. It was unusual then to have a car... I was the only one in the village then that had a car, now I'm the only one that *hasn't* got one! I had no trouble with a young lady then... I always had one to go with me!

Anne. Didn't someone offer to sell you a house in Goveton once?

William. Oh yes, the farmer at Longclose said, "William, do you want to buy a cottage, 'Rose Cottage'?- fifty pounds!" ... 'course I wasn't married then and I wasn't interested.

Freda Penwill

Born 6th March 1910

Died 18th October 2005

Recorded on 14th January 2004
& 16th April 2004

Freda. I was born in the pub at South Pool; it was the 'Union Inn' then. The toilets were right over the stream and next door to the pub. I remember it was a two-seater and quite high, I remember having a job to climb up there; and I used to go and hammer, or unlatch the door, and invariably there was somebody sitting there... they used to say, "Oh Freda, what are you doing? You mustn't come in here!" Then, after that we had this 'Elsan' thing which was smelly and horrible!

All those houses, right down through the village, nobody had any sanitation at all, no hot water, none at all.

Next to the pub lived Mrs. Caunter, a marvellous old lady who used to keep ducks galore. It would be nothing for her to kill twenty ducks in a morning; she'd start about four in the morning killing them, 'course the poor old things would be screaming. She had a little shed she used to pluck them in.

They used to have 'rent dinners'. I've heard my mother say that she'd cooked a turkey and a huge round of beef, and perhaps a leg of lamb or mutton, and then the spare bedroom Mum used to turn into a dining room. All the farmers used to bring their rents, most of the village too. Most of the farms were owned by Captain Hallifax in those days, he was at Halwell House, well then the Molesworth-St. Aubyns lived there; they were there during the First World War, I know.

I was only three when I went to school. I know I thought I was quite clever because they had frames with wire and coloured beads, and I could count up to twenty. I thought I was much cleverer than the rest of them, some couldn't count up to ten. We used to have slates then you see, with horrible slate pencils; a pencil of slate, oh they were horrible, scratchy, yes I can remember that.

Mr. Chase, the schoolteacher would have 'magic lantern' parties, and when we'd finished the boys would take us home with the lantern.

Steve. Did you get travelling salesmen coming into the village?

Freda. Oh yes, Baker Bob used to come from Beesands; he lived at the extreme end of Beesands and when Hallsands was washed away I remember he couldn't come then, because all his bread and that was washed away. I remember it very well; I was six at the time - I remember going out there on a Sunday to see it.

The butcher used to call with a horse and van on Tuesdays and Fridays. Henry Cleave he was called, from Slapton. He used to go all around: Hallsands, Beesands, Prawle... it was about eight o'clock in the evening sometimes, before he got there.

Steve. There was a lot of cider drunk then.

Freda. Oh yes, an enormous amount - we used to have two hogsheads and a half I think it was, in a shed adjoining the house; 'course Dad, in the winter, would love to chop up wood for the fire, because, you see, he'd be drinking all that time! A hogshead is the biggest one - a big tall one, taller than I am now; it used to be tapped just before Christmas.

We'd love to go to Ford Chapel on Good Friday because they had a wonderful chapel tea; beautiful cakes, huge slab cakes from 'Parkhouses' in Kingsbridge…oh, about the size of that tray - you don't get lovely cakes now like they used to make. Mum always used to have one in the house, I think it used to be about seven pounds in weight and I think it was four and sixpence she used to pay.

We'd all go in the Chapel… forty or fifty of us, all sat around. I think tea used to be ninepence a head, we'd have lovely splits and butter, cream and jam, and then have evening service afterwards!

It's all been torn down sadly like some other chapels, but I remember going to one or two weddings there… and two or three funerals.

Celia Shepherd used to walk to Molescombe from Pool, and she always wore a little shawl over her shoulders and a man's peak cap. My mother was in the pub then and Celia used to start the day on a glass of ale. She used to have a half-pint glass, I think it was a ha'penny then in those days. The Prettejohns used to live at Molescombe, quite a big family, and dear old Celia used to go and do a whole day's washing for all that family for a shilling, and then walk all the way home, and have another glass of ale… poor old soul!

In those days there were carriers, there was no other means of getting to and fro. There was about six or seven carriers on the Quay at Kingsbridge, all lined up, covered vans. They used to go from Pool on a Monday, Wednesday, Friday and on a Saturday. They'd bring back anything you wanted: boots, shoes, reels of cotton… you could get anything, and sometimes there might be about six passengers. It wasn't a very comfortable ride, you'd have the rabbit hampers you see; hampers of rabbits used to go away by train to Birmingham and Manchester, 'course there were porters in Kingsbridge station, there were two or three of them. I remember one of them had white hair, snow white and they used to call him 'The Ferret'.

I can hear them now shouting, "Ferret, are you there?"… they'd want him to give a hand with these hampers and put them in the goods carriage.

When I was about eight, in the First World War, I remember seeing a Zeppelin going over. I was in the bath in front of the fire and Mum wrapped me up in a blanket and carried me out to see this thing. I heard that it dropped several bombs in London and then crashed.

There was a dinner, in appreciation for the soldiers, just after the First World War. They cooked in the copper where the beer was brewed; they used that for all the plum puddings, and to cook the meat. I remember four or five farmers carving… I can see these huge rounds of meat, you never see them like it now. They had this frozen custard…a kind of ice-cream I suppose. I remember seeing these great blocks of ice in a sack, all in sawdust. I'm not sure how they did it, but Mum and Mrs. Elliott had a machine there that they made this custard in and then froze it.

In 1918 I was very ill, in bed with 'flu: during the epidemic. I can remember Dr. Webb coming to see me, 'course the Doctors used to ride a horse back then, there was no car. Doctor Webb hadn't come when it was eight o'clock in the evening, so Rose Parker put a candlestick in a bucket, lit the candle and walked all the way around the village to everybody that was ill, looking for Doctor Webb. He'd been out since seven o'clock that morning… he'd been to Beesands, Beeson and all around there, on horseback, looking after sick people.

Apparently they didn't expect me to live or some darn thing, but anyway, I cheated the crows and I'm still around now !!

I went to Moorhaven as a nurse in 1928, and I did twenty-three years there.

I started in 'E' Ward, the Infirmary ward. The Matron would do the round and she'd put her finger round the door: "Sister, was this dusted this morning?" - and the nurse would be for it if it hadn't! She was very strict, but you learnt by it.

I always remember the 'Newcastle', the big battleship…the bay was full of ships to preserve Plymouth and the people… and the searchlights that went up were marvellous. I remember one night, I was Sister then - I'd been Sister for some time - I was in the 'pads' with about fourteen

patients because that was the safest place to be. I'd previously been out on the terrace watching all these searchlights going up - you could see to read a newspaper on the terrace. I was in 'C' Ward then, it had a beautiful view over Mothecombe bay. I didn't want to go in the underground cellar because … I've thought about it so many times since… you see, all the central heating pipes were underneath and, well, if a bomb had dropped on one of those we'd have been scalded to death; it's horrible to think of it.

Ralph Pepperell

Born 16th November 1907

Died 19th January 2005

Recorded on 30th January 2004

Ralph. I had three brothers and four sisters, and I was the youngest. They didn't expect me to live because I was so weak. In those days they used to insure children for a penny a week insurance, to cover any funeral expenses if they died early. Well, the Insurance Company wouldn't accept the premium for myself.

I was born in Robinson's Row, Salcombe… two bedrooms, a kitchen and a sitting room. The daughters went out to 'service' when they left school and there was four boys left. Some of us used to sleep down in the lounge at night, and Dad made a leaf for the table, to extend it so that everyone could sit and have a meal at the same time. We had candles in those days, no electric light. I remember a representative of the Gas company came and said would we like gas installed in the house and I said, "No, I'll have electricity!". He said, "You'll never get electricity up here".

There was an outside tap in the courtyard out at the back, and shared between four cottages; one tap, no water indoors. Mother used to cook with an old-fashioned 'Lidstone' oven and grate… coal. I've never known anyone cook such nice meals as my mother, we used to have rabbit every Sunday… delicious!… the way Mother cooked it, with suet pudding.

Steve. *Where did you buy your clothes?*

Ralph. Mother used to make them. I remember one year she made me a lovely suit with knickers that buttoned up below the knee, and one Sunday morning when I was going to Sunday school I fell in a pool of water… wasn't she angry when I got home.

Steve. *What do you remember about the First World War?*

Ralph. I was only seven when it broke out. My eldest brother joined the Navy. He got mined up in the Baltic and stepped from one destroyer to another that came alongside and all he had was a blanket. They struck the mine at night you see, he was in his hammock. Then he travelled up to Scapa Flow and from there to Plymouth with only the blanket. When he got to Plymouth they supplied him with a new uniform.

The other two brothers were in the boatbuilding industry and they were building whalers for the Navy, they weren't called up.

Steve. *Do you remember the old aeroplanes?*

Ralph. Oh yes, bi-planes… we used to go over to Prawle on Sunday afternoon and evening watching them training… taking off and landing, and on one Sunday one pilot was too low, his wheel caught the hedge and he landed with his nose on the ground and his tail up in the air.

I went to school in Salcombe until I was eleven, then I won a Boarding scholarship to Kingsbridge Grammar school; that's where the Cookworthy Museum is now. The boundary was Gill's paper shop, we weren't allowed to go further than that, but one Saturday lunchtime we all trooped down to a shop about six, ten yards beyond the boundary. The Headmaster came down the road and found us out of bounds and he said, "Go up into the Long Room". About ten of us got three strokes across the backside with his walking stick!

I think there was five of us in our dormitory; there was always some pillow-fighting going on. The two rooms there, the doors were opposite each other and we used to have a pillow-fight with five in one room and five in the other - until we were told to stop it and go to bed.

Steve. *What was the food like?*

Ralph. Oh, all right - except Mondays, you had horse flesh on Mondays; it was bluish in colour, not appetising at all. The Masters were: Brown for History, Wykes used to teach Mathematics; Wood taught Latin and Broders used to teach French.

Steve. *Did you like learning Latin?*

Ralph. No, no couldn't understand it.

Steve. *What sort of games did you play in Salcombe?*

Ralph. The most exciting one was putting a bottle or a tin on the water at Whitestrand and trying to sink it with the stones the Council left there. They used to dump the stones there for road making and we used to use them.

I remember distinctly the tragic accident of the lifeboat. I was at school then, 1916. The Headmaster was notified and he closed the school and sent us all home. Father was a lifeboatman at one time, when they had the old sailing and rowing boats.

Steve. *When did you do your sailing?*

Ralph. Before I left Salcombe. I won eight trophies in three years in three different boats.

Steve. *When you left Grammar school, what was your first job?*

Ralph. I was a Clerk in the District office of the Pearl Assurance company in Kingsbridge, and after two years they wanted to transfer me to the Head office in London, to train as an actuary, but with the smog and smoke in London I decided not to go.

I got a job with a builder in Salcombe, as a carpenter. All the four butchers in Salcombe used to send their saws to Dad to sharpen, and he used to give me the short ones to sharpen. I could sharpen a saw when I was fifteen. There was only one person I've known who sharpened a saw better than I could and that was Harold Finch; he'd been a forester in Canada and then he came back to Salcombe.

I left Murch's and went to Birmingham and studied. The first year I paid the tuition fees but for the five years after that I did so well that I got free admissions. When I finished the final year I got 100% in Statistics, and for Dynamics, 100% Maths, and 93% for Surveying. They asked me to join the teaching staff then, and I did twenty-two years, first at the College of Advanced Technology, which was converted into Aston University. My fellow student got a job as a Lecturer in Houston, Texas, and the last I heard of him he'd been made a Professor.

Steve. How did the Second World War affect Birmingham?

Ralph. There were raids and I was mostly supervising the making of decoy crates filled with wood shavings and creosote, to put on isolated sites around Birmingham. When a raid came they set fire to them to attract the bombers to bomb there instead of bombing the city.

Steve. Tell me the story of your friend with his binoculars.

Ralph. Oh yes, when he stayed with me he didn't open the window and as he looked through them with the binoculars everything was distorted and he said, "Ralph, those cows over there have got six teats"… I said, "Yes, it's a special breed they developed in this part of Devon: four for milk and two for cream!"

Steve. And that was because the glass was old?

Ralph. Yes, when they make glass now they make it on a bed of mercury to get a true surface, but the old glass in the house was distorted so when you looked through it, say, looked at a down-pipe, it seemed to have two or three bends in it; that's why the cows were distorted when he looked at them!

– ❖ –

Bill Widger

Born 28th November 1906

Died 5th January 2008

Recorded on 6th February 2004

Bill. I was the eldest of nine and we had to walk from Cole's Cross to East Allington to school. I went to school for four years without missing a day - that was an achievement in they days.

I had a medal, size of a five-shilling piece, and each year they sewed a bar on the ribbon. A girl called Bessie Quick went to the same school and 'er'd 've been eleven years without missing… 'er lived in the village, see.

The Headmaster was called Buswell then… we were always pleased to see a traction engine coming with the thresher… oh aye, all at the gate to look at 'en.

It was a very good treat, in the summer time, down on the lawn at Fallapit; the whole school would go down there and have a tea party, lemonade to drink… different lemonade than it is today. Mother used to make her own lemonade: buy the crystals and put hot water on them to dissolve them. 'Eiffel Tower' lemonade it was called… a nice taste that was.

Me uncle lived in Addlehole, see, and kept cows, and he had a milk round, used to go Kingsbridge every day. I used to go and help deliver from a horse and trap if I was staying there.

He had a fairly high trap and the churn stood in the back of 'en, and you drawed the milk off out of a tap, without having to get up in the trap. People would come out with their jugs, and some you would deliver with cans.

Some, they'd be 'fraid to show their self, they'd put their hand out around with the can... perhaps they wad'n dressed proper, see!... 'fraid the boys would see something!

Milking was all done be hand; generally farms had a dozen cows perhaps. You'd get out early in they days, not wait 'til the sun got up! If you were a labourer you used to come to work 'bout seven; you see, the horses would have to be fed, get the cows in and start milking...no milking- machines then. The milk used to be separated, each farm had a separator. The cream would come out one spout and the milk out the other. They used to rear calves with separated milk and the cream had to be made into butter to sell, used to make it up into pounds and half-pounds to take to market at Totnes; 'twould be sold by auction - the best butter would make the best price.

Steve. *What games did you play when you were a boy?*

Bill. 'Hare and hounds', used to play dinner times, another was 'Paper chase'; you dropped bits of paper and they had to follow... we went all out around the farms, but us was told off if us wad'n back be school time.

Lord Ashcombe owned Fallapit House and used to come there several weeks in the summer. He lived up Reading and Fallapit House was his country estate, see... not only that, he owned ever so many farms around East Allington. He had several working for 'en and he would drive round and inspect the farms. There used to be a 'rent day'; they used to come up 'Fortescue Arms' to pay the rent, once a year. I remember seeing the farmers down there congregating when us was up school on rent days.

Steve. *Where did you get your water from at Cole's Cross?*

Bill. From a well, yes, you had a windlass with a chain and bucket on it... you had to put 'en down and wind 'en up to get your water.

When we were living at Churchstow I walked from there up to Paignton to visit my aunts. I was still a youngster then, going school... used to go Kingsbridge Show, that was an outing... it was up Highhouse Farm then.

In Kingsbridge there was Bowman's Garage up top of the town - motor repairers, really. Then there was Quay Garage down the bottom that used to supply cars, and next was Ryeford Garage that supplied a make of car called 'Clyno'. Several farmers out and about had them; a compact little car, nice to look at.

I left school when I was thirteen, I'd done all me attendances, see, that's why I could leave earlier.

In they days most corn was cut with a binder, though I have cut it with a scythe... difficult pieces. You'd generally have three horses in a binder, especially if 'twas on an awkward or hilly field. Two horses would do a level field, and the same would apply with ploughing. I bought me Fordson tractor in 1941, they was just coming in on farms in about 1940, after the War started, but it was difficult to get them. I used to grow a fair bit of corn during the War; you was compelled to grow more. At harvest time us used to drive to the corn ricks with horses and wagons; about three or four horses going all the time; one with the folks up the field loading the sheaves, one would be coming down with a load, one unloading, and there'd be the empty one down there ready for me to take up again.

I was interested in steam when I was going school, used to see Goodman's come there with a thresher; 'twas a fine job to see and hear this engine coming up from Venn, 'course he'd be puffing coming up from there.

Goodman's had four traction engines, four sets: that's threshing-machines and engines. Their depot was out Holset, East Portlemouth, that's where they worked from. Certain drivers had a district... I knew the one that had East Allington district, called Jimmy Yalland, from Chillington. The thresher used to go around to different farms and he'd have, say, four ricks. He'd pull the thresher in between them and thresh them all before he moved on. It was a dusty job sometimes, but it needn't be if it was picked up in good condition.

The farmer used to supply the dinner; sometimes you'd go in to dinner and sometimes you'd have home-made pasties brought out to the field, see... have cider if you wanted it, or tea.

We used to take the sacks of corn with horses and wagons into Bonds, merchants down on the Quay. He bought it and we'd deliver it fer 'en in 'West of England' sacks; they was two hundred-weights, you had to be strong to carry 'em. The boat used to come up there, the 'Steam Packet', used to come up to collect things - 'twad'n only corn, 'twas anything they wanted to shift down Salcombe way, or Plymouth.

Fred Jeffery

Born 28th April 1915

Rose Jeffery

Born 20th January 1918

Recorded on 27th February 2004
& 19th October 2006

Rose. I was born in Keyham, Devonport, and came

to Salcombe when I was about four or five. We camped out on Millbay Sands for the summer because we had nowhere to live. Then eventually a cousin of Dad's in Salcombe let us stay with her... and then Dad got a house in Church Street.

We'd moved around because he was in the boat-building trade, I suppose in the Dockyards, because my brother was born in Kingswear when Dad worked for Philips in Dartmouth, and two of my sisters were born at Southampton when he went there to work. Kitty was born in Weymouth, 'cause he worked for Philips over there, and I was born in Plymouth. He came back to Salcombe then and set up his own business.

Gran Cook, that's Dad's mum, she lived to be eighty-eight I think, and she always wore very black clothes with a little 'poke' bonnet, long black skirts. I never saw her in anything but black.

I used to have 'cocoa sops' for breakfast: you cut up bread, put in sugar and cocoa and then pour boiling water over it... and a drop of milk. Mum would buy a four-penny sheep's head and make a lovely stew out of it... the tongue and the brains; I always say that's where I got all my brains from! Well, if we had a rabbit I always used to have the head and eat the brains and the tongue. Sometimes we had cooked meat and vegetables, or fried potatoes and cold meat, something like that... not pizzas and stuff like they have now. We used to fetch our milk from the farm each morning in cans.

When you had chilblains on your toes you'd dip them in the 'charlie pot'... that's the best thing because it contains ammonia, I've done it myself. If you had a cold they used to say to rub your chest and the bottoms of your feet with camphorated oil.

I went to school at Salcombe Infants School, which was in Courtenay Street. I remember in the morning we took a penny to Mr. Rich the baker, and had a hot currant penny bun for our lunchtime. As we went past the shop there was a grating over the bake-house underneath... and the beautiful smell of the buns cooking. Then when I was at the Girls School we used to come to Kingsbridge from Salcombe for cookery and laundry lessons, and Mother used to say, "I can't give you your father's dirty shirt, here, take a clean one out of the drawer"... you had to take your own laundry in... and Loddiswell used to come in the same day.

Steve. Fred, you went to work at Longclose?

Rose. Yes, from the time he left school at fourteen until he was sixty-five... fifty-one years.

Fred. I got half a crown a week...five bob a week... ten bob.... couple of quid... and it was thirty bob I got married on. It was all horses and carts... the binder...

Rose. ...and sowing seeds with a 'sillup'.

Fred. ... and the old scythe - nowadays all they got to do is use their fingers, just press buttons for this and that.

We used to keep twenty cows, milking cows, and a few younger ones, outdoors... hand milk 'em!

Rose. They had names didn't they, 'cause you had to keep a chart of their milk, so they had to have names... Buttercup and Daisy. It's all numbers now; everybody's a number these days.

They used to let 'em out to come down here in the fields after they'd milked 'em: didn't need to drive 'em, they knew exactly where to go... leaving their visiting card as they went up past! Mrs. Johns used to be there billowing her apron to try and shoo 'em on, to try to get 'em in the field before they did what they wanted to do.

It was all orchards down here, you had to get out in the morning and pick up all the apples before the cows came down, else they'd eat them. They were lovely eating apples, 'Royal Red Streaks'.

Steve. Did you make cider up here at Longclose ?

Fred. Oh, yeah, that was when I was going 'school, years ago. They used to crush the apples down and had a 'umpteen-gallon' trough catching the juice coming out... and before us went to school us used to go up, have a glass, and swig cider as it was coming out.

Steve. You started young!

Rose. Yeah ... and been at it ever since!

Steve. Do you think things are better now?

Rose. Well yeah, tractors can go on... the horses had to stop... you've got to compete, I suppose, in these days.

We had to feed the horses and they had to be looked after, so that was work before you started.... yes, seven days a week job you know. We never had a holiday until Peggy left school, apart from our honeymoon.

When we lived down 'Brook Cottage' you had to go out and fetch the water on washing day. We had a great big iron boiler to heat up and first you would put in a lot of whites and bring it to boil. Then you had to rinse it, and 'blue' it, and mangle it to squeeze out the water... if you didn't look out you could break the buttons - unless they had rubber buttons. Sometimes I was working here 'til nearly five o'clock... still working, doing the washing... now you put it in and switch on and it washes itself.

The toilet was out over the brook, the people next door used to come down the little path, outside by our back door, to get to theirs.

I first worked at St. Elmo, for one season, and then I went to work at Bowringsleigh. I can remember having one of these big trunks with all my bits and pieces in; not a tin one, but one of these big brown ones with wooden ends on it. I went there as under housemaid, there was another housemaid over me and then there was the head housemaid, Miss Bowden. Then there was the housekeeper, the cook, the kitchen maid, the butler and the pantry boy... and there were men outside.

We had a half day off in the week and Sunday every other week. I slept right up at the top - all the rooms at the top the staff used to live in - there was a back staircase and a corridor going along to the bedrooms. Some of the boys slept out over the stables, I think; there were stables there in the yard.

Every morning when they used to milk the cows Miss Ilbert would fill up several glasses of milk, and mid-morning we used to go and pick up a glass to drink. I shared a bedroom with another girl - just a bed and a wardrobe or a chest of drawers. We didn't have much clothes anyhow; you had your uniform on all day so you didn't need much clothes… only when you went out, once a week, for your half day and had to be back by nine o'clock… so coming back across the lawn I used to put my watch back…"Oh, sorry Miss Bowden, my watch must be slow"!

We would get up about half past six, I think … you were supposed to finish downstairs before breakfast. Once they'd had breakfast you weren't supposed to be doing the downstairs rooms then. You had to clean all these big rooms with a 'Bissell' brush… either that or a hard broom, which raised the dust… no carpet-sweepers or electricity in those days.

There was all this carved stuff and a lot of brass to clean. Then you had to go upstairs and do cleaning up there, while they were downstairs. It was hard work, you had to go in the bedrooms and black-lead the fire-places.

In the evening you had to put the Lady's clothes out, lay it out ready for her to wear to dinner… their underwear and their shoes… and if that dress wasn't right she'd ring the bell and you had to go down and get a different one.

I used to wait at table sometimes… and when the table was laid it looked beautiful, the candles and the silver… and the glasses. Then go round and turn the beds down, back 'three-corner-way', and pull the curtains.

We mended their clothes, darning and things like that… you would finally finish at bedtime, nine o'clock or something like that.

Steve. What uniform did you wear?

Rose. In the morning it was blue dresses and a white apron, and in the afternoon a brown dress and an ecru apron… everything went to the laundry.

Steve. Bowringsleigh is a huge house, isn't it.

Rose. Well, yes… a great dining room and another big room… the study and a little passage to the back door and the staff quarters. Then the Mrs' study and the door at the other side that went to the drawing room, a great long room… from there was the billiard room with doors leading out onto the lawn. There was a room where she used to do the flowers…then upstairs; at the far end of the bedrooms was a nursery, and Mr. Tim's room, which nobody was allowed to go in - that was the son that got killed. There must have been some guest rooms 'cause they had guests come there. I used to have a

photo of the house, it had a big tower, and a chapel. We had morning prayers in the dining room, but we never had a service in the chapel.

My brother was killed in the War… he was the apple of their eye, 'cause there was only one boy with four girls. Dad never got over it and more or less died of a broken heart; he never worked again; that was 1941.

My brother was thirty-six and had a wife and two children… he was on the 'Gloucester', they never stood a chance. Evidently he was in the supply branch, which was right where the bomb dropped…. he was the oldest and I was the youngest.

Steve. What about rationing in the Wartime?

Rose. Well, out here you could catch rabbits, and you had eggs and things like that. We managed on our bit of offal that was about, and you could grow your own vegetables and stuff like that.

– ❖ –

Winifred Easterbrook

('Auntie Winnie')

Born 14th March 1912

Recorded on 17th March, 2004

Winifred. I was born at Town Farm, East Prawle;

one of twins. My mother had twelve, but only raised four; they all died in infancy, or when they were born. I suppose years ago they never had the care like they have today. I only remember one, a boy born after Jack and me, 'course they had big families years ago. Mother had another lot of twins, twin girls before us.

Steve. *Did you have a village midwife?*

Winifred. Yeah, somebody in the village would tend to that person… an older woman. Sometimes there were complications; they just had to deal with it as best they could. I don't suppose they were very hygienic and all that, not like today; the same as Mother with those children… perhaps they died as soon as they were born, you see they didn't have the care or the cleanliness.

They had big families then, even when I remember there was always six or seven, you see. They had no sort of preventatives, they were often living in just 'one up, one down', but they managed, it wasn't like it is today. Hygiene standards were much lower than today, you wouldn't wash your hands very often in hot water! You just couldn't do it!

I remember the First World War… I remember the planes, 'cause the farmers gave up a couple of fields to become an 'aerodrome', and it's still called 'aerodrome' now. There was men from the village that was in the War, several people here that went was maimed and came home. My cousin Bert, whose father was the shoemaker here, he went to War and was shot right through the face. He was missing, presumed killed, and then a message came through to say that he was found, but wounded… but he survived it.

My father was a farmer, born and died in the same farmhouse… and *his* father was a farmer before him, that lived there. My mother was born at East Portlemouth and taught in the village school, an under-teacher. She played the organ in the village church there, and I've still got the same organ now… I suppose when they had a pipe organ, I daresay they gave it to Mother. It was at home all my young life, and what lovely evenings we used to have with it, with the hymns. The headmistress of our village school, Miss Langdon, taught me to play.

We had the piano and the organ at home, and Mother could play the fiddle; in fact, all her brothers could play the fiddle… I had a wonderful childhood.

I remember Mother's father, Grandfer Stone…he was lovely, he used to grow early vegetables out on the cliffs at Portlemouth, and used to go to Salcombe to sell them. Well, everybody grew their own stuff in their gardens, and everybody kept a pig… and fowls and ducks.

In Prawle we had two shops, two public houses, a dressmaker, a shoemaker - which was my uncle - a proper shoemaker, learnt his trade… a blacksmith and, of course, we had travellers come with pots and pans, and paraffin oil. I've still got an 'Aladdin' lamp here now, and we always had to have candles. Two bakers came from Frogmore and East Portlemouth, and the butchers three times a week. Everything was brought to the door then. People couldn't afford cars, a lot of people only went to Kingsbridge once a year, for Kingsbridge Fair.

We used to have Prawle Fair on Whit Monday and Miss Pritchard used to come from Kingsbridge with her pony and trap, and all her 'fairing' and glorified 'ice-cream'… custard and all that, and well… a sixpence would buy more than you wanted, 'cause farthings counted as well. Then in the evening there would be a 'kiss-in-the-ring', out in one of the fields. They'd come from Beesands, all around, and then somebody would come and knock you out… you'd go running and when they caught you they'd kiss you… 'course you could easily slip up in a cow dab as you was going around!

Steve. What about harvest time?

Winifred. Oh, that was the time... taking 'drinkings' out in the field. Mother would make big currant buns - rock buns - and sandwiches. We'd put a white cloth in the basket, packed with cups, and go out in the harvest field with 'drinkings'... a big copper kettle where they'd put a potato in the spout, to save it splashing out. Then you'd see the rabbits come out; this was in the days of the binder you know.

Steve. Quite different today isn't it!

Winifred. Oh yeah! That'll never come again, will it... stitches in the field, 'stooks' they call it, which were left to dry out.

When it had to be threshed two men would come with the threshing- machine... about six o'clock for breakfast... and then we'd get help from the farmers around; we've had as many as eighteen to dinner... a great big round of beef, and perhaps apple pasties or something after.

There were no tarred roads years ago. They used to bring a load of stones, and I can remember a roadman would be sitting knocking up these stones to put on the road. He would sit there all day with a bag on his knees breaking up these stones for the road; then a steamroller would come and roll them in.

Eventually my people had a greengrocery business in Dartmouth where they sold their own vegetables.

I remember going to Dartmouth with two horses in the trap, and the fore-horse was called Polly; she must have know every blade of grass on the way. I remember too, going to Dartmouth Regatta in the horse and van, when I was young with my twin brother, and they'd make a bed with potato bags for us in the van; we'd soon be asleep, 'cause you see, it was four or five hours each way.

Children left school at fourteen, but I stayed on 'til I was fifteen because Miss Langdon wanted me to stay on and be an Assistant. Well, when I was fifteen my people took the shop in Dartmouth, and I had to leave school then to be the 'Missus' at home with somebody to help me, a girl that lived in. We had cows of course, and a separator... made cream, and I could make butter.

Steve. How did you make the butter?

Winifred. Yes, well you got a wooden butter bucket and then scalded your hands in real hot water, and then get 'em cold under a tap with cold water... then you were ready to turn the cream, with your hand. It was separated cream you see, and you'd turn it with your hand until gradually buttermilk drains out of it. Then you tip that off and wash out the surplus buttermilk with cold water, and mix in some salt. It's ready then to make into a round, or we'd do it square with 'Scotch hands', and put a pattern of a cow on top, with a press. It was sold around the village, and people would come with their jugs for milk and cream.

We'd kill a pig, and that was cruel... a living pig tied to a pig's-form, and then the pig-killer would come and cut his throat; then down at the barn at the bottom of the court they'd hang the pig up, cut it open, and do all that. We used to make hog's pudding; my mother would cut up the pig, joint it up and salt it in, in what they called 'standards', great big earthenware pots.

Steve. Where did you get your water from?

Winifred. ... down at the well; three parts of the village have got their own well where people had to go to fetch their water in buckets... this one out here never went dry. We had a tank next to the Rayburn, you'd tip the water in and that always kept warm. We used to fill that every night... it had a tap at the bottom. You were always careful how much you used 'cause you'd have to go and fetch some more.

A lot of women would go picking sticks from the hedgerows 'cause you had to light a fire every day in the Lidstone stove. On washing day you had to light the 'copper' and when it boiled you put the clothes in to boil.

I worked hard, made cream and butter, and we had an acre of peas in a field, 'cause my people used to go to Dartmouth market, and I used to go and help in the shop; by then they had a car.

I was in Dartmouth when it was bombed during the Second World War... a split second and it could have been our shop... a split second and it could have been me... terrible, frightening... a busy Saturday morning in Dartmouth, and there was people killed in the street; 'twas silent, people were listening for trapped people in the rubble.

Steve. Was there a lot more trust of people then?

Winifred. Oh, you'd go to Kingsbridge and you wouldn't lock your door, now I don't go up in the garden without I lock the door. Gypsies used to come around with their wares, all sorts of things: linen buttons, wooden pegs that they used to make themselves and sell. You see, I've lived in the best of times.

– ❖ –

Phyllis Hutchings

Born 9th July 1913

Recorded on 2nd April 2004

Dolly. We was born there opposite Coleridge Lane, in Chillington; there were six of us, four girls and two boys. Us all had 'do our bit. We used to go to Darnacombe Farm to see Grandpa and Granny Mitchelmore… it was a hell of a long way, mind you! … and Phyllis, 'er used to be pushed in the pram. That was to collect the blankets for washing, and when they lived at Kernborough me and my brother had to pull the old pram up Tanpits Lane, with a bit of old rope tied to the front…'ell of a long way, and 'twas steep… and 'er was molly-coddled in the pram.

Steve. Do you remember anything about the First World War?

Dolly. 'Course I do, my Daddy was in the First World War… Ypres, in France, he was away nearly all the war. He had shrapnel in his eye and he got shot through the leg.

We lived at Torcross when Daddy was in the Army, and was there when Hallsands was washed away. The waves were so big that the sea joined the Ley… and the water came all down the chimney and was all around our feet and up the stairs. At that time Mummy had a new baby, my younger sister.

At Christmas, if you was lucky, you had a sugar

Dorothy (Dolly) Parsliffe

Born 5th July 1911

Died 21st January 2009

mouse in your stocking and a few nuts. One year when Daddy was coming up the stairs, he slipped and dropped the nuts. Oh dear! Father Christmas lost his nuts!

We had one great big bed that Daddy bought when he came out of the Army and us used to sleep two at the top and two at the bottom…

Phyllis. …everybody had someone else's feet in their face…. and 'twould be two of us in the pram usually too, a boat-shaped pram!

Dolly. My mum she used to made 'ogs puddin' for sale; she done a lot of pigs' bellies …you know what that is - 'ogs puddin', yes, you've never tasted nothing like it.

Phyllis.… made with groats. I can see Mum now, with a stick pulling 'em inside out.

Dolly. … 'er had an ol' pokin' stick… and 'er used to pull the pots, like this…

Phyllis. Yeah, down over the stick… then put 'em in salt water, and then, next day, put 'em in another lot, before you filled 'em.

Dolly

Dolly. … and after school, I used to come home and get that 'ogs puddin', and with an old market basket on my arm, walk down Torcross and Beesands. Us 'ad our proper customers there!

Mum used to bath us nightimes… four maidens… and do our hair up in rags, for curls. Then we had a toilet down the bottom of the garden… with a bucket and a wooden seat… and newspaper and brown paper all up on a nail… sometimes there wad'n a bit of newspaper and the brown paper was a bit stiff! I used to go out and scrub that old thing, Saturdays.

Phyllis. … scrub the seat , clean out the bucket, do the floor…

Dolly. …nobody else didn't like it… and then when us was out there one of the younger ones would scratch on the door and frighten us, 'cause the rats used to get in and we used to be scared stiff.

Phyllis. We emptied all our rubbish in there, what Dad called 'the pit' and then he used to use all that for the garden.

Dolly. Daddy used to have a nice onion and do'en for breakfast, I used to like that.

Phyllis. Mum used to put an onion in the fire 'til the juice was coming out - you'd let it cool off a bit to put in your ear for earache. Then she used to make this ointment… we used to go and pick penny-pancakes and primroses… a lot of things… done with 'sweet oil'.

Dolly. … houseleek… and ground ivy, to make Mummy's ointment, boil it and strain it.

Steve. *What was it used for?*

Dolly & Phyllis.…anything…anything …sure to cure!!

Phyllis. Me and my brother Bert used to go up Frittiscombe Lane to a field and put in mole traps. We used to skin the moles and tack 'em on to a board, and when they were dry we sent 'em away for coats and that… and we'd get money for 'em. We were always paid in coins, no notes back than.

Dolly. I was paid in farthings when I worked in the laundry, they were very tiny coins.

Phyllis. I've got a 'third of a farthing', I don't know how long ago they were used; but a farthing was a quarter of a penny, then it was the ha'penny, the penny…tuppenny-bit, thruppenny-bit, and sixpenny-bit. After that it was the shilling, then the florin: that was two shillings.

Dolly. Half a crown, that was two and six, and next up it was a pound. After that there was a guinea: one pound, one shilling. Yes it was all coins, until later on when the ten-shilling notes were brought in…but we used to call a sixpence a 'tanner' and a shilling a 'bob'.

Phyllis. On Market days we used to be scared stiff, 'cause the blimmin' cows would be coming in the kitchen. They used to walk all their cattle from further out, to Kingsbridge Market. Grandad Mitchelmore used to go in to the Market Hall where they sold butter, cream, rabbits and that. Butter was sold then for one and nine a pound.

Phyllis

When we were young I was always dressed in blue and Dorothy in red. We had hats alike, but different dresses … and petticoats; Mother used to make our underclothes, it was like crochet, but it was knitted.

Dolly. When we were 'in service' Mummy did our washing… there was always a line across the kitchen for drying clothes….and our caps: she used to turn them and make the frill around the front with a 'goffering' iron. She took in washing for other people as well.

We used to go Stokenham, 'Old-time dancing'; but Mum used to take us up there, us wad'n allowed to go alone… in case us went astray!

Steve. *Tell me about your first job?*

Phyllis. I worked for Squire Pitts; I was kitchen maid and that was hard work, 'cause everything was made there … jams, …sponges was made with strawberries, and cream from the farm.

On shooting days it was pasties and rock cakes.

Everything was grown there… all your vegetables and your fruit, and we bought all the crab and lobsters living… we used to cook them, and massive great turbot, we'd cut them into about three pieces and all that long neck piece used to be stuffed. Then there's all the birds: woodcock, pigeons, pheasants… and there was always rabbits.

I got nine and tuppence… and had to buy me own uniform, the big apron and the light blue dress, black stockings and shoes… 'mob' cap. That was in the morning, then in the afternoon your little fancy apron and frilled cap. In the morning all your cleaning and that had to be done, then you'd change over to afternoon dress and small apron.

You used to have to sprinkle salt or tealeaves on the carpet before you brushed it with a hard brush! The tealeaves would clean up the dirt off the carpets… the dust and that!

I was there for four and a half years and then I went to Teignmouth for twenty-six years. I had the same money there for cook-general as the cook got at Squire Pitts; I had nine and tuppence out there, you see, and she had twelve and six - so I went to Teignmouth fer twelve and six; I thought I was made.

I was in Teignmouth during the Second World War, and when they bombed Bitton Street, which is the main road from Newton Abbot, I was down in the town and stones were flying everywhere… it was terrible.

I married and lived in Teignmouth, well I was down in the town living, but at night I used to walk up nearly to the golf course to sleep at my mother-in-law's, and we watched the bombing of Teignmouth from up there. The planes came in one day each side of the Pier, low, almost touching the water. There was a girl on the Pier that day, that had a new dress on. They said, "Everybody get down on the floor"- but she wouldn't, you see she didn't want to spoil her new dress…. she was killed; went right through her, yeah, she was about fifteen and lived near us.

Near where I lived they dropped a bomb and they were trying to find all the people that were in the house. There was a boy missing, about seven or eight years old, and they brought him out on a stretcher. As he went by, he put up his thumb… they'd found him under the table!

Bill Elliott

Born 6th September 1911

Died 8th November 2008

May Elliott

Born 1st May 1911

Died 21st June 2004

Recorded on 30th April 2004

Bill. We started at Charleton school when we were three years old and later Dorothy, Fred and myself walked from Charleton to Kingsbridge school for two years … there wad'n no buses much in they days.

I started work on the farm at South Huish at the age of thirteen. It was hard work, all horses… cor, the miles you walked, following horses!

Steve. Do you remember what your wages were on the farm?

Bill. Fourteen shillings a week… we paid three shillings a week rent, and thruppence a pint for our milk. I used to push-bike from Charleton to Thurlestone every day until 1933, when we got married and there was an empty cottage there… got married on the Saturday and went back to work on the Monday morning.

May. You was biking to South Milton to work and then back to Strete to me.

Bill. Yeah, used to go up to Strete, Wednesday nights.

In those days we grew our own vegetables: you didn't see vegetables in shops like you do now, not until years later. The grocers used to come round; and Moyseys from Kingsbridge…and we used to get our bread delivered from Lapthorns at Frogmore.

May. When I left school I got a job working on a farm, in the house. My sister-in-law was in Lady's Service and when she left to get married to my brother I took over there as cook-general for two old maids in Strete… in what was the Vicarage after. I used to only get out every other Sunday, and Wednesday for half a day. They used to do a lot of entertaining… teas and things. When I left to get married I was getting thirteen shillings a week.

Bill. I done twenty-seven year farm labouring, then I got a job with Costains, building the sea wall at Torcross. When that finished I went on rabbit-trapping, done a bit of gardening, and then I joined a gang laying the water mains from Prawle to Portlemouth. Then the Kingsbridge and Salcombe Water Board wanted to do their own work, by direct labour, so six of us got together and our first day with the Water Board was when the Lynmouth disaster was, and, cor didn't it rain!

Well, we carried on and took the water from Diptford Green to Avonwick, all hand digging - 'paid by results'. We done ten year at that, pick and shovel… that was hard work as well! I done twenty-four year with them, and my last ten year was driving the JCB.

My grandmother lived 'til 'er was ninety-nine… proper strict 'er was. She used to go around delivering youngsters, that was her trade. She wore old black frocks, right down to the ground… and her white apron.

During the War we took in two evacuees, a brother and sister from London, the Old Kent Road.

They were all up the Village Hall and they came to these last two, brother and sister, and they didn't want to be parted, so me and Mother said, "Right then, you come with us".

May. We had the children for two years, he was about twelve and Eileen was about ten… we still hear from Eileen now. Then we used to take soldiers' wives… we had two sisters come down, 'cause their husbands was stationed in Stokenham.

They came for the weekend, and we've been friends ever since.

Bill. We were evacuated in 1943: six weeks and everything had to be moved out; all the threshing-machines from outside the area came and threshed all the corn, and what a game it was! Everything moveable had to be moved. They supplied transport, you see, and they supplied all the boxes and barrows to put all your gear in, then the lorry would come, pick your gear up and away we went, the last day of November... and we came back the last day of November, we was away exactly twelve months.

May. My brother moved our chickens with the tractor and trailer... and the cat!

Steve. What was Strete village like years ago?

Bill. A lovely place Strete was... there where the car park is now, on the left just before you get to the pub, was a blacksmith's shop, his cottage and the Reading Room, well, two rooms; Boys' Club and Ladies' Club... and 'twas all burnt down when the Yanks came, 'twas all blowed to bits.

– ❖ –

Gladys Login

Born 26th October 1905

Died 4th March 2006

Recorded on 30th April 2004

Gladys. I was born in East Prawle.

Steve. You worked at South Allington House, what did you do there ?

Gladys. Oh, keep the house for Squire Pitts... wait table... clean the silver... do a lot of darning, evenings... used to have to darn their stockings! I was housemaid, made all the beds and kept the bedrooms clean... and the old Squire, mornings when you took up their hot water in their basin, he would tell you what suit he would want you to put out to put on. In they days they had a little tennis court down there...used to have tennis parties in the summer, you know, have their game of tennis, then you'd have to serve afternoon tea to them. The cook would prepare it, but you'd have to serve it. We had little pay; I suppose they used to keep us in food, but we didn't get a big pocket of money.

My husband was a Login, whose parents got washed out of Hallsands... you know, when the village was destroyed. His father was a fisherman; well, they managed to save their boats and things and then they went in and out from the little cove down below here, Ivy Cove, and the family lived in the first cottage here. My father used to go to sea with his father... they had a little boat and used a little cove called 'Lanty Cove', just after you leave Prawle Point, for the fine summer months. In the winter months they used to rent bits off the farmers where they could go trapping; catching rabbits

40

with 'gins', and they'd make their nets then, in the winter.

I was married in 1926 when I was twenty-one year old, and I've lived here ever since. My husband went to sea on the early tide on the morning we got married. We had a little service over to Stokenham church: there was four of us: my father and me, Frank - my husband, and his brother, Cecil. Then we walked back to East Prawle, and my mother had a cooked lunch for us 'times we got back… some roast beef.

Mr Jameson was the taxi-man, he came up after tea and picked us up… with our belongings and a bit of food, and brought me down here to Lannacombe with Frank… and that was that!

Steve. You're miles from anywhere here aren't you?

Gladys. When I was first married the butcher used to come once a week… the baker… the grocer man… ol' Lil Pritchard with her fruit, and a draper-man would call: 'Britton', from Kingsbridge.

Arthur Irish

Born 22nd July 1903
Died 2nd November 2004

Recorded on 25th June 2004

Arthur. I was born at Edmeston, Modbury. I remember Father used to grow a lot of apples, and made cider. I remember being sent out to start the old engine for the crusher, to crush the apples, and the pulp went down a chute.

Dick Moore used to lay down the layers of reed or straw, in the 'press', and Harry Kerswell threw the pulp on to it as it came down the chute. It took five cartloads of apples to make a pressful, and what was left after pressing was called the 'mock'.

Son Jim. They used to build it up in the press with straw to hold the crushed apple together. They had one big engine that used to drive all the farm machinery, threshers and all of it.

Arthur… 'twas a difficult engine to start, for a small boy. I had to pump 'en to get the vaporiser hot enough so that if I sent 'en backwards on the backfire the flywheel would come forward again. Anyway, I had to put oil in the pot that oiled the bearing every time the piston rod dropped … that would drop one drop at a time on the bearing. I had to lean in over and one day I got caught up… luckily I had a poor old weak coat… I gave meself a fling and landed on the floor.

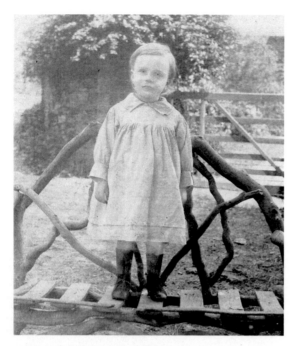

When I was very small I used to wear lace-up boots and something like a dress! And when I went to bed I used to wear a calico nightshirt. I slept in a pull-down bed, and I had to wash in a basin with cold water… occasionally it would have ice on it. There were eight of us in the family, and we had to behave, our parents were very strict. I was taught by my sister from the age of seven, and she was strict too and had me carrying the bottles of ink and the exercise books into the schoolroom - one of the rooms in our house!

Steve. You had proper lessons with your sister at home?

Arthur. Father organised that. He wouldn't allow me to walk by myself in all weathers. He said he wouldn't have it and he got the School Inspector to agree to it.

Daughter Vicky. She taught some other children as well, from one or two farms.

Arthur. When I went into Kingsbridge to the Grammar school I was ahead of a lot of the others; I'd done all the tables and the spellings, but I hadn't done any algebra or geometry, 'cause my sister didn't know any. I had 'six of the best' across the backside because I didn't understand it, and didn't bring in the homework done in the morning… because I was doing pretty well in the other subjects they thought I wasn't trying when I didn't do the algebra.

When I was at school in Kingsbridge I saw a lot of the horses being loaded up down on the Quay, to be taken away… that was during the First War, see. During the Second World War I was in Aveton Gifford, and Aveton Gifford hill was very narrow then, before it had been widened. There were thirteen American tanks and they couldn't get up the hill because it was icy. They linked them all together and they pushed and pulled each other to get up the hill.

I was married in 1932, at Loddiswell Church - so that's seventy-two years that we've been married now!

I used to go out working horses, 'drawing voyer'.

Son Jim. I'll explain. When you plough steep fields the soil tends to get down to the bottom; more so in those days because they practically always turned it down the hill, as it was easier work for the horses. So then, every so often they'd haul this earth to the top of the field. They had wooden butts: two wheels and a 'skid' in front and the horse used to pull them with trace- chains. They used to load them up with shovels at the bottom and the horse used to haul it to the top of the field and then they would tip it out; 'course in those days they had about eight men working on a 300 acre farm- there wasn't much machinery then, 'twas all horses.

Arthur. I enjoyed my working life on the farm, I always did - I never wanted to go on holiday. To do a job, and to do it better than I did it the last time, was all I wanted.

Hubert Tucker

Born 4th February 1922

Recorded on 12th July 2004

Hubert. I was born at Fallapit Farm, East Allington. I used to work all sorts of things off the water-wheel in Fallapit. The water-wheel was a marvellous thing; the pond used to be on the left and the channel where the water used to come through, there was a drop of about twenty-five feet. The damper was like a wheel with two teeth there, and you turned the damper up to let the water in to start the wheel… you had to let in a fair drop to get 'en going, and once he got going you'd shut the damper down, 'cause once he's rotating it doesn't take much water to keep 'en going.

The gearing's fantastic, see, you've got smaller wheels coming off 'en and you wouldn't hear a thing once he's going.

It was iron cups bolted onto elm platforms… elm will live in water for ages, and the bolts that bolted the cups onto the wooden pallets was all brass, 'cause brass don't rust; if anything went wrong they could take 'em off.

On the way up to the farmhouse there was a piggery…used to keep about eighty or ninety pigs, and George Hannaford used to come down and kill two pigs every three weeks. It was brutal, they tied 'em up and cut their throats, that's how they used to do it.

There was a proper boiling place, you know, a copper for hot water and that, and he used to hang 'em up , and next morning, when they was stiff, it was my job to take these two carcasses in the town wagon into Mill Street, that was Edward Donovan's butcher's shop. It *was* pigs in they days; ten, twelve-score pigs, not the little things you see today.

At the farm there was a little door in the wall and that's a butter-house, it's still there, it's built in under the ground, under the copse, and they used to keep the butter on blue slabs; all the shelves were these great blue slabs. The butter would keep there; but it was made in the dairy at the end of the stables.

My father was a cider drinker, and of course, so were the men. We had four constant employees and before the men went out at half past eight Father would say, "Hubert, fill the kegs". Each man had a keg that would hold six pints… it's a miniature barrel and they'd have a keg of cider every day.

My dad was a wonderful cider maker, he really was… he used to put raisins in it and all sorts of things. If it was a bit pale he'd put raw beef in it; that would bring the colour up, you see.

At one time we used to take the apples to Harleston but later years, just before the War, we took it down to Minchley, down to Holbeton, they had a more modern pound. At Harleston the apple was pressed on reed, but down at Minchley 'twas all done on cloths, with an automatic screw worked by an engine. You'd see the juice run out to a vat which was all white-tiled, 'twas like a tank underground. Then you'd pump the juice out into ten-gallon barrels on a trailer and bring it home. Ten days before I had to clean all the hogsheads out, that is sixty-four gallon size… a 'pipe' is a hundred and twenty gallon, and a 'puncheon' could be two hundred gallon, a huge thing that was, but we only had one of them, the rest was chiefly hogsheads.

You'd fill them with a 'tiller', a wooden funnel with bands like a barrel and you'd leave it for about a fortnight to work, and all the rubbish would work out: because, if you didn't gas would form and bust the barrel, you see. When it had finished working Father would doctor 'em up a bit. He put a ten-gallon barrel in when my brother was born in 1917, and bunged it down…. and he tapped it when he was twenty-one… and believe me, 'twas like dynamite!!

We had three orchards down Fallapit; we had various cider apples… Bickington Grey, Blemheim Orange, these apples were all pounded separately, but honestly, that cider was like champagne!

A gentleman called Robinson lived at Fallapit House, he was the editor of an American newspaper, and he was quite a wealthy man... oh, it was a beautiful place, really, gun room and billiard room he had there too... used to have a lot of parties there. He had two cars, one was an American 'Packard', a huge car it was, about four-litre... and the gardens were magnificent. He had four gardeners there in the Thirties, and, of course, that lovely pond with the island in it... lean-to greenhouses, all well looked after... winter gardens ... and the rhododendrons, Lord Ashcombe had planted them everywhere.

Tollditch used to be a sawmill and I used to watch the horses down in Nutcombe Woods... they used to cut the trees down and drag them up with horses, up to the wagons and load them at the bottom of the little lane. They had to go up Nutcombe hill from Fallapit gate right up to the main road at 'Firs Cross'. One wagon used to have six horses to take those trees up and then there used to be nine horses, and the three horses used to come back and hitch on the front of the second wagon, to get the two wagons to the top... 'cause then three horses could take it into Kingsbridge then. The wheels were much wider and more substantial than ordinary farm wagons and used to

have drags on 'em, 'droogs' they called 'em, hanging on chains -'cause they used to go down Belle Hill you see... wonderful to see: six horses, one before the other, going up Nutcombe hill; it was a wonderful sight...and a lovely sound too.

As a boy I was a bit of a tearaway really, and Father decided I needed more discipline so he sent me to Kings College Taunton, a Military School. I was there for four years...and it was tough!

I passed out as a Non-commissioned Officer at the age of sixteen - but my father needed me at home, and I was able to come home, as farming was a reserved occupation, you see. Not that I wanted to, well I was enjoying myself: I mean at that age it's all an adventure and you don't think that you're going to get a bullet through you....but, it's a costly adventure, because out of the twenty-two Officers in my Company , thirteen were killed in the War.

Steve. Tell me the story again about the moorland farm!

Hubert. That was when I was sheep-shearing as a contractor for Mr. Lock, and he sent me to this farm up to Bovey Tracey. It was up across two fields and when I got there and knocked on the door out come this lady with button-up boots... one over the other, come up about two thirds of the leg... so she rung this bell, and down he came from the moor-ground and he said, "Boy, I didn't know you was coming today". I said, "I sent a card"... He said, "Postman don't come here very often!"

Well, we sheared the sheep and finished quarter past four, so she said, "Young man, have a cup of tea before you go!" So I went in the kitchen and the hearth fire was over there, and, well, they didn't have a saw ... they used to bring in the poles, and as they burnt so they'd shove 'em on... you had to walk over 'em. 'Er said, "Have a bun?".... anyrate 'er knelt down and 'er pulled this great brass knob on a steel tray, out from underneath the hearth... and 'er had bread, buns and cake in there....cor, they smelt beautiful!.... it was the wood ashes cooking it from the top, see.... and they buns was beautiful! I came home and said to Dorothy, "I've been somewhere today, they'm living two centuries behind!" That was about 1964-65. It was a proper old moor farm 'cause the stream came down through the middle of the court to a trough; they had running water all the time.

Wilfred Login

Born 28th April 1925

Recorded on 13th September 2004

& 5th February 2007

Wilfred. I was born at 'New Houses', a quarter of a mile down a steep hill from East Prawle; it's near the beach, 'Horseley Cove'. They built the five cottages for the coastguards and the head coastguard had his own house at the end.

One of my grandfers was a fisherman, and the other grandfer was one of these … what you call 'fish hawkers'. He used to have a little pony and trap and he used to go to Hallsands and buy fish off the fishermen coming in, and then go around the village selling it.

My father's family, the Logins, were all washed out of old Hallsands. They lived in two cottages at the far end of the village, right over against the cliffs. My father was a young man at the time and he was fishing with his grandfer. Father's father was in the Navy at the time, and he was allowed home. The old fishermen knew about the tides and came to the conclusion that there was going to be trouble… and they prepared right away. They had a meeting and said, "Right, out we go!", and they carried all their stuff up to the top of the cliff.

I've got six sisters: three older sisters, I'm in the middle, and three younger sisters…and two stepbrothers! We used to live in a two-bedroomed house; one of me stepbrothers used to sleep in the sitting room, and we had two double beds in our room, nothing else. Every bedroom had a grate in they days, with a mantelpiece… and that mantelpiece was used to put the candle on. It had cob walls and was beside the farm. There was a barn where they used to fatten their bullocks in the winter, and they was tied up in there: they'd never come out, they'd be stood in that shed for about four months. They'd just get mangolds and hay and straw… and to tie them they had a chain around their neck, down through a loop and a block underneath so they couldn't pull it through. That chain used to go up and down and what a clatter! cor like thunder!… right next to my bedroom…and we used to hear the rats running in the ceiling, but they never came down in the house.

Steve. *Well where did you hang your clothes?*

Wilfred. What clothes! … we only had one set of best and one set of working clothes… and all that best was in me mother's wardrobe, there was only one wardrobe for everybody. Me father didn't have no best clothes, he never went anywhere to use best clothes!

We had one wardrobe and one chest of three drawers, we only had Sunday clothes and school clothes and I used to have to wear nail boots made by the cobbler… and leather leggings. They'd last me three years… he made the boots big enough for three years growing! I only had two pairs of boots made in me school days…but it was happy days.

Mrs. Elliott lived down at Walland, that is down a little narrow lane, right down in the valley from West Prawle. Well she took to me and sent her husband out to ask me in one day. So I went in and there she was sitting by the fire in the hearth… the fireplace was about a good eight feet…ten foot say, wide and two could sit in there, one chair on each side. There was a big hook coming down the middle of the chimney with notches on and you could put your cooking pots on whichever heighth you wanted. She had a big oval iron pot, I reckon he'd hold about three gallon of soup… she'd sit there and if she wanted some soup she'd just scoop it out with a gert big iron ladle…it would be there all the time, and there'd be plenty of meat in there… rabbits… and potatoes, vegetables…. keep putting it in, it was strong!

It was smoky in there too, sometimes a puff would come out into the kitchen. I was fourteen then, so that was in 1939.

All the farm labourers' houses had a passage through; you'd go in one front door to two sitting rooms in the front, one on one side and one on the other. Then you had a kitchen and back kitchen each out at the back. Outside you had a big yard… you'd got your toilets and the old water pump, they all had to use the pump. You used to have to pour some water down, in the top, to 'prime' it, to get the water flowing.

Each house had the same each side, you both used the same staircase to get to your bedrooms… you could lock your doors, but, of course, all farm labourers knew each other, they didn't worry.

The cottage would belong to the farm, and whoever came there to work would get a cottage, and when he left the farm he'd have to get out.

Steve. You could be walking from your kitchen to your sitting room and you'd meet somebody from the other family.

Wilfred. My grandmother's house was like that - they went to the right, the others went to the left… but they were all 'Aunties'.

Steve. Were they real aunties or did you just call them that?

Wilfred. No… like the whole village of Prawle, ninety per cent of the people were called Auntie or Uncle by you, because it was a small community.

I can only remember going to Kingsbridge twice before I was fourteen; that was to two Kingsbridge Fairs. The first time I went to Plymouth was when I had to go for my medical, when I was eighteen and I had a motorbike. You never had to go out from Prawle: Kingsbridge was a foreign place to go.

I used to go bird-baiting, because there was a Depression on, and there was no work; we couldn't catch any fish because nobody had any money to buy anything. It started, I think, in 1929/30 and it went on for six years. We never got no meat, the butcher didn't come round because nobody had money to buy meat. I used to catch starlings; you know, for a youngster to have to kill a bird! Father showed me what to do. I had some weak 'gins', that's rabbit traps; they were very weak, wore-out ones, 'cause the others would break the bird's leg, then they'd fly away. You just put a bit of food on top of the plate and as I caught a couple I had to pick 'em and catch a couple more. I'd pick 'em and clean 'em for me mother, and then she'd make a pie out of them, it was nice.

Starlings is black meat, thrush is white meat, like chicken… 'course there was a lot of birds then, not like now, cor, thrushes, blackbirds, everything you could think of. You'd see some fields black with starlings in they days, just like a black cloud going along.

Through the Second War my stepbrother used to go out and get seagull eggs at Gammon Head, because you couldn't buy eggs, you see, they was rationed. They weren't allowed to be sold to anybody around locally, so we used to have seagulls' eggs.

Powleslands, bakers from Slapton, used to come and he used to give us one and sixpence a dozen. Me and me father used to go out and get dozens of eggs … two baskets each on our arms. It was just over two miles to bring these eggs back… walk all the way. Mornings was best, 'cause they'd laid the day before - in the afternoon they'd usually lay. They only lay three eggs before they stop laying, so if you found three eggs you'd take two and leave one. Always leave one in the nest and they'd lay on top of that one; never empty a nest, you'd always leave one egg and then you'd get another one alongside of 'en the next time.

'Poop' Codd, he used to live behind Locks Farm in Prawle, one little house built of cob and thatch, and he used to have a ladder to get upstairs. It had one tiny window in it. Downstairs it was very small with the ladder going up… but there was only a floor where you went up to sleep: that's why, when he was drunk he wouldn't go upstairs to sleep, he was afraid to go up there. I would say it was about ten foot by ten foot. He had a little tiny 'Lidstone' stove and one seat, that's all he had.

He used to go, "Poop, poop, poop"; that was his speech - but he was a jolly old chappie.

I used to work on the farm on Saturdays, and I'd milk the cows… I used to like separating. The separator was like a cone inside, made up of twenty-one plates fitted over the cone and the milk had to pass right through.

The cream would separate and go one way and the milk out the other chute; it was marvellous how it sorted it out.

When you took it to pieces to clean, well, the farmer used to just put it in a bucket of water and wash the last cream out, but I used to sit down and lick every bit of that raw cream off…cor, it was lovely, but very rich mind.

I had a big accident when I was seven. You see, this old bike was a wreck and he didn't have no brakes on 'en, and we had to go down this steep hill. When we got to the bottom and turned the corner there was a big lorry getting cauliflower out of the field… and of course I landed on me head. I had a fractured skull, I was unconscious for three days… Doctor came, but he couldn't do nothing. He told me mother, just had to wait… you had to pay for the Doctor then. I had a big cut and all she bathed me with was raw cow's milk, not boiled or nothing…just as it came from the cow: that's how we used to get our milk in they days.

The wheelwright would make gates and hurdles for fencing and the blacksmith would shoe horses and make all the farmers' implements. There was what they called a 'spurtang' that used to be dragged to rip the ground up; like when they had sheep in the turnip field, it was hard and they couldn't plough it, so they'd go over it first with a 'spurtang', and these big feet would rip it up before they'd plough it with horses.

The wheelwright used to do all the woodwork, that was the middle of the wheel, the hub and the spokes, and then a wooden band around with the spokes let into it, all chiselled out by hand. Then they had to take it to the blacksmith's shop on the Green where there was a big iron circle, bigger than the size of the wheel. The iron was about an inch thick with a hole in the middle… up through that hole was a chain. They would chain the wooden parts down on the top to hold it tight so it wouldn't move. Then the blacksmith would get a couple of boys in to help him with the bellows. I've been there times pumping the bellows…and he made the big band from flat iron, I reckon about eight foot long, and he made holes in the iron band so it could be screwed into the woodwork. He'd put it on the forge, and they didn't burn coal at the time, it was all 'douse'.

'Douse' was the barley iles, the fuzzy ends of the barley. When it was threshed they all broke up and it goes in 'douse'

from the threshing-machine, and that's what he had to get, 'cause it don't blaze, it just smoulders, red hot ashes.

All that band had to be red hot, then he had iron tongs, and open up all the front of his workshop to get this thing out, and he'd have about twenty buckets of water all around outside.

That iron had to go right down straight onto the woodwork, everybody would be hammering to get it down quick. Then, as soon as the iron touched the woodwork they'd all have a bucket each and tip it as fast as they could to cool it off, else it would burn the wood.

In the winter I used to have to cut willows with me father. We had groves where we grew the willows for our pots - little old damp patches in the valleys which belonged to the farmer, and we had to pay the farmer 'couple shillings for that. You had to keep it clean, you had to look out for bindweed in the grove, because that would grow up and catch hold of the willow and pull it right down. It would spoil the willow… instead of going up straight it would be curved down around. It took us two days to cut the willows, then we had to carry them up to West Prawle, and a lorry would collect them from there.

Wilf at the tiller, fishing off Prawle with his father

47

We had a plague of octopus that came in from Africa, carried by the warmer water. We had a hot summer in 1952, and in 1953 the octopus came in by the thousands. We went on for three years hardly catching anything; you'd have a couple of nice crabs in your pot but there was only the shells; they just sucked out the crab flesh between the joints, they were useless. Then I went to work on the farm.

– ❖ –

Fanny Andrews

Born 15th October 1904

Died 20th January 2008

Recorded on 17th September 2004

Fanny. I was born at South Milton, near Thurlestone, and came to Aveton Gifford when I was eight. We lived three doors from the pub - that was the 'Commercial' then, before it was the 'Taverners'… and my mother walked miles and done a day's work, to the farms around…doing washing and scrubbing. We slept four in a bed, two down the bottom and two up the top!

We used to have hot hair-tongs and fizz our hair up when we were young…put 'em in the fire…

and burn your scalp sometimes! … we liked to have our hair curled.

We used to have wooden hoops and skipping ropes, play hopscotch and all sorts in the road then, no cars to go through, no cars at all. We walked in and out of Kingsbridge and done the shopping… and I haven't travelled around anywhere else, but they were more happy days than they are now.

Daughter Shirley. We had eight shops in Aveton Gifford: Post Office, a bakery, butcher… we could get everything we wanted. We had a blacksmith at the end of the village and as children we used to sit and watch the horses have their shoes put on… and we could buy coal up this end… and Hannah, that's my father's cousin, she used to make tea-cosies and things like that, and sell them in her front room window. All the shops were in someone's front room; we had three that were general stores.

We had a lot to do with the Church. The Church played a big part in our life: we celebrated all the special days, and every Whit Sunday we used to be given a new white dress and bonnet.

Fanny. My mother used to clean the chapel and when people died she used to go around and 'lay them out'…. and she died when she was ninety-eight.

Me and my mother used to pluck and draw chickens for the whole of the month of December, and the whole house used to be covered in feathers!

At the end of it we might get half a crown, and a chicken given to us for our Christmas dinner.

Me and my mother had a Lidstone stove which had to be black-leaded, and if the wind blew down the chimney, the room would be filled with smoke and soot!…you couldn't see each other!

Everybody wore aprons over their dresses for many years; nowadays people don't own an apron. We used to wash our hair in rainwater…leave the bucket outside the back door to catch the rainwater, and use soap … clean your teeth with salt on your finger!

Fanny. Then the Jerries came and bombed us!

Shirley. Yes, after the bombing people were afraid and they used to put the kids in a pram and the people used to walk out of the village.

Fanny. … she was a baby in a pram then, and my son was running around. We'd go up the road, anywhere we thought was shelter, just by the hedges… anywhere out of the village.

You see, all the doors and windows went !!… and only one little girl was killed, at the Rectory…. well really they tried to protect her but she was suffocated.

– ❖ –

Kathleen Weeks

Born 1st February 1911
Died 7th November 2006

Recorded on 20th September 2004

Kathleen. I was born in Dodbrooke and then me parents came out this way…there was six of us: three boys, three maids. We lived in a bungalow at 'Firs Cross', East Allington …. us had to pump water in the field and us had chicken and that up there… 'twas happy days. You could come down East Allington and leave your doors and windows open. There used to be tramps on the road in they days and they wouldn't harm a fly; they'd ask you for a drop of water, and you'd give it to 'em and on they'd go.

When us used to live down Greenhill was the best, we all used to play over there; one of me school friends used to live down 'Chute Row', 'er was called Winnie Lane. We used to do all sorts, skipping and that … and Doris Weeks … 'Pip, Squeak, and Wilfred'… Doris, Winnie Lane and me… I can't remember which one was which… and us used to go 'Band of Hope' over Chapel… no such thing now…happy days I'm sure.

Mr. Holmes down here had the baker's shop, you'd have your hot cross buns made four o'clock in the morning by 'e.

Then there was the Post Office and they used to sell clothes and all sorts of things, used to go over Sunday mornings and get the cream… used to have lovely cream. Then there was Beat Penny and Bill, that was a shop you see; he used to come around with the coal as well. You used to get your milk over Lister's farm.

There was a blacksmith up where Sopers are now… and George Efford was over there, he used to sell bikes, all sorts of things, tyres, and the radio job… used to go there for batteries. They had taxis there too, oh 'twas a lovely shop. His wife would be out brushing all outside be eight 'o clock mornings, geddout do, yeah.

We all had our jobs to do before school: picking sticks, yes, us used to walk down, me and Ethel Luscombe, 'er had to do the same, pick a 'burn' of sticks… 'twad'n no use saying you wad'n going 'do it, like they do now, you had to do it.

I left school at fourteen and went out to work, 'twas the gentry style, caps'n aprons and all that game. I used to have to work Sunday afternoons cleaning brass…Sundays!! I've worked all me life and I keep on saying "I've never had a holiday"… never!… worked, scrubbed and cleaned… scrubbed floors, mind you, yes I had to work, no playing around !

I used to go over me granny's, they was all musical, all played the accordion. Grandfer Yeoman used to give 'em the music… and dance he would! … yeah, lovely days, they didn't have nothing, but they was happy. We used to go over in the harvest field and catch rabbits, come home gone ten o'clock at night.

I had eleven children then meself, so I never used to sit down; like now you sit down and watch telly - you never done that, you was working all the time, washing and….'course Henry was good in the house, he'd clean the boots and shoes and line 'em up be the wall ready for the morning: they don't do that now, they don't black and shine shoes, that's gone out 'adnit.

I used to work over the pub and had to wash the spittoons; they used to spit in 'em, and I had to clean 'em!

Steve. *Can you remember anything else about the village?*

Kathleen. Well, it used to be alright when you smelt the loads of dung! Old Florrie Tucker used to live down the bottom there and 'er used to chitter 'bout 'em making a mess… 'course they used to bring the cows all through the village, didn't they. What a mess it used to be, but you didn't think about it… my goodness me, it's different now.

I remember one Christmas-time I walked from East Allington to Totnes and bought a new teapot. Then the cover blowed off and went all the way down the hill and I had to go all the way back to get 'en! I've walked and done shopping in Kingsbridge, yeah, carry it all the way back. I wouldn't do it now, 'tid'n safe; you was safe in they days!

I remember Doctor Webb would come out on horseback to see my mother, well we used 'go beach with a pony and trap sometimes, go Bantham and places, and take a picnic!…yes, will never do that no more! I said 'tother day, " 'twouldn't be fast enough for 'em now would it".

50

Lilian Prettejohn

Born 10th March 1914

Recorded on 4th October 2004

Lilian. I was born at Beesands and was one of eleven: nine girls we were and two boys... yeah lovely! ... lovely times together. We used to go down on the beach when we were kiddies, down under the rocks... we used to be in the water all day long.

Steve. Could you swim?

Lilian. No! none of us. My sister Liza, she was the oldest; she was born at old Hallsands and then they moved to Beesands. We used to live in a thatched cottage down at the bottom, and there used to be a Chapel joining it. It's all gone now, washed away all of it.

I heard my auntie say that when they lived down Hallsands, and got washed out from there, I think they got seventy-three pounds as compensation.

I used to go to Beeson every morning to fetch the milk and give it to the people in the village... sometimes a quarter pound of cream or pound of butter on top. I had two cans, one in each hand on a little wire... walked about a mile and a half - for sixpence a week! You can't believe it.

My father was a fisherman, and my mother used to go washing for people; she went up across the fields, to Middlecombe.

We had to walk to Huccombe School; we never had hardly anything on our feet, just worn-out boots; it was hard days. I wad'n much good at school... and my daughter 'rinned' away from school one day... rinned home!

When I was fourteen I left school and went to Beeson on a farm, to work for a family called Honeywills... bag on me back and off!

I had to sleep in up there, that was what was called 'in service'. I had to do everything... scrubbing the steps, on your knees, out through the kitchens; all blue stone... and scrub the great table. They had five children and I used to have to scrub their boots off and blacken 'em. I used to clean the silver and all the knives and everything on a Saturday night, and I've never had a holiday. I left there because I went up in the field in the night : we used to go up hanging out the clothes on the line at midnight, up in the field, and I stepped on a piece of wood with a great nail in it that went right through me shoe into me foot.

My brother Tom used to go up on top of the hill and look out for fish, and he'd take his hat off and just shout all 'round... he'd shout, 'Ey boat'... and 'course we'd all run down, wouldn't we. They used

51

to go out and shoot the nets around and we used to pull 'em in: two lots, one each end like... lovely times... that's why my arms is aching now I think... pulling they in. Then we used to drag it along on the beach, helping the men. We used to catch mullet, bass, and salmon; we used to have a licence for salmon. I remember going to my mother's funeral, coming back and catching three outside our place.

Dad used to go out fishing in an old boat with no engine in 'en... sails; and come home with nothing sometimes; that was awful poor days really.

When we had the bomb dropped on Beesands, during the War, my husband's sister-in-law had her leg blown off, and I saw that happen... and then 'er had 'er little sister come up just for the weekend, and her little boy was playing with the water at the tap outside.....and there was his little body... and there was his little head, yeah, true. I shall never forget that... that's why I get upset sometimes. Several were blinded and my nephew got shrapnel near the brain, it used to give him fits; he was about seven. I had my husband's brother's little boy put in me arms; he had an eye injury, and then there was a mother and tiny baby killed as well... it was dreadful, really. My sister had a First Aid place there, and of course they hit that, didn't they.

Frank Crocker

Born 4th November 1917
Died 15th November 2005

Recorded on 15th October 2004

Frank. I was born in Beesands, in the thatched cottage at the far end; 'course 1917 was the year that Hallsands was washed out. I've lived here all my life, except during the War. In those days there was twenty or thirty yards of grass out in the front where the wall is now, and then just a foot drop and you was on the beach.

Steve. Did the sea ever come right up to the houses?

Frank. Oh yeah! We had the sea in our house twice.

I went to Huccombe School... had to walk there, about a mile and a half, and I left there in 1931 when I was fourteen and no bigger 'n a rabbit! We did mental arithmetic, writing and spelling.

The most children we had was eighty-four, from Beesands, Hallsands, Kellaton and the surrounding farms: they all went to Huccombe School.

When I left school I had a rowing boat and a few pots, close to the shore, and that's how I started. I caught crab mostly... and then we used to shoot lines in the summer, then you'd get ray and conger and used it for bait. At one time we sold plaice and turbot to 'Trouts Hotel', Hallsands, to Ella and

Patience… they were running it then… but crabs was the biggest trade.

Steve. What did you do in the winter months when it was too rough to go out to sea?

Frank. Make crab pots; we used to grow all our own willows in beds over at Hallsands, and in the winter time you'd go and cut them, bundle then up, bring them home and make the crab pots. I've made thousands in my time; you'd get a mould, twelve holes in it, and you'd stick in twelve rods…

weave the funnel, drive a stake in with strings on, bend 'em back with your arm, tie 'em back, get your shape and 'ring' from there. I could make one in about four hours; we used to make about eighty, and one year, me and me brother, we made a hundred and twenty.

We had to make enough money in the summer to last through the winter.

Steve. Did you ever get into any danger out at sea? Could you swim?

Frank. We were out there scores of times when we never ought to have been and not very many of us could swim. We lost two boats in my time fishing here: fifth of November 1937 two brothers got lost… Phil and George Prettejohn… and twentieth of January 1953, my brother-in-law Harry Patey, and Bob Lynn, they got lost… they never found anything at all… we were out both days.

I retired in the late 1950's… well, I think I was the last one that was fishing here, they all moved to bigger boats in Dartmouth and what-have-you.

I suppose everybody wanted to get bigger and make more money; that's what it's all about today id'n it, money comes into everything

I was twenty-one when I joined up and because I was a fisherman they put me on the minesweepers; and was on them for five and a half years. I had two year on the River Mersey, twelve months in Iceland; then I came back and went to Swansea. Then we came round and went up to Dover and joined in the Invasion of Normandy. We left Dover harbour at five o'clock on the fifth of June 1944 and invaded on the sixth. We had to be the first to get in, with the minesweepers, so were steaming flat out all night.

Steve. Did you have, in the back of your mind, the thought that you might not return?

Frank. You didn't think like that, you just take it as it comes, like. It was a job that had to be done. I used to say to me mates when we got paid, "What's the use of taking money out there? If you get blown up 'tidn no good to nobody, you may as well spend it"…..I sunk a few pints in my time then, I'll tell you.

Bill Stone

Born 4th November 1904
Died 22nd April 2006

Recorded on 18th October 2004

Steve. *What is your earliest memory?*

Bill. My father was a farm manager, and we had to walk our cattle from Prawle to Kingsbridge, to market. I was ten year old and I asked Father if I could stop home from school to go with the cattle, and he said, "You'll have to be out six o'clock to walk to Kingsbridge"; it must be ten miles. It took several hours... the cattle would get tired and lie down... right through Charleton, to the market : sell the bullocks, take 'em up the railway station... and they took 'em away.

Steve. *Where was the market then?*

Bill. In Church Street, next to the 'King of Prussia'... 'twadn very big, just rails for sheep... and this little place where you sold the cattle.

Steve. *Then you had to walk home again!*

Bill. No, there used to be another neighbour taking sheep with a horse and wagon, and he used 'take us home!

But we got caught once. We walked to Kingsbridge and took 'em to market and the butcher bought 'em... well, they didn't go by rail... 'twas Butcher Hannaford out Torcross...us had to take 'em back there!! Then the chap that had the horse and wagon came out there and fetched us, see.

Well, 'course it's different now, they do silage, but us used 'grow mangold and turnips... but now that's finished, that's how its altered in my time. Yes, silage has come to stay I think...too much work hoeing mangolds.

You'd cut corn in August, cut it with a self-binder ... turn out the sheaves, then you had to stand them up for drying in sixes, see... that was a 'stitch'. When 'twas dry you'd pull 'em down for an hour, air 'em off, and then go out an' pick 'em up, make a rick for the winter when the thresher comes. That rick's got to be thatched in then... Oh geddout, now the combine comes in and does it in no time.

I used 'do hedging with a shovel and digger, see, well that's gone, they go 'round with a tractor and do three times so much as us would. In they days, mind, 'twas all work and very little money; now it's different, it's no work and plenty of money!

In the Thirties when us came down to 'Thorn'

54

you couldn't sell nothing… that began in the 1929 - 30's Depression… couldn't sell anything if you went to market.

I can remember the First World War…us had the Air Station out Prawle, and weekends I used to go up with Jack Tucker and pick up the swill with a pony and a little trolley. They wouldn't allow just anybody in to fetch something - unless they was with somebody. I could go in, cor geddout, I seen the aeroplanes upside-down up there… I heard bangs, us would run out 'top of the cliffs at Start Point… there's a ship going down … yes, blowed up… us used to run out and see the ship going down… yes, somebody had hit 'en… Yes, I can mind that!

Steve. Can you remember your Grandparents?

Bill. Yes, Granny and Grandfer, that's Father's mother and father. They lived out the old Coast Guard Station, out Prawle. That's some years ago when I used 'go out there… but they didn't have much money, they'd buy a few herrings or something for their tea. Granny done a bit of milking, I can see her with her white milking hat, like a bonnet… and Grandfer he was on the farm.

Gwen Tucker

Born 15th April 1928

Robert Tucker

Born 18th January 1930

Janet Tucker

Born 13th December 1939

Recorded on 18th October 2005

Janet. We're five brothers and two sisters all together, and six of us were born at Chain Cottage, Allaleigh. I was the only one born here at Instart, East Allington.

Robert. Chain Cottage is along the road from Allaleigh, towards Tideford- but it's all a tumbled-down ruin now; one part of the house had a slate roof and the other part was thatched.

Janet. During the War we were evacuated from Instart, half of us children went to Auntie and Uncle at Coomery, and the other half went to

Robert, Janet and Gwen Tucker

55

Venice farmhouse, with Uncle Robert and Aunt Sarah.

Steve. I'm interested in Lower Venice at Allaleigh because my family lived there in the mid eighteen-hundreds, that was my six-times great-grandparents, James and Sally Pedrick!

Gwen Tucker

Gwen. Lower Venice farmhouse is a ruin now too, but I remember it as a working farm. It had a huge open fireplace, with the crooks hanging down and the oven at one side of it.

Robert. Our Grandfather Tucker went there at the turn of the century, so Tuckers have farmed in Allaleigh for over a hundred years; but at Lower Venice it's steep ground, and all the work was done in those days with horses, no tractors. I remember Uncle Rob wouldn't use a horse and cart, he used a sledge or a butt... you could put bags or bales on a sledge, and a butt was more like a cart, to hold roots.

Janet. Uncle Jack used to use a butt to take the milk out to the stand at the bottom of the lane, for the milk lorry to collect.

Gwen. Uncle Robert had a lovely garden up at the back, and used to grow lovely strawberries, and there was any amount of damson plums in the orchard. His wife, Aunt Sarah, used to take them to Totnes and 'hawk' them around the town: selling them from a basket.

Robert. When we were little we didn't travel very far, so we didn't know relations that lived at Harbertonford.

Robert Tucker

There was a quarry opposite Chain Cottage, but they never did any quarrying while we lived there. Father used to go blasting all over the place, because that was his job.

Father was a quarryman and used to take contracts with Devon County Council to supply stone for road building and repair. They used to blast the stone out... they'd have a steel drill and drive it into the solid rock. One man would hold and turn the drill and the other one would strike it with a sledgehammer. When they had drilled the hole they put in a pound of gelignite, tamped it down and detonated it. Then they'd break down the blasted rock by hand, first with sledgehammers and then the special two-pound hammers. Of course they didn't have goggles in those days, but they had some crude wire-mesh ones to protect their eyes from flying splinters of stone. The stone would be 'yarded up', measured into cubic yards, and then it would be loaded by hand into horse-drawn carts and, later, onto small lorries; that would be in the Thirties when lorries were coming into use. They loaded it either with a Devon shovel or a special fine-toothed stone-fork. It was taken to the site of work, spread by hand and rolled in by the steamroller. They were building roads then, 'cause in 1929 there was no tarmac through the village of East Allington, but when we went there in 1938 there was tarmac by then.

It was dreadfully hard work but Father told me that when he was doing his quarry work, a man used to walk from near Sherford out to Allaleigh… and they'd work from seven in the morning until six in the evening, and then walk home again. Father said several men would walk from Dartmouth, which would be about six miles, with no complaint, delighted to have a job of work to do to earn a bit of money. He employed about half a dozen men and then stone-crushers were invented, and the Quarry at Buckfastleigh undercut the 'little men' and forced them all out of business: it was in the Depression in the Thirties, you see. The old man who farmed here during the First World War told me he could remember when the Royal Naval College was built in Dartmouth… and he said a lot of the work force came from Harbertonford; they would walk to Dartmouth, be there by seven o'clock, work from seven 'til six and then walk home again.

We came here to Instart in 1938, and then we were evacuated from here in 1943. We were away ten months and when we came back it was amazing how the weeds had grown. Father had left a field of swedes and they went to seed, and the seeds kept coming up for twenty years…. what an amazing thing nature is. Those seeds can stay in the ground all that time and still germinate, which reminds me of the 'Flanders' fields in France, you know the poppy is the symbol; poppies grew where no-one in living memory had ever seen them before… in shell holes.

Everything on the farm was done with horses then: you'd cut the grass with the horse mower and sweep the hay with the hay sweep. It was all pitched up loose, made into ricks and the ricks thatched… and then in the winter cut out with a hay knife. The corn was all cut with a binder then stooked up to dry; then picked up and made into ricks, to be thrashed through the winter. I remember an old boy that lived at Harleston Cottage told me that when he was a young man they used to cut the corn with a scythe… and that a day's work was to cut two acres of barley. Can you imagine telling someone to do that now!

Gwen. If you got thorns in your hands or cuts or anything on your hands, we would use 'Lysol'- wonderful stuff! You can't get it now… and if your hands were festering, due to the washing powder for the dairy utensils, you would go to the Doctor then and he would give you 'Gentian Violet'… and now you aren't allowed to have that.

Another remedy : we used to drench bullocks with 'red water', with urine from the chamber pot… boil it up with rusty old iron in an old crock ..and give it to the bullocks for a drench. Father done that.

Janet. There was a little chapel at Allaleigh, just before you turn the corner at the bottom, before you reach the stream. It's an old tumbledown shed now, but they used to hold Chapel meetings there.

Steve. Apparently there was a meeting house or chapel at Coles Cross?

Robert. That's right, I remember when I went to school there was still stained glass windows there. The one at Harleston was a just a tin shed, and I remember going there when the Reverend Lucas was the vicar at East Allington. There were several large families living at Harleston then, so you only needed three families of nine children and the place would be overflowing.

Janet Tucker

Mary Hibbs

Born 11th August 1914
Died 27th November 2007

Recorded on 1st November 2005

Mary. I was born at Jaspers Farm, Cornworthy and I remember going to school when I was four. Our school was at the top of the village next to the Church, but we didn't have any playground, 'used to play out in the road. There was two class rooms and two teachers, and oh, it was cold in the winter time. They had an old boiler thing that would never go right, so it was ever so cold, and we could wear our coats. I hated school because there was a lot more to do at home... there was all the animals to see to. I used to love to do the animals... cleaning out the cow houses and the pigsty. I loved all that... and harvest time was really magic for us children, because they had the binder to cut the corn and we used to help to stook it all up. Then Mother would bring out a roast meal to the workers in a flat-bottomed wagon... roast beef and whatever, and all the veg, all out in the middle of the field, and sit on any sheaves there, to eat our roast dinner... it used to taste lovely!

There was the old Abbey in Cornworthy, the Priory, and they used to say that there was a tunnel going from the old Abbey to the church... but whether there was or not I dunno!

We kids used to go in and up the steps and look out over the village... we used to love going in there and looking out, but I don't know if there's a lot left of it today. They used to say that there was monks living there, which I reckon there was.

I remember the rag-and-bone man: well the dogs always had bones, and they'd collect the bones and pay a penny or tuppence for them - I think they must have rendered 'em down or something.

At Tuckenhay there was a paper mill where they used to make the paper for those big five-pound notes, and they used to collect all the rags... that's what they were made from. The mother of one or two children that went to our school used to work down there with rags, and we used to walk down to Tuckenhay and take her dinner down.

I remember coming down when we were kids at Sunday school, we'd come down to Torcross.... I thought Torcross was hundreds of miles away! We'd come down there by pony trap, bring a picnic and go on the beach; we used to think that was marvellous.

I think the First World War broke out on the 4th of August 1914 and I was born on the 11th. After it was over I remember going to the school room to get our mugs with '1914 - 18 War' on it. I can remember that... and when the Second War broke out in 1939 I lived here in Beesands, in a dear little cottage just along the road from here, that was bombed. The dear old soul that lived next door, her grand-daughter was putting her little boy to bed and they were both killed. She was called Bullen, and her little boy was called Brian. Then there was another lady who was staying next door on again, and her husband was in the Navy. They came up here to get away from the bombs in Plymouth, and her little boy was killed... 'course they were out playing on this Sunday night and they said, "Oh, aeroplanes"; they were waving....oh, it was awful!

Then the lady that lived here, her husband was killed, and her young daughter Phyllis; it was her first leave from the WAAF and she was leaning in the window talking to her mother, who was in here. Her father was sat on that stone outside, and they were both killed by the blast… and that dear little boy that was killed, my neighbour, he was only a few months old.

Then further along, on the road, there was another little girl, her Dad was in the Army; she was called Mary… and she got …. oh it was terrible! And looking back you wonder how the devil you lived through it, but you did.

I happened to be lucky 'cause my husband's father and mother kept the pub then, and my niece came in to borrow an apron and she said, "Oh, come on Aunt Mary, we're in there having a sing-song", so I threw me book down and away I went with her.

Not long after the bomb dropped, and the cottage was completely demolished. My husband was home on leave from the Air Force and he was out the back of the pub in one of the sheds repairing a motorbike, so 'course he was alright…. but to see all your belongings and all your bedding strung up on the barbed wire all through the village… oh, it was terrible. But I thought, 'well, at least I'm alive…!'

Then Cyril, my husband, died in the War: he was in the Air Force, so that was another blow… but his family were so good to me that I didn't want to go back home then.

Steve. Has Beesands changed a lot in the time you have lived here?

Mary. Oh, a heck of a lot, the wall has changed it. You used to walk across the road from your front door and there was a little green lawn out there, and then step down onto the beach. I think it was 1960 they started bringing boulders here, but when it was an awful rough sea the boulders would move. We used to have shutters up to the windows and a little door that used to slot down, and, oh yeah, the sea still used to come in. We had a galvanised garage out the front and that one got washed away…it was very frightening. The wall has made it a lot safer, 'cause I used to get so scared.

Looking back we didn't have the luxuries that they've got today, and I think they were hard days, but they were good old days because there was no television or anything like that. I don't remember ever having an ice-cream, our 'high day' was when Mother used to make lemonade from crystals… and that was the only drink we had other than water out of the tap. I think we grew up tougher, that we didn't have all the germs like they've got today, 'cause you were immune to them.

– ❖ –

'Kitch' Hancock

Born 14th September 1914

Died 24th April 2009

Recorded on 1st November 2005

Kitch. I'm Ernest Kitchener Hancock really, see… but everybody calls me 'Kitch', I don't know no other; ever since I can remember I've always been called 'Kitch'.

Steve. That's because you were born at the beginning of the First World War?

Kitch. Yes, 'date of birth is September 14th 1914. I was born down North Cornwall, near Boscastle, and well, when I say we're Cornish, half our farm was in Devon, the other side of the river. We could call ourselves either really; 'twas two or three farms in one. Back in they days farming was worse than 'tis today: you asked Father for a shilling and he'd say, "You had one a month ago!"

We didn't have no money but we had a big farm, and loads of grub - see, kill a bullock or a sheep; you know, we lived well, but no money, and if you went to market you was lucky if you had a bid for your cattle…. we was ticking over! Oh, I could write a book about it!

Steve. You came from a big family, didn't you?

Kitch. Yes, thirteen: nine brothers, four sisters… and I was the youngest of the lot, I was the 'nizzledredge'. I had five brothers, no fat about 'em, great six, seven-footers, shoulders as wide as that table… it's funny why I was so much smaller that the others!

We had a strict upbringing: see, our mother died when I was only about four year old, and me oldest sister reared us really… it shook the family up. We had a great big farm and we had about fifteen great big heavy carthorses that we used, to do the ploughing and that… and about eight or ten ponies - 'cause there was eight or nine brothers, and we all had a pony, a nice big horse to ride.

Our kitchen was about ten times this size, you'd just about want a pushbike to get 'one end of the kitchen to the other… stone floors, Delabole slate, and a 'cloam' oven… open chimney, and in one side there'd be like a oven, made with firebricks. You'd bring in a faggot of wood and burn 'en and get 'en red hot, and then you could cook your roast dinner and bake your cake and biscuits after, all on the one heat like. When it came out 'twould be beautiful… a lovely way of cooking.

It was about late twenties, early thirties, in Cornwall in the Depression; nobody hadn't got nothing, nothing at all. We had about five to six hundred acres, say, two or three farms wrapped in one, 'cause farmers hadn't got the money. I remember Father had three farms rent-free just to keep tidy, then that gave us extra work, worse luck! Oh yes, we used to have up 'hundred and fifty odd acres of corn every year. I mean, 'twouldn' be a big acreage for today with tractors, but we did it all wi' horses, you see. I can remember five farmhouses out of seven in the parish empty, nobody in them. We used to look after the ground and perhaps use the yard to put cattle in, but nobody in the houses… lovely big farmhouses, nobody in. Mind you, they didn't fall down, 'cause they were well built.

When I got a bit older we couldn't get no money. I took up this 'all-in wrestling'…cor, that was vicious back in they days - they meant it! … if they could break your arm they would. We used to come up to Plymouth from down Cornwall, and if you won you'd have, I think it was about a fiver. But you'd earn 'en 'cause you'd go home and next morning you'd be black and blue. The most ever I come home with, I went to Bristol once, and I come home with twenty-some-odd quid! That was when wages was about a pound a week.

We moved up here in 1945 and I was Chauffeur then to Sir John and Lady Seale, for twenty-five years. Driving then wad'n no trouble 'cause there wad'n much traffic and you couldn't go very fast. If you done over forty miles 'hour Lady Seale would say, "We're nicking along, aren't we Hancock"! - but when they were asleep then I'd give 'en the whip!

You could change gear if you wait…you'd put the clutch in and you'd go…'one-tock-two'… that's how long it took to put 'en into next gear, if you tried to before 'e'd grate.

The Model 'T' Ford only had two gears, see, you pushed the clutch in hard and that was low gear…and if you was coming uphill, by the time you got half way up, your foot would ache and come off… then you'd be out of gear altogether, and you'd grind to a halt… you'd have to push him in again.

Steve. Were your teeth a trouble to you in those days? What did you clean them with?

Kitch. Never heard of cleaning teeth, you just left 'em. If you had toothache we used to have a dentist, he used to go into Launceston and you'd get there, in somebody's yard, sit on the shaft of a cart and he'd take out your couple of teeth, just yank 'em out!

Things have changed so much, a lot of youngsters today won't know what an old farm-yard looked like, 'cause they altered, they ended up as building sites; oh, I think it's sad, I don't like it, no, I like to see it how it was.

– ❖ –

Henry Lidstone

Born 9th November 1919
Died 6th December 2008

Recorded on 17th January 2006

Henry. When I was born in Derby Road, Kingsbridge my mother died, so I was brought up by my grandparents until my father married again. My mother's maiden name was Quarm, and her father had a shop at the bottom of Fore Street, where Pritchards are now.

Father was a butcher, called Henry the same as me, but they used to call him 'Harry', and he and my grandfather were 'Lidstones the Butchers'.

I worked in Father's butcher's shop for years, from leaving school at fourteen until I went in the Army during the War. I went in the 5th Devons first of all, before they shifted us into the Anti-Tank Regiment, and I was in Kent for most of the War. I didn't go abroad until just after D-Day when I went to France and then Germany. I was at home on leave when Kingsbridge was bombed the first time,

Henry Grant
Lidstone

Henry's father, Henry Grant Lidstone, and brother
Peter outside the family butchers' shop

when 'Eastmans' butchers and 'Lewis the Jewellers' were hit. I was out at East Allington with my brother delivering meat, and we were up by the church there and heard the explosions. We said, "It's Kingsbridge" … when we came back it was absolute chaos. The second time they hit Kingsbridge was where Woolworths is now, but I was away then.

They used to milk cows at the bottom of Duncombe Street, well around where 'Codds' the plumbers were after, and they would drive the cows up every day past our shop, right up through Fore Street and down Duncombe Street for milking.

At one time there used to be 'Oke's Garage' at the top of the town, where 'King's Market' is now; we used to get our petrol there. Later they went down into Bridge Street, where the 'Anchor Centre' is now. Well, when you think about it there were five or six garages in Kingsbridge then, where you could get petrol, and yet there weren't many cars! … now there's only one petrol station in Kingsbridge, for all the cars around today!

Before the Second War we still did our own slaughtering in a slaughterhouse near where the

Health Centre is now, just this side of the railway line. We had a rail-crossing there and Father used to rent about eight or ten fields there. I remember once, when we used to take the cattle across the fields, and one ran away and we had to stop the train.

We could always tell the time by the trains when we were in the slaughter-house. In those days it was the old steam trains, and we knew exactly what train it was; 'course Market days they used to have special trains for carrying all the livestock away.

Of course, everything was delivered in those days and I used to do a lot of deliveries… on a bike at first; one of those bikes with a basket on, to go around the town. I would have to go up the town and take the orders, come back, then Father used to cut the joints, and I had to go back again to deliver them. We used to salt beef and pork in brine tubs… we used to salt tongues as well.

Years ago they used to take the meat around and cut it in the horse van, and I remember going with a horse and wagon before we had the motor vans. If you went around Kingsbridge the old horse would stop every time you came to a customer…

he knew exactly where to stop. We used to keep them in a stable down behind the shop.

When I learnt to drive I used to go miles in the van, two or three times a week - to the villages and all over the place. You see, there was no freezers, you used to put it in a larder or something like that, so you had to have it fresh.

After the War they stopped slaughtering, because it used to be delivered by lorries from different areas... that was the end of slaughtering for us.

Mary Crispin

Born 18th March 1924

Recorded on 23rd January 2006

Mary. I was born at No.1, Homefield Cottages, Sherford. There was a school there in Sherford and I went there for a while, until I was about ten or eleven.

After that, when it closed us had to go to Charleton School.

There was two playgrounds: girls and boys, and toilets there, and two classrooms, one for the juniors and one for the seniors. It was full: they used to come from Harleston and Stancombe and all around, they used to walk... some used to come up from Frogmore.

There was a blacksmith, after the school building, on the left, then the Church. We used to go to the Chapel, which used to be full, and the old lady, Miss Schofield she was called, she'd get up lovely parties for us.... tea parties, and presents. She used to travel in a horse and wagon from Chillington in all weathers... thunder and lightening, yeah, with a 'hurricane' lamp.

I remember one Christmas they gave me a turkey to pick on me lap, and I got half way through it, and this thing walked off, he was gone! cor, I was gone too!... I runned home... I runned all the way up home, left the turkey on the floor; ..'twad'n dead, poor old devil.

Steve. *Talking about characters, you talked about 'Fishy Tucker', why was he called that?*

Mary. Ol' Ned, he used to go round with fish years ago, see... pony and trap... and his wife used to walk to Frogmore for cider; 'er used to say 'er was going down for Ned and when it came to, 'er was having it for herself, yeah! 'twad'n for old Ned 'tall! Oh, pretty goings-on out there, used to be... and 'Buffer' Wills, what he used to do: come in town, do some shopping and go in 'Matthews' up Fore Street, a food shop, you know, and he'd say,

"What's your cheese like?" and of course they'd cut 'en off a piece fer to taste. From there he'd go to another shop and ask, "What's your cheese like?"... he never bought any!

Aunt Lizzie Langworthy was a relation to me, 'er had a shop down 'Brook', sold sweets and that; us used to help ourselves when 'er wad'n looking... shame really! 'Er had an old place out the back where 'er kept 'er money... times 'er got out there, us would scramble for some sweets and out the door.

Steve. *Wasn't Homefield haunted by a dog?*

Mary. Well, yes, there was a dog there at Homefield, 'cause I goes there one day to smooth it down and it disappeared... oh yes... several have seen that. Don't go going out there in the dark 'cause it's still there they reckon. There was several parts of Sherford that was haunted.

Up on the right was the 'Pound House,' they've turned it into a house now. Well, Mother used to go down the farm to help do the washing and that, and help milk the cows... and one day I said, "I would like a glass of cider". So Richard said, "Go in and get a glass and go up the Pound House and help yourself". I got up there and next day I goes up again, up I goes and drinks some more cider; 'course you had to stir it, you see... I stirred it around and up came this rat, dead rat!

Ough ! that finished me! I goes down and I said to Richard, "What a thing, you've got a dead rat up there in the cider". He said, "Well, do you know what, they reckon if that goes in the cider, that's what flavours it, they reckon!"

Steve. *Can you tell me about when 'Bowden' was bombed?*

Mary. Oh, yeah, I worked there for the farm manager, Mr. William Bullen, and was in the barn and had to come out to feed the pigs, 'twas about quarter to five. None of us heard anything 'cause of all of the machinery working. When I came out it was all down on the ground... ruins... the farmhouse and the buildings... all gone.... and there was bits of people, you know.... a little baby, and the soldier, he was home on leave, he got killed as well... and his wife, she was still living but she died when they got her to hospital. The Manager's wife was still living and she was in the kitchen where the others was to, but she lived to tell the tale. It was a big shock... I often think about it you know. I went to get me bike in the garage and there was Mr. Bullen: he was killed as well, he was rolled up like a ball he was, I could see that he was gone.... not much I could do. I just went home - I was very upset, and, of course, Mother was worried 'cause she'd heard it.

Steve. *You were telling me you were machine-gunned once!*

Mary. Oh yeah, we were out in the field loading up sheaves, and Miss Burdett-Coutts told me to run over be the hedge - but I wouldn't 'cause I wanted to stop with the old horse, I was so fond of animals... that's when they bombed Kingsbridge... that's where they was heading for, you see!

– ❖ –

Alwyn Staddon

Born 26th June 1910

Died 12th September 2006

Recorded on 31st January 2006

Alwyn. I was born in Kingsbridge, my father had 'Victoria Boot Stores', practically opposite the Town Hall, and we lived there. It would be Victoria who would be Queen at the time, I can't think of any other reason.

The first lighting I remember was a funny... a sort of gas, and it was only in the best room, you see. It had little tiny gas-light lamps... my father had gone to the expense of having a gas light put in!

The first car that I can remember was a little saloon car and it belonged to a Miss Kitchen, who was the editress of the local Gazette; that was in the First World War I believe. I remember distinctly my father coming into the shop and saying something like, "War has been declared!" Father had a big room at the back of the shop and during the War it was commandeered for the use of the troops, they slept there. There were a lot of troops in Kingsbridge and I remember seeing them marching through the town. When the First War finished I was only eight.

My father learnt his trade, started as a workman and he knew shoes inside-out; you couldn't tell him anything about shoes. He went to London for a time and managed a shop up there. In Kingsbridge he didn't repair shoes, just sold them. He used to do hob-nailed boots, especially for farmers... and football boots. He used to get up about seven in the morning and go down and sweep the pavement: that was his first job before the girls came in. My father used to do a lot of business, especially on Wednesdays and Saturdays when they used to keep open 'til ten o'clock at night. If there were customers about he stayed open longer; of course they were out to oblige customers, the service was different to today. Mother worked in the shop, she specialised in the women's trade. Everybody knew everybody in those days, nobody walked up and down the town you didn't know. I well remember my father coming into the shop saying, "There's a stranger coming up the town".

My mother and father were rather fond of Torcross, and our summer holidays would be spent

out there. First of all they used to hire a horse and carriage, from a farmer, and in those days people would put up summer visitors in their homes, so my father would book up the bedroom with two little cots in it for my sister and I. Then, later on, when the motorcars were coming in, my father would hire a motorcar from Leslie Oke, to go out as far as Torcross for our annual summer holidays!

All I wanted to do was play the piano: if I could have made a living at it I would have done. I learnt from a Mrs. Veysey Stoneman. Veysey used to have a grocer's shop and a gramophone shop: 'His Master's Voice Stores'; he was the first man in Kingsbridge to have a gramophone as far as I know. His wife taught me to play the piano, I started at six and at the age of eight I passed my first music exam... you see, it was customary in those days to have a piano.

I've given piano recitals in Plymouth and down in Truro, up in the suburbs of London... I've played up in Scotland, in Northumberland, Blackpool and all over the place. I've got dozens of programmes somewhere.

I went to work for Lloyds Bank when I was sixteen and a half, and when I went to Totnes branch my father bought me a car so I could go up and down to work. I was there for four years and then they sent me to Newcastle-upon-Tyne! After that I worked in branches in many places; around here locally, and in London too.

Pat Farleigh

Born 4th June 1924

Recorded on 23rd February 2006

Pat. I was born here in East Prawle, down in the cottage which was the Post Office, the cottage that my mum lived in since she was orphaned at the age of six. She went there to live with her granny, because her mother had died of TB, and a month later her dad died… they were thirty-four and thirty-five years old.

Granny Hannaford brought up seven children of her own, as a widow, and then Mum and her brother. The eldest sister went out 'in service' when she was thirteen, and another daughter died at twelve of TB; Mum was the baby.

I've lived here in the village all me life and when I was a girl all the cottages were lived in by people that were born and bred here, they went down the generations - but Prawle idn't like it was. Us was allowed out in the winter for 'hour after tea; we'd play 'hare and hounds', go over where the ricks were and down around the willow grove - we didn't have no watches then, we used to guess the time … but if us was late getting back in us would get jawed!

I cycled to Kingsbridge for a long time, for music lessons. I started when I was eleven, until I was fourteen. I went to Mr. and Mrs. Adams, to learn piano; but some weeks I 'mitchied' and I didn't go, I used to go around the shops, or go to me cousin's house and spend time with the kids.

I think it used to take me forty minutes to go in; I used to cycle Ford way and come back the other way through Stokenham; but it used to take me longer coming home 'cause I had to push up all they hills, and I only had an ordinary bike, you see,

no three-speed or anything.

I was sixteen when the RAF came to Prawle; we had Royal Artillery with 'ack-ack' guns. We had the Devon Regiment here once, the Buffs, and the Royal Marines came to train for Dieppe. So there was eight hundred services here during the War, and, actually the camp was over West Prawle to begin with, that's where the original camp, the Radar Station was. Then they built the Camp over here on top of the hill and moved in. It was eventually closed in 1957.

I've done for the Post Office for fifty-five years, dear, so that's a good service, id'n it. I was twelve years as Assistant to me mother, and forty-three and a half years as post-mistress. My mother had taken the Post Office over in 1915, from Mrs. Beer, and I took it over from Mum in 1950: so it was in our family all that time, seventy-eight years!

When I started with Mum she was earning thirty-nine pound a year, and I had half a crown a week… two and sixpence. After sixteen months Mum wrote and they raised it, and she gave me a pound a month… but do you know, I used to save out of that! When you think of it now… what a difference, id'n it. We had to do postal orders and pensions… and savings…. the Savings Bank was one of the main things… and telegrams. We did telegrams for years, you see the first Christmas Day when the Service personnel were here I was still delivering greetings telegrams when 'twas half past one in the afternoon, because we had so many, you see, and somebody was getting married once at Muckwell, and I cycled to Muckwell eight times that day with greetings telegrams.

When we went decimalised I was going to give up, 'cause after 'pounds, shillings and pence' all my life… but we went to Kingsbridge in November and January, just before it come in in February and we were given books to work through. I was the only one out of the lot that could balance the books … 'course it was easy after that.

Freda Widger

Born 8th January 1920

Recorded on 28th   February 2006

Freda. I was born at Sloutts Farm, Slapton, down in the village; it was a working farm then, but all the farms in the village have been sold off, because you can't drive cattle through the village now, like I used to do.

My mother's parents kept the Post Office at Slapton, and her father was a shoemaker and mender. They lived opposite the church, that's where the Post Office was in those days.

We had Powleslands, the bakers in the village, beside the 'Queens'; they delivered bread around and I can remember one of the very early vans they had, it had solid tyres to it. Weeks had a garage there, where the Field Centre is now, and they supplied the village with electricity before the mains came in. We used to take the accumulator for the wireless there in the horse and wagon, to get it charged up. We only had one to start with, then you had to wait for that one to come back again, but in the end my father bought another one so we could change them over. We children learnt to do it, how to open up the box and change the coil. We were one of the first in the village to have wireless and when there was anything special on, people would come in and listen to it.

We were evacuated in December 1943, and it hit my mother very badly, clearing out, 'cause a lot of stuff had to go in store, and we had six bedrooms at Sloutts. We had to move all the animals, the implements, hay, straw, mangold… every day for weeks my future husband came over to do that before we moved out. We had to sell quite a lot, they had a market for all the animals they didn't want… but who wanted them? - because all the farmers around the area had to go and nobody wanted to buy them. We took just one cow for milk for ourselves and the rest had to go. We had to start again when we came back, you see, and quite a few people didn't come back at all, they settled somewhere else!

We were the first to come back, in November and lived with my mother and father at Sloutts for three months. Slapton was like a ghost town, very eerie! We were married in May 1944, a week before D-Day. We knew we had a farm to go to but Poole farmhouse hadn't been repaired. It was in such a bad state, the kitchen ceilings were down… it was very badly knocked about..

At Poole we had shell-holes in the front lawn and you got paid for every shell-hole in the fields. You had to go around and count 'em all up, and if they were big ones you counted them as two. We had over two hundred in one field, so we didn't pay any rent for two years, because we had so much compensation to get back. They were still finding bombs when they were working on the ground, ploughing and that… it was very worrying.

George Brimacombe

Born 24th December 1913

Recorded on 17th March 2006

George. I was born at Chillaton, between Tavistock and Lifton, but later we lived at Boar's Hill, Combe, near Bigbury. It was a smallholding at one time 'cause there was a shippon there to tie up cows and all that.

It was very old, cob walls and thatched; there was one big kitchen, and outside the back door there was a stream running…. we always had salted fish for Sunday breakfast and that was put out there with this little stream running on it a day or so before, to get the salt out of it. The toilet was down the bottom of the orchard, built on top of the stream!

I had a new bike when I was at Boar's Hill… six guineas, from a bike shop up Brownston Street in Modbury, 'Rudge Whitworth' it was, with coupled brakes and dropped handlebars.

I lived there until I left school at fourteen, and then I went 'live in' up the farm house at Lixton, Loddiswell. Me parents still lived there until Father retired.

I remember the water-wheel working at Bigbury Combe, and that water-wheel used to do the threshing, reed-making and combing, drive the mill and even drive the separator. They had two ponds: one small one, right beside the water-wheel,

another big one up in the field, and when you was threshing you had to go up there and turn on some water because it took a lot of power to drive the thresher… sawing up wood with a saw bench, as well. There was a wheel down in the bottom floor and a wheel up in the barn… you had to set the right speed, you know.

Up Lixton I used to be indoors mornings, scrub the floors and clean the boots, skin the teddies… and twelve o'clock I went out to bring in the cows, tie 'em in. Then after dinner I used to go out with a 'oss and cart draying cabbage, turnips and mangolds. I was the farm boy and I used to get six shillings a week. I used to dray the dung out… what was it, seven paces apart we made the rows; pulled it out with this digger thing. A cartload would make six or seven heaps. Two fellows used to come in from Churchstow to spread the dung with forks then.

They had a plough, harrows, cultivator, chain harrow… then there was a grass harrow with spikes, all horse-drawn. The hand tools was an 'eavel', that was what they used for cleaning out the stables, and heave the dung in the cart… and for spreading it out in the field. There was teddy diggers, and hoes for hoeing mangolds and turnips; … a hook for paring the hedges - all had to be done be hand.

I had a motorbike when I was seventeen… twenty-five pounds: it came from 'Pikes' down Plymouth. Me first car was an old Morris 10; high wheels… a hundred and twenty pounds, I think it was… we got it up 'Eveleys', Exeter.

I remember in the stables at Bigbury Combe there was nine horses: Trooper, Violet, Prince, Hector, Madam, Damsel, Tiger…. later when I went to Elston I had four horses in the stables there: Trooper, Lion, Jessie and Prince… two of them were dray horses from London, from the breweries… huge great things they was, and that one in the picture, Violet, came up be train from Lifton where I used to live. I had to go to Kingsbridge and bring her home. She was in foal and when the sale was she made a hundred guineas; that was a hell of a price for a horse in they days… and the colt made fifty-seven guineas.

I was working at 'Tufflands', towards Bigbury and was exempt from the Second World War. I didn't have to go in the Army 'cause I was on the farm, so I had to join the Home Guard. We used to have to do duty in the Home Guard, mock battles and all that, they used to do. Anyway, when the bombs hit Aveton Gifford, some dropped in the marsh, and all the mud and the eels was up in the street! I saw the church go up, and I said to the farmer, "Aveton Gifford has been bombed, I want to go back home". One little girl was killed at the Rectory, but no one else in the village.

Claude Solomon

Born 29th November 1923

Recorded on 12th June 2006

Claude. Father came up from St. Austell, as he had come home from the First World War without a job,

and Captain Holdsworth out Widdicombe House took him on for a time. See, they went away without a guarantee of a job when they came back, not like the Second War when employers were compelled to take 'em back.

He went back to Cornwall and later we came back again, when I was six weeks old, and he went to work for the Ilbert family at Bowringsleigh: he was a footman on the coach, and as he got older he became the butler. We lived at Piers Cottages, out on the Thurlestone road, then we moved down to the Lodge and he worked at Bowringsleigh then until he retired.

Mother was a Crispin, her forefathers built the Grammar School, a long way back; I think they were Quakers. The family home was Rickham, out at Portlemouth, but the Crispin family also built the baker's shop here in West Alvington. My grandfather used to deliver bread with a horse and wagon.

In they days everybody knew everybody, and it was a happy atmosphere. There was no TV's or anything like that, you made your own entertainment: played in the woods, built little camps and things like that, and I joined the Scout Movement. Even at school we used to be able to play anywhere… go over the copse dinner times, hear the school bell ring and dash away back to school. Now they've got to keep an eye on them, for safety's sake. You can't trust anybody. We had two schoolmistresses here, Mrs. Thoroughgood and Miss Hilldick.

We lived at the Lodge for a few years and I went to Kingsbridge school from there. I was able to save a bit of money and bought myself a bike; see, that was the attraction then - ride down so far as the gates at the bottom Lodge and put your bike behind the laurels and track up to school or whatever. You could leave a bicycle anywhere then and nobody would touch it; now, if you left it outside he'd be gone.

I worked at Bowringsleigh for a while when I left school and then I joined up when I was eighteen. I was away with the Eighth Army from 1942 until it was disbanded in 1945, and that opened my eyes a bit I can tell you! Home here during the War Mrs. Thoroughgood's husband was in charge of the LDV: that was the Local Defence Volunteers, but they used to get called the 'Look, Duck and Vanish'! Then, later on they became known as The Home Guard.

After the War I went bus driving for Western National, driving the Dockyard workers to Plymouth at five o'clock in the morning. One particular morning I went to start the bus, swung the handle and it came back and broke me arm, so after that I went farming. I went to work at Cross Farm, Woolston, in 1949 and spent the rest of me working life out there. That was when we came here to Lower Street to live and we hadn't been here long when our neighbour came down from his garden and he said to my wife, "Here you are my biddy, here's a lovely big cabbage for you".She said to him, "I don't want your old cabbage!"…well, see, she'd seen him going up there every morning and pouring his 'upstairs water' over them !

In those days hundreds of things hadn't been invented - even the plastic bag; there was nothing like that when we were younger. When we went shopping you had a straw-made bag, a three-cornered thing with a knot in the middle of the handle. I bet there's one down the museum; you'd sling 'en over your shoulder and away you'd go! 'Somerfields' wad'n invented then!

Hilda Tucker

Born 2nd November 1920

Mollie Dudiak

Born 25th May 1928

Recorded 19th June 2006

Steve. *I'm here to talk to you about the place you grew up in, in Fore Street, Kingsbridge.*

Hilda. We were born down in Langworthy's Passage, which was down behind 'Timber House', as we used to call it, which was where the entrance to the car park is now. There was a cycle shop and a grocer's shop there, and in behind that were houses, on each side of the path. We went down over cobblestones to where we lived, right at the bottom. There was a huge yard there and there were two more houses down round the corner on what is now all car park. The toilets were right across this yard, and in behind Mr. Kennard kept horses and chicken and that. Next over was Brunswick alley where there was a little sweet shop and then Brunswick Place, but the whole area was condemned, and demolished under the Slum Clearance.

The cottages were very small and only had a little scullery, a kitchen with a coal fire, and we had a little bit of garden and some sheds where we had a 'copper'.

They used to have nice ballroom dancing in the 'Albion Hotel' and you could watch it from the yard.

Mollie. 'Reynolds and Clarks' was a three-storeyed wooden building, and we lived through the passageway and down behind, where there were six or eight cottages; but there was no outlet down the other end so when the restrictions came in it was condemned, because if there had been a

fire in the building all of us down the passage wouldn't have been able to get out. The opening was big enough for a horse and cart to go down, and we lived down the bottom where two cottages had been made into one, because we had a big family of eleven children. There were massive, high stone walls with stables on the other side; that was why we couldn't have an opening to get out, it was occupied by horses. There was no comfort: stone floors, flag-stones, and in the kitchen was a big wooden table. There were four little bedrooms 'cause Mum had got permission to have a doorway knocked through upstairs between the two cottages - but it was still cramped. Three of us slept in one bed and I was always 'piggy-in-the-middle' because I was the smallest. We left there in 1935 when it was condemned.

Hilda. We were living over in Wallingford Road when the bomb dropped in Fore Street. I remember they kept the children in the Picture House, 'cause my brother was in there and they had to wait to get out. There was another alley called 'Headland Place', about where Woolworths is now, and that was destroyed in the War, when they had a direct hit. Eastman's the butcher got bombed too, and further down that passage was the Congregational Chapel. They thought my father was in there but he wasn't. He used to go and wind the clock in the Congregational Hall and the Town Hall clock. When Plymouth was being bombed we used to go up to Darky Lane and watch, but my brother used to be scared stiff.

Len Tucker

Born 24th September 1920

Died 25th March 2008

Recorded on 19th June 2006

Len. I was born in Greenhill, East Allington, but we always called it 'Chute Row' because there was a trough in the wall; I think it's still there, where the water used to just pour out into it. I can remember going to school when I was three and a half. Us used 'go up across the fields from where us lived... you'd go up through the churchyard and into the school. I used to 'mitchy' a lot!... we used to be walking up to go 'school and the jackdaws were nesting in the Church tower. At a quarter to nine they'd pitch on the hands and go in... 'course they'd stop the clock, and we used to wait until it started again!

71

I was an apprentice plumber when I left school at fourteen and I served me time, seven years, with Scobles; they were the biggest firm then, in Kingsbridge and around the area.

When the War began I had to go and register and have a medical down Plymouth, then I had me calling-up papers…. and that was that, you had to go. I was in the Air Force for a while, then I went on a gunnery course on the Isle of Man. Then I done two and a half year, in the desert, in the Middle East. I saw some action out there; it was at the time that Malta was under siege, and we came down from the desert and got sorted by some officials. I was a Corporal then, see, and because I'd been on the gunnery course I got put on this merchant ship, in charge of the twelve-pound 'ack-ack' gun, on the back end of the boat. The Commander in charge said, "If anything hits us you'll get blown somewhere, that'll be the end of it … you don't have anything to worry about!" …. I was just twenty years old then.

I had to come back and finish me apprenticeship with Scobles then, and I spent most of me life working for them ….. built every house on the Rack Park estate. See, when the War finished we built houses everywhere, in every village around Kingsbridge, say twenty here, fifteen somewhere else…East Allington, South Pool, West Alvington… all the council houses.

I learnt to drive with Scobles, then I joined the Fire Service, and I drove the fire engine for twenty-seven years, regular! We had a brand new Rolls Royce, 'OUO 474', that was the number of 'en. We had one or two bad fires here… in my day you stopped there from start to finish, all night and all day!

Tom Putt

Born 28th October 1916

Recorded on 29th June 2006

Steve. I believe you and your family have had some very sad experiences in your life.

Tom. I was born in Salcombe on the 28th of October 1916, which was a very significant date, as my father was drowned the day before in the Salcombe lifeboat disaster: he was Thomas Henry, the same as me.

It was during the First World War and the lifeboat was called out to a boat in distress near Prawle Point. It was a rough night and they set out in terrible seas; 'course it was rowing in them days. When they got to the boat they discovered the Coastguards had rescued all the men, but not having radio in them days, they didn't know until they got there, so really they needn't have gone.

Anyway, as they returned to Salcombe they got outside the Bar and the sea was breaking over it. They had a talk about what they should do; should they go on to Plymouth, or turn back to Dartmouth, or make a run for it up Salcombe Harbour? The majority was for coming home, so they made a run for it, but they were caught broadside on by the Bar breaking and tipped her over; 'course there was no self-righting in them days. There was only two men that survived it, a lot of the rest were washed up at Rickham.

In the meantime I was born that night; the birth was brought on by the tragedy; I wasn't due for about another three months.

My Mother was Edith Dignam, and she had a particularly tragic life. Firstly one of her brothers was drowned in the harbour here, he was only seventeen. I remember she always talked about it. She was married first to a coastguard, and they had two children; well, her first husband died of some disease, her second husband was drowned, and her third husband, William Henry, was my father's brother, and he was killed with her when Salcombe was bombed. I also lost my first wife and my little son then. My little boy was born in September 1942 and my wife had had him down with my mother, down in Church Street. My stepfather and my stepsister's two stepsons were in the kitchen / living room having their tea. Mum and Grace and the baby were in the sitting room, and these planes came over and dropped the bombs right on our house. My stepsister got out, and the dog; my stepfather and the two boys were killed in the living room, and Mum and Grace, and the baby were killed in the sitting room. I was up in the

Cairngorms then, so I had two days travelling to get home, and I didn't know what had happened until my sister and brother-in-law met me at Kingsbridge Station, and told me on the way home...the baby was five days old - I never did see him.

Steve... and what happened to your stepbrother?

Tom. Well, it was 1918, and he was in the Navy, up at Scapa Flow, and he went sailing for one of the officers, crewing for him; and I don't quite know what really happened but he was drowned, he was about twenty-three.

I met my second wife, Eva, in Easingwold, Yorkshire, while I was still in the Army up there, and we married and lived up there for a while. After several years she said she would like to come to Salcombe to live so we moved down with our two eldest children, and she was quite happy here.

Steve. I read a newspaper article about an apple called 'Tom Putt' !

Tom. Well, I understand there was an old Reverend Tom Putt from Gittisham, near Honiton, and there is an avenue of beech trees there, and the area is known as 'Putt's Corner'. It's said that there's still a big portrait of the old Tom Putt up in the staircase of the Old Vicarage, which is now a hotel. The apple is named after him and is red and rosy... like Tom Putt!

Gladys Santer

Born 15th June 1906

Died 20th March 2009

Recorded on 10th July 2006

Gladys. I was born at Lower Hutcherleigh, Blackawton. It was a very long house made of cob; it must have been at least two hundred and fifty years old. There was the wide path leading up from the courtyard, up through some trees, where the carriage went from the house to get to the beautiful pillared entrance, on the way to Blackawton. It had lawns bordered with double crocuses, and they looked so pretty.

We understood that Squire Grant and his wife and three daughters lived there, many years before my family. He owned Middle and Higher Hutcherleigh … all that area. When I was a child I met a lady who said she was a workman's daughter, born in one of the workman's cottages down by the Lower Court, all joined on to the cattle and pigs' houses. It was where we used to play, where the cattle used to be. There was a beautiful orchard of two or three acres, with several pear trees and plum trees of different kinds. We children gathered the apples… picked them up and put them in bags. The walled garden had wide stone tops where we used to sit and read a book… we had plenty of freedom, and scope to enjoy life.

In 1914 the owners decided to build a new house, and we moved in there in about 1915 or 1916.

I went to school in Blackawton, a mile and a half each way. The country schoolchildren would take their lunch and sit on the churchyard steps to eat it, and then go to the village tap to have a drink… we were quite happy. Now things are so different, aren't they, they wouldn't dare to let children do that.

When I came home from school my work was to take care of my younger brothers; that was when the new house was being built. One day when I was out with them I heard a terrible noise, it was like a monster coming. I rushed them to a gate and we went through a field to where we could see. I saw it was a big steam lorry all loaded with bricks, a 'Foden' steam wagon, and it was noisy, you see I'd never heard or seen anything like it in my life. It was generally very quiet, only horse traffic, you see.

Once a year the wagon would be fitted up safely for us, and we would go to Torcross; there'd be Mother and Father and seven children. We'd take a big kettle, and at Torcross a cottager would boil the kettle for sixpence, and we were able to have our tea on the sands… that happened once a year. Our horse, Mabel, always went home nice and quick, because every year she had a little colt that would be waiting for her evening meal, so she always went home smartly, you know!

I'll tell you something that used to interest us: old Mr. and Mrs. Noyce, I suppose grandparents or great-grandparents of the ones now in Kingsbridge. They would come along with a horse and open wagon, and they would be selling all tin things… and kettles, plates, saucepans; and there'd be two bags at the back, one for rags and the other for bones, and we'd save all our big bones from cooking and they'd go in their bag. They travelled from Kingsbridge as far as Blackawton and back.

Steve. It's a bit like today's recycling!

Gladys. Yes, the rags would be used for paper, and the bones would probably be boiled up for glue.

On Sunday mornings my sister and I would see that Mother's veil was all right and had no little holes in it and, of course, we all used to wear gloves.

It was about the time that some ladies were discarding their veils, and Mrs. Noyce said, "I don't wear veils and gloves, I've given that up!". She was modern!

Steve. What can you tell me about Oldstone in Blackawton, that old ruined place?

Gladys. Well, there were three ponds up there, and when my mother was a young woman, long before she was married, it was on the papers, down in Plymouth, that one of the Squire's daughters was found standing up in the mud in the pond… some say she was drowned… and a young man who had been staying there had gone away to America.

One of the village girls took me to see what they call the 'shell cave': that was near the big house and they said a hermit had lived there. The walls were lined with shells, all around, and some were used to line the roof. One day we took our lunch and saw it and then went back again to school. The house was a mansion and it burned down.

When we were old enough we had to hoe mangolds; there'd be about four of us hoeing mangold, turnips… and setting potatoes, putting them in, that was always done about Easter time.

I had to pump the water from the well, it was something that fell to my lot and I hated it; even the boys have said it was hard work. I loved to hear the drips as they came down on the roof above, to say the tank's full. It was something that you couldn't refuse - if you were told to do it, well you did it, although I used to hate it.

I remember the blizzard of 1927, 'cause my sweetheart, as he was then, couldn't get back home to Totnes, so he had to stay with us, and I remember the men were all queued up outside the baker's shop for bread ... we did have some hard winters back then.

My husband was a colporteur, he used to go around with a box on his bicycle delivering Bibles and other Christian literature, and also things like writing paper and envelopes, that the rural people would find useful.

Jack Patey

Born 31st March 1921

Recorded on 10th July 2006

Jack. I was born at Lower Batson, which, in 1921 apparently, was in the borough of West Alvington, not Salcombe... 'Batson was a borough town when Plymouth was a fuzzy down': that was an old saying.

My father's father was a ship's rigger, and he died young and left my grandmother to bring up six children on her own. His family were all shipwrights and Naval men... I'm told they were hard men. My father died at thirty-four and left my mother with four of us.

My mother was a Thornton and her uncle was the skipper of a ship built by Date in Kingsbridge, the 'Anna Maria'. Her first skipper was washed overboard and he drowned on his first voyage. My great-uncle took over the ship, and my grandfather had gone to sea with him when he was eight, because he'd lost his mother when he was very young. He was the ship's boy: they had a lot of brass on these old windjammers, you know, and that was his job for the first voyage, to clean all that, and then feed the birds on board... and one day he was feeding the fowls and he thought to 'eself, 'I wonder if the old cock bird can swim?' He throwed 'en overboard and he drowned! 'course he got in trouble over that.... and of an evening he used to go down to the crew's cabin and hear 'em telling their yarns and that. He crossed the line on his first voyage as they went to Brazil, and they had a stow-away on board, a coloured man who wanted to get back to Brazil, and they had 'en in chains.

My grandfather jumped ship in Southampton; he'd been away for a couple of years and he didn't want to be away on a ship any longer.... he was a young chap of ten years old. Well, the Police caught up with 'en, so in the end his brother labelled 'en - put a label around his arm and sent 'en back to his father!

I drove the last horse around the 'pound' at Batson Hall Farm when I was about eleven, I reckon. Well, boys used to do that, but I was the last one to do it. The farmers used to bring their apples to the pound and unload them from their carts. The horse was hitched up to three big bits of wood in a triangle, and he had plenty of room to go around... I used to sit on the wood and drive the horse around. It drove the big cogwheels of the crusher that champed up the apples and sent them down into a big container. Then they'd shovel out the pulp into the big press.

My brother was a boxer, he held the red ribbons for two or three years in the Middleweight Division in Catterick Camp, Yorkshire. He lost the sight in one eye with boxing... but boxing was a popular sport back then... well, he had his first fight in Salcombe, in what used to be Rosebank Garage, just alongside the Church. He was fighting a bloke down there, he was only a boy, you know, and my brother had a terrific punch on 'en, and, well he could have killed that bloke that night with one punch.... that's what the other boy told me, years after. He said he was concussed and couldn't remember going home that night.

Old Jacob Terrell - or 'Job' as he was known - lived to be a hundred, and he died about three days after; that would have been about 1932. He had a grandchild one year old when he was one hundred years old and they had this 'ere do down Batson to celebrate. Jackson, down Horsecombe Farm, gived out strong cider, 'twas in a rum cask... they were soon on their hands and knees!

I didn't have to go in the Army, I was exempted as I was on a farm, and then I was badly wounded home here. I was out in a field with me horses corn-harvesting; it was September the 8th 1942 and the boats were going out to sea, they were getting ready for the invasion, and a Focke-Wolfe came right in to bomb a ship, see. I had cannon shell through me back and I walked half a mile holding me lung in me hand. I had an eight by six wound in me back, and they could trace me all that way from where I was wounded. It killed one horse and the other died within twelve months, I think. When they opened the ambulance doors in Plymouth, and saw I was still living, they said they wouldn't have believed it. I was in and out of hospital for four years.

I'd been under machine-gun fire three or four times before, when I was working me horses over at Snape's Point, where they were coming right in.

After that I did gardening for people, and finished up at Snapes Manor, in charge of the gardens there.

Steve. So really you had a worse injury than some in the Army received!

Jack. My brother was in the Royal Corps of Signals and was in action at Dunkirk; he was one of only three that came back in his lot... he came through the War and never had a scratch.

Wally Tarr

Born 9th April 1926

Recorded on 10th August 2006

Wally. I was born here at Inner Weeke, Loddiswell and when I was about eight or nine years old we moved to Outer Weeke, the house just at the end of the yard here. Then when I got married in 1953 we came back here - so I didn't go very far!

Steve. Tell me about the Saddleback Hill.

Wally. That's how we have always known it, 'Saddleback Hill'; but it's not as high as it used to be. Years before the road was tarmaced it was stones and stuff, and in 1937 when we were at home with Mother and Father, she used to take in visitors. There was a bloke that was a mechanic for Donald Campbell, and he came down here with a long car, I think it was an 'Alvis'... and what happened! He came up over the hill and the car got stuck on the top! They always say, 'One side you'm going up to heaven, and all of a sudden you'm going down to....!'

Mother used to make butter, and Father used to take the butter and eggs up to Jack Guest in Loddiswell. Later we started selling milk and I used to take it with a horse and cart, mornings, out to Knapp Mill where the churns were collected. 'Course the churns have all gone and it's all tankers now; and they had to go a long way to get a lorry load of milk as there were so many small producers. It's sad as many of them have given up milk production and the ones left are getting bigger and bigger.

Steve. *Do you remember any of the working mills around here?*

Wally. Yes, Avon Mill, where the Garden Centre is now: it used to be called Holman's Mill, and further down stream there's Hamley's Mill, now known as New Mill. Near here was Knapp Mill, but that was just ruins. Father used to take corn to Hamley's Mill to have it ground, and Mrs. Hamley used to do the milling. It was done by a millstone powered by a water-wheel… but that's all gone.

Steve. *Did Father pay you or were you expected to work for your keep?*

Wally. When you wanted some money you'd say, "Father, I want some money please?" and he'd give you five bob perhaps, and if you asked for more in a fortnight or three weeks time he would want to know what you'd already done with the five shillings!

I joined the Home Guard when I was fifteen; you really had to be sixteen, but I put me age on so I could get up to Loddiswell with the boys that I went to school with. Well, towards the end of the War, I had this form that I was called up to go down the mines, somewhere in Wales… they called them the 'Bevin Boys'. I went to Plymouth and passed me medical, but they found that, because I was in agriculture, I could get exempted. You see, food was wanted more after the War actually, because the troops were coming home and all Europe was starving… so I didn't go.

In the Home Guard we did a lot of marching, and rifle practice… no wonder they called it 'Dad's Army' … it was a bit of fun, but there was a serious side to it.

You know a lot of people can hardly imagine how farming has changed… you can't remember a binder working with horses, can you? - and then the tractor came in and took over. The combine harvester did away with the threshing-machine, and things are still changing!

– ❖ –

Bill Lethbridge

Born 8th May 1920

Bet Lethbridge

Born 27th February 1924

Recorded on 5th October 2006

Bill. I was born at Frittiscombe, at Stokenham, the second oldest of ten children. I went to school there at Stokenham, the old school at Carehouse Cross; we used to walk there every day from Frittiscombe.

When we used to cut corn with horses and a binder, you'd go round and round until you get a bit left in the middle, and all the rabbits would get in there, you see, there'd be any amount in there. Then you'd have a rare bit of sport catching rabbits, the dogs would be tired right out by the end of the day.

Bet. When us was harvesting at Pinhay's Farm, South Pool, where I was born, us used to catch a lot of rabbits, and I'd say to 'em down village, "You wanna a rabbit?" … "Yes, if you skin 'en". I'd skin a rabbit and sell 'en for sixpence… and do errands for people for two or three pennies. I saved it up 'til I had three pounds, seventeen and six pence, and I bought a bike; I was about eleven then, I reckon.

Bill. Father had a threshing-machine and steam engine, and me and me brother used to drive round the roads, threshing for other farmers.

Sowing seeds in they days was done with a 'sillup', strapped around your neck. The real name is 'seed-lip' and it's kidney shaped, and you sowed the seed by hand. You don't see none of that now, it's all done with a tractor now.

We had to milk be hand then, see, no machine for milking then… carry the buckets, took 'em to the dairy and tipped them into the cooler. You'd let it run down through the cooler into the churns, and then take the churns out and load them on to the horse and cart.

We took 'em to the milk stand every morning, and wait for the lorry to come round from Totnes to pick 'em up - seven days a week.

Bet. I used to have to milk three cows before I went to school, and used to either ride me pony or me bike to Frogmore: Miss Adams used to teach at Vine House there, she had nine pupils. Then I went on into Kingsbridge; Stanbrook House, up top of Fore Street, where the teachers, the Misses Parkhouse were very strict.

I remember when they had the Post Office at South Pool, we used to go in there when stamps was a penny ha'penny. Miss Bevan used to run the shop and you'd go in there on a Saturday night, and they had a big round cheese there on the table… and the old cat used to be up there asleep on top of the cheese! I always remember that.

There used to be a carriage drive years ago from Fallapit House to Buckland-Tout-Saints. Lord Fortescue used to drive a carriage and pair down the drive and came out by that seat at the bottom of the hill, go down the road and up behind Tollditch, right down there through the fields and the woods, and out Flear Mill… up round the corner and in to Buckland.

Bill. When we were evacuated from Frittiscombe in 1943 we went to Uncle's farm at Loddiswell. The Americans had set up camps around there and left just before D-Day. My little brother, he was the youngest of all of us, he was about seven, went with two other boys into the fields one afternoon and found a hand grenade in a rabbit's hole. It exploded and killed my brother, and seriously injured the other two; one of them died the next day.

After the evacuation we didn't go back to Frittiscombe again, we went to Stancombe, over Sherford. Then Bet and I got married in 1945, and

in October 1946 we came here to Nutcombe, and we've been here ever since.

Steve. *I was looking at those hooks in your ceiling.*

Bet. That was for hanging up the hams, they would be all salted and put in linen, and they'd be alright for six months. There was an open fireplace there, and I've still got the chimney crooks that used to hang down, to boil up the cast iron kettle and a big boiler for hot water.

I remember going down Chillington when the War was over; they had Tommy Luckes's white horse, and they'd painted him red, white and blue!

– ❖ –

Edna Tucker

Born 3rd October 1921

Recorded on 30th October 2006

Edna. I lived at Coombe Cottages, East Allington when I was a girl, the first one inside the gate. It was three cottages then, but it's all into one now. We had two bedrooms, no water, no bath … the bucket toilet was past the other two cottages, down by the sheds - no flush… and the water was down there at the end with one tap for all of us; there was no water *inside* the cottage at all.

Candles and lamps then, that's all there was, you couldn't run down to the toilet in the night, no, you had 'charlies' under the bed!

We didn't have a sink in the kitchen, we had washing-up pans. We used to wash ourselves like that: in the kitchen with a pan of water, and when 'twas cold Mother would put it in front of the fire in the other room. There was an old tin bath for us to strip down and sit in, to have a soak, once a week.

It's different today… they don't know what hard times it was then, and yet we were happy … no fridges or nothing like that… Mum used to put a net over the meat, and us used to stand the milk in a drop of cold water in a bucket, to keep it cool.

When I left school I went and lived up Mounts in a farmhouse, cleaning and 'doing'; I was fourteen years old. I used to do the separating, feed the fowls, pick up the eggs and wash them, do a bit of cleaning and dusting.

Steve. What choice of jobs did you have when leaving school?

Edna. You didn't have no choice, not shop jobs or anything like that, you just went out 'doing' for people. You couldn't get into town very easily, either you walked or you had a bike.

Steve. Where would you have your hair done?

Edna. Only had your hair cut, couldn't afford to have anything different. Bill Lethbridge used to do it, 'e charged sixpence to have your hair cut… girls, boys, anybody at all, sixpence each.

Steve. What about if you needed any dental treatment?

Edna. Oh, just too bad … 'used to go school dentist then, didn't we, he used to come up to the school every so often - us used to dread it, yeah, if we could stay away we would.

Steve. How did you get rid of your rubbish years ago? You didn't have a dustcart coming around!

Edna. Some stuff you used to be able to burn in the garden, but we used to take a lot of it down the lane in a wheelbarrow, down to the Quarry pit; down the lane on the right-hand side… anything at all!

Steve. What do you remember about Fallapit House?

Edna. My mother used to work down there, when the Robinsons were there.

She was down there for years - and loved it; she used to walk from Coombe every day, and walk home nightimes … dark as a bag! No torch or anything, Dad used to come partway and meet her.

She was in the kitchen, cooking and washing. They used to have parties: "Oh lovely", she said, "to see the people dressed up, 'twas beautiful to see them come in their posh cars and their evening dresses". It was a beautiful place, 'course they used to have a place there where they

79

had monkeys, and banana trees… oh, 'geddout do', when I used to go down there 'er used to take me up to show me… a proper hot-house, you know… and different coloured birds… I loved to go up and see them.

Us used to go down Nutcombe bottoms and pick crab apples to make crab apple jam. We'd walk down there with the children, pack up our tea and they'd love it. We used to spend hours down there: the little bridges, and they'd paddle in the water… oh, we've been there many times on a Sunday… took some food and a little kettle, have a fire…'course you can't do it now.

We were living down Greenhill when we had notice to get out because of the Evacuation. I'd just had my second daughter and wasn't out of bed when we had notice to clear out. I had to get out of bed and me husband and me auntie packed all our stuff up, and we went up to Mounts, which was on the edge of the Evacuation area. We were up there and they was firing shells in over us, pitching just over us… it was frightening, they were firing 'em too far you see, until somebody reported it. When we came back from the Evacuation you never seen anything like it for rats, it was living with rats 'cause the grass was so high and there wad'n no cats around to catch 'em, 'cause all the cats had been taken away. They cut the grass down and poisoned 'em then, see.

Then we could go to the Parish Hall and get bits and pieces that they used to give us, to help with our homes again… you could get blankets and pans, soaps and buckets and all that. You could get brushes and tins of paint… to do it yourself, they supplied it.

Ken Holmes

Born 18th February 1922

Recorded on 16th November 2006

Ken. I was born at Laburnum, East Allington, a smallholding in they days.

My grandfather Holmes was the Estate Carpenter for Fallapit Estate. I left there when I was three.

Steve. You started farming at a very young age!

Ken. Yes, Father died when I was twelve and my Grandfather Baker helped my mother to carry on the farm until I left school at fourteen. It was before the War and things were very hard. When I took over I had two horses and a single-furrow plough, and a few little implements… it was a hard life, long days.

There was a bit of leisure… I've been to a pantomime in Plymouth, sat up in the 'dicky'-seat behind Wilf Rogers, he used to take us…all open. They used to have a kind of taxi that took people on trips to Bantham or wherever; and there was a decent bus service then, it used to be tuppence from Churchstow to Kingsbridge.

There were boundary stones originally, mainly there for the roadmen. They cleaned their stretch of road as far as the next boundary stone, a flat stone in the hedge. They're not visible now, they're grown right in the hedge, out of sight. They showed the boundaries of each parish and the roadmen worked up to them.

When the War broke out in 1939 the War Agricultural Committee came round and… "We shall want this field ploughed and put into corn, and this other field ploughed up". Before you ploughed anything in those days, you'd do up all the hedges, and I can remember hedging and casting up all around the fields, and then eventually get the plough out with the horses and start ploughing. You could do about an acre a day if you got there about nine o'clock in the morning.

It was a major step up when the mechanical age came in, from the War onwards really, when things got better financially. Things have changed so much, I've always said, "It'll never change so much in such a short time again".

Milk was our main income, we got up to about twenty-five cows at one stage, that was about the most we had. Then pigs came into it, 'cause we used to have about twenty-five sows, and reared all the offspring up to pork or bacon weight, whichever was the most profitable. I got a good name for me pigs; we used to send them to Newton Abbot market - every week, for ten years. All the butchers knew my pigs and I got me name: 'King of the Pig Trade'!... I was quite proud of that.

I saw the bombs drop on Aveton Gifford. We were getting in hay with horses and wagons and I stopped on the brow of the hill, and with the same this plane went over, and I saw the bombs leave the plane. When they went off it frightened the daylights out of the horses.... and my mother was down there that day, she went to have a dress altered. She hadn't been down in the village for years, and she picked on that day to go down... but she went in under the table and she was alright.

Eddie White

Born 18th April 1910

Died 21st January 2007

Recorded on 21st November 2006

Eddie. I was born in Old Road, Harbertonford, and I've lived in Harbertonford all me life. I was the eldest of seven, and we only had two bedrooms; one big bedroom and one smaller one where three or four of us boys used to sleep together... we made sure we kicked each other out one time or another!

Grandfer White was the village cobbler, and in those days Harbertonford woollen factory was in action and Gran was one of the weavers up there. Grandfer wore a bowler hat and Granny used to have a two-piece costume that nearly touched the ground - because they didn't show a leg in those days if they could help it!

I was a small boy and she used to send me down to the back door of the 'Red Lion' with a bottle put in a piece of paper, for a sixpenny brandy.

Steve. *The Woollen Mill was a big employer I should think for the village.*

Eddie. Yes, and he had the Buckfastleigh Mill as well... there was a woollen mill there and he was the owner of that. They employed, I suppose, eighty people up there; they all had different jobs, and they used to have young boys for to carry the wool, until in later years they had apparatus: push a button and up they'd go; but before that they used to carry it up. They used to make blankets, and 'collar checks' for horse collars. You see, where the collar rests against the horse… it's a kind of blanket, for when the horse is pulling, they didn't hurt themselves.

I went to school in the old school-house next to the pub here in Harbertonford; that's where I got my education, and our teacher, Miss Melhuish, she used to wear drawers which buttoned round the knees.

I used to be in the Church choir here and at home we had a gramophone and used to play all sorts, like the 'Big Band' music…Jack Hilton and his band, and Henry Cotton.

It was hard times because there wasn't the food about, but I never felt hungry and we were always healthy. Mother used to cook a lot of potatoes, smash 'em up and put some fat mixed in with it… and that would be a meal.

We had to go up and fetch a bucket of water out of the pump up the hill. Me and my sister used to take a bucket and fill 'en up, and of course, 'er was shorter than me and we'd be leaking wet by the time we got home.

We used to play marbles and spinning tops… whose would go the longest… and when we were a bit older we'd go up in Mr. Finch's field and kick… well, 'twould be somebody's hat or something… simple entertainment!

There were five shops in the village, it was often a front room where they used to buy and sell things… in one she'd have iced fingers….and had to shake off the mice droppings!; we never used to think nothing of it… I've seen mice running all over the buns.

I do remember that every Easter we all had new suits, from Stoyles in Totnes.

Father was in the Army in about 1898, and he was at the Relief of Peking. Then he came out and got a job as a carpenter, and then of course, the First World War came and he had to go again. He went out to France making bridges and that, and when he came home on leave he always left his mark behind!!

My youngest uncle, Uncle George, was killed in the First World War… he was eighteen. He was in the Boy's Brigade and he got on well and got to be a Sergeant. He then got called up and went to France, and within a fortnight… they weren't quite sure whether he walked on a mine or what, but he had his legs blown off. He was at Edinburgh Hospital and my Gran had been no further than Dartmouth from Harbertonford, so she said to the family, "You lend me a few shillings", and she went up to see him; she stayed a week and he was getting better. He said, "Mum, I'm getting better, you go on home". Three days after she got home she had a letter to say he'd died. Eighteen year old! … I remember him well because we lived with them and I used to sleep with him; he was a boy and I was a kid, if you like.

I was a Corporal in the Harbertonford and Harberton Home Guard. I know they laughed at us, but we were very serious mind you, no nonsense. We did house-clearing, wood-clearing, lots of things we had to do. It used to be a joke in the village, but it wasn't a joke when we got on the job. We used to be at work all day and then be on guard at night… see, summertime we'd harvest 'til nine, and I was two miles away, I had to walk home; I worked at Stancombe Farm on the old Harbertonford road.

I worked at Stancombe Farm for forty years… Dad died a couple of months before I was fourteen … he died in the January and I started there on the first of April. There was a sign post then at Luscombe Cross, a great big lump of granite with, I think, 'T', 'B' for Totnes and Brent, and 'D' for Dartmouth.

When I was getting married I had thirty-two pound saved in the Post Office, so I said to Edith, "When you go in to Totnes you go in a furniture shop and pick out some furniture". Well she picked out a double bed, a wardrobe, a tallboy, another cupboard for clothes, a two-leaf table, four dining chairs, two fireside chairs and a dresser… and she brought back two pounds!

Bernard Steer

Born 25th October 1927

Recorded on 16th January 2007

Bernard. I left school at fourteen and went to work at Stears, the bakery on the Quay. I worked for Ralph Stear on the van for about twelve months and used to deliver out around all the villages. Funnily enough, all these villages had bakeries, but, because the War was on, you could only have bread delivered at a certain time of the week because you couldn't have bread from the same baker every day. During the War white bread was light brown because they put back most of the 'M'-grade flour, which was dark. It wasn't like wholegrain bread today, it was finely ground and was just a kind of tan colour.

There were several other bakers in Kingsbridge: there was Ryders in Church Street, Stears, Hannafords, Pearces… and Ellis' in Duke Street.

Ryders was where the passage goes up to the Eastern Backway, the first shop there, and the ovens were in behind so when we were kids, and if it was cold, we would warm our hands on the wall by the heat of the ovens there.

When I was eighteen I was called up to join the Navy, the War hadn't ended then, in 1945. I was working for Trants Millers then, in the office, and when the papers came through he called me into his office and said, "Look, I've got these papers, but I can get you exempt"… and I said, "No thank you,

I'd rather go", because, although it was wartime, I thought to myself it would be an experience, and perhaps see and do things that I probably wouldn't if I hadn't gone.

The War was coming to an end but I stayed on for three years. Then when I came out of the Navy they offered me a job to go back into the Mill to learn the milling side. The job I was on then was, what they called, the 'centrifugal' floor, that was the very top floor of the mill. Right down below was the floor at street level, that's where the 'Roby' diesel engine was situated. It had a massive great flywheel, and all the main shafts came out from there. The platform there was where the lorries would unload wheat, which was mostly in big 'West of England' sacks. It was tipped into what was called 'the well', and then transferred to the holding silos. When they wanted to mill that wheat it was transferred to the other end of the mill where it went through a process of washing, screening and cleaning before it came down to the mixers. You see, when you are doing all English flour you would have to mix in some 'Manitoba' wheat, Canadian or Australian wheat - to give it strength, or else the flour wouldn't rise.

When the cleaned grain was ready it was weighed and sent down to the roller floor where it went through a process of cracking and breaking through different-sized rollers; some were fluted, some were smooth and it went round in a flow, sifting and cracking, sifting and cracking until it was fine enough for flour. It went up to the next floor where there were purifiers, then up again to the centrifugal floor where I worked.

The mill was a five-sack plant, which meant that we were taking off ten to twelve bags an hour, and each bag weighed a hundred and forty pounds.

There was also a wheatings chute for fine bran and another chute for rough bran. You had to put the bag up over the chute, pull a belt around it and put a clip on it. Then put the lever up to let the flour come down.

It started off on the bottom floor as grain and after it had been through all the processes it finished up back there as flour.

There had to be exhaust systems and the dust all finished up in the cowl… there was a big box up there underneath the cowl, and that would fill up with all the dust that was drawn off the machines. That had to be cleaned out about once a month. We'd take out about twenty or thirty bags of the stuff, and that had to be gradually mixed back in with the wheatings for pig feed - nothing was wasted.

Every so often the place had to be fumigated, because there would be a build-up of flour moth…. It would be like big wads of waste cotton, so everything had to be brushed off and the machines cleaned down, and then everything was finished for the weekend. Then all the doors and windows were sealed, one floor at a time, and canisters were set off to kill all the moths.

The finished product went to all the bakers around; Powleslands of Slapton, Thorntons at Portlemouth… all the bakers in Kingsbridge, Ivybridge, Plymouth… and we used to send truck-loads of flour to Wales and other places on the Kingsbridge railway.

I worked there from 1949 until about 1953. I came out before the mill packed up, which would have been just a few years after that.

Dorothy Taylor

Born 27th August 1910

Recorded on 22nd January 2007

Dorothy. I was born at East Charleton, but it was different then; no traffic, it was just quiet. There was a shop there, the first house in the village, after West Charleton. There were two farms, Cornish's and Fairweather's, and in my younger days Sarjeants were at East Farm… and where the Garage is now used to be allotments, where my father had one. We got our water from a tap just a little way away from the house, and we used to bath in a galvanised bath, once a week. I used to have 'hand-me-down' clothes from our cousins, but occasionally we would have something new. They couldn't afford it; Father only used to get thirty- two and sixpence a week… Mother used to give him the two and six for his spending money. We always had to wear a hat; I had a 'tam-o-shanter', a little red one, and I had one I wore on Sundays when we used to go to Sunday School at Frogmore - we weren't allowed to go without a hat.

When Grandfather Elliott died we went to live with Granny then, and she lived 'til she was ninety-nine. She was a nurse in her younger days and used to go around delivering babies. Granny used to make a yeast cake and she used to make the bread. I was the eldest of eight and I had to do work in the house to help out; as each new one came along there was more work… washing and that.

I had me tonsils out when I was just about going to school; the hospital then was in Duncombe Street, and

Doctor Cowper lived there afterwards. I worked for Doctor Cowper later on and once, in the dining room, I said to him, "This is where I had my tonsils out!" - they used to use chloroform then to put you out.

The first car that I remember in West Charleton was when the vicar had one. Everybody else had a pony and trap. All the farmers had stables to keep their ponies and traps in … I had to walk… until I bought a bicycle! I bought it from Mr. Steer when he had a cycle shop up Fore Street, and I used to pay him half a crown a week to pay it off. We didn't used to go anywhere, well, I went to Torcross for me birthday once, Granny took me out to Torcross by bus - but I never went to Dartmouth.

I had to leave school at fourteen and go to work. My first job was for Cornish's at the farm… for six shilling a week. I had to wash the stone floors, and wash the buckets and separator after they'd finished milking - but my mother always collected my money, I never saw my wages. If I wanted any money I used to have to ask Mother for it. I stayed at Cornish's for about two years. Then I went as housemaid for Mr. Wykes, the Headmaster of the Grammar School in Kingsbridge. I had half a day a week off, and every other Sunday, to go home… but I got to keep my own money then.

Steve. When did you learn about Australia?

Dorothy. Oh, when I was young I'd never heard of it. Not until my youngest daughter emigrated there, and in 1978 I went off to Australia for twelve months; it was the first time I'd ever been abroad and the first time I'd ever been in an aeroplane. Since 1978 I've been out seven times, but when I was a little girl I never imagined going anywhere like that; I didn't even know where Australia was. When I was eighty I went up in a hot air balloon down at Ugborough…and a helicopter, when they were doing rides from the rugby field in Kingsbridge.

Sabina Berryman

Born 30th July 1910

Died 7th June 2008

Recorded on 29th January 2007

Sabina. I was born at Lipton Farm, on the outskirts of East Allington, then we came to Whitlocksworthy when I was about five, on Michaelmas Day, September 29th. I had a sister and a brother older, and a sister and a brother younger than meself, so I was in the middle. In the kitchen there was an open hearth and we burnt faggots of sticks, and Father used to bring in great poles; I don't think he liked sawing them up. Mind you, it was all right, we used to put the kettle on the two logs to boil. The kitchen was so big it took me an hour to scrub all the blue flagstones.

We made our own entertainment, I can tell you that; 'twad'n made for us, not like today. I was a real 'tomboy', everything me brother done I done: if he climbed a tree I climbed it… and how many times I've torn me clothes, and go in and look at Mother with me dress caught up in me hand!

Us had toys, but not like they have today, I can tell you. I had a rag doll, but I was never much for dolls you know. I was happy being outside, we had a lot more freedom then, when we was little.

Father kept some sheep at Upton, a mile away, and we used to walk up there on our way to school… count the sheep and then go another mile to school across the path fields.

When I got bigger I had to help to make butter, all by hand…. and when I left school I did a little milk round: Thurlestone Links, the cottages and the big houses down there on the front… with a pony and governess-car, that was a pony trap with seats each side. I used to have a four-gallon churn of milk; 'twas heavy and I used to have to lift it up on the cart meself, and deliver in cans… we supplied the cans, and the bottles when bottles came in.

The Links Hotel was built in 1911, but I remember the wing being put on for the ballroom, and I can remember going there to dances and whist drives. I loved dancing: the Quadrilles and the Lancers… and the Charleston. The Links Hotel brought a lot of visitors to the village… it was the elite. The Links Hotel had the first bus and us would run up the lane to see it go by.

At Horswell House then were General and Mrs. Alexander. We used to have lovely fetes there and they always gave a Christmas party, every year… they were a real Gentleman and Lady, and I remember always curtseying to him!

When we wanted anything in town Jim Johns, the carrier, would bring it out… and you used to have things 'on appro', that meant 'on approval', so you would try it on and if it didn't suit you could send it back.

I've walked miles after horses working down ground for my father. It was all heavy horses then… I can remember Flower, Tiger, Lion … Madam and Tommy and…oh, Harry Foale…us

named him after who Father bought 'en from!

I can remember when I first got married, cutting all my husband's grass with two horses and a reaper… oh, it was hard work before I got married and it was hard work after… but it's all mechanised today idn'it.

Dorothy Mingo

Born 18th September 1920

Recorded on 8th February 2007

Dorothy. I was born in a little cottage near the village of Belstone, near Okehampton. Then we went to live with Grandma: Mum and Dad took part of the farmhouse. There was no-one else around, the nearest house was about two miles away across the moor.

Dad was a farmer there, and a Range Warden as well. He used to clear the ranges, move the cattle over the moors, back from the firing zone. It was the Royal Artillery there, Government- controlled, you know. It was very hard, but happy times. We'd make our own fun; we used to get the calves tame, and then get up on them and ride them around. I didn't have a childhood really, and I was old when I was young, if you know what I mean. It was tough - Dad made me work when I was eight… dropping potatoes. I had to take the bucket, and it wasn't a plastic one like now, I could hardly lift them. First of all I had to sow the manure, I could do it along with me hand, and then put the potatoes so far apart. Then Dad would come along and split the furrows with a small plough pulled by one horse.

I had to hold the chickens for Father to kill'em, because I was the oldest I suppose; but it didn't worry me, see, it's life id'n it.

Steve. What would you do if you needed a Doctor?

Dorothy. They didn't go to the Doctor like they do now; they couldn't afford it 'cause you had to pay. I remember one time I had to walk to the next village to fetch a bottle of medicine for me auntie; it was two and sixpence then and I dropped the bottle and broke 'en, but the Doctor just dismissed it... put me up another one and didn't charge, 'cause I was so upset.

I left school when I was fourteen and went to work on a farm. I used to help fry the breakfast for the farm labourers, on an open fire.

I joined the Women's Land Army in 1941, when I was twenty-one. We were conscripted in; we had to fill out a lot of forms and get our uniform before we came away. The uniform was overalls with braces, in a brown 'muddy' colour. We wore green jumpers, ties and a badge... sort of 'plushy' round hats, and they were fawn... and a little fawn blouse. Then we had a big overcoat that weighed a ton, and it came to your knees.

So I was sent to East Allington, to Lower Poole Farm, in January 1942 and Mr. Bond met us at Kingsbridge station. You see, some girls went to

hostels and worked on the land from there, and some went to 'live in' on the farms. We did everything that a man would do; used to do hoeing turnips and mangold, and I used to feed the calves and the pigs, and we did other things like picking poultry, casting dung and all that. It was an awfully long day; we had to get up early in the mornings, there was milking at six o'clock.

You had somebody from down here to see that you were looked after alright: Miss Ilbert it was, she used to come and see us sometimes... and of course, they were worried at home because I'd never been away from home before. We were treated very well and we had wonderful food; Mrs. Bond was a good cook... she was really wonderful.

I was there from January 1942 until the Evacuation in December 1943, when I went home for a while and got married. I had met Gilbert down here; he was at Higher Poole, working for his grandparents.

Hazel Stephens

Born 15th January 1922

Betty Tabb

Born 24th September 1924

Recorded on 14th February 2007

Betty. We were both born in Slapton and we've both lived in Slapton all our lives, except through the Evacuation when we were moved out.

We've always had to work, from when we were old enough. I remember coming home from school I had to go down every day to my grandparents to get their water in from over Carr Lane… fill all their buckets and whatever they had. Then there was another old lady in the village, just up above us, and I used to do the same for her… fetch her water every night.

Hazel. The children today wouldn't do what we did. We had to go right down the bottom of our garden to fetch water, there was a well there, and it still comes out of a pipe there. I wouldn't use it now, but in summer you'd get really nice cold water.

Betty. We used to get ours half way up Brook Street. We used to go down to the beach to get seaweed to lay on the garden in the winter; the worms would pull it in then; it's good for the garden you know. I can remember Charlie Perrin used to live over Brook Street and he used to pick winkles down in Frogmore Creek. Then he would cook them, and come around and sell them by the pint. We used to have a little pin and get them out… with a little bit of bread and butter… lovely!

Hazel. … and watercress… we used to pick that and sell it, it grows down here in the stream, down the bottom.

We were lucky, we had Miss Wingate's shop in the village where you could buy anything; you could get bedding, sheets, towels, knitting wool, shoes, and anything there. That was just below the Gospel Hall and when the Ropers took it over from her they even used to do fish and chips. Then we had the Post Office, which was a shop as well, over at the Round House.

Betty. … and two bake-houses, Jarvis was at the Round House and Powleslands was over

next to the Queen's Arms. We had a cobbler's shop down where I live now, and opposite was Downing the tailor, and I've heard that when he used to make a suit he'd walk to Plymouth to get the material and walk back. There were also two butchers: Rogers and Cleave, and there was Miss Treeby, years before, who had a sweet shop down there.

I can remember when there was a cider pound here in the village, and there was another one down at Start. We used to go in there and pick up just an ordinary bit of straw, to suck up the juice.

Steve. It's unbelievable to think you had so many shops in Slapton!

Betty. There was a policeman, Betts, here in the village… a doctor's surgery up Brook Street at Rose Cottage; I think the doctor lived in Chillington and came here twice a week. We had a nurse living in the village, so it was jolly good.

Hazel. Well, you couldn't go anywhere, there weren't any buses about. You didn't go to town, hardly ever. We didn't get buses in to the village until after the War - before that you had to walk out to the 'Sands'.

Our parents worked hard, yes they certainly did work. I think the only leisure time they had was the Sunday School outing, that was once a year.

It was our treat, that was what we used to look forward to. We used to go to Paignton and we'd make a dive for Woolworth's, 'cause everything was sixpence or less.

Betty. You could get a lot for sixpence, couldn't you.

Hazel. We used to go down to the beach when we were children, we'd be out there every day during holidays… all day, in and out the water. After school in the summer, we'd pick up our things and out for a swim. In the evening the men would be out there fishing for mackerel… you'd see them out there pulling their nets in with the mackerel and that… we lived on the beach in the summer, we really did.

I had to help my Dad on the fruit and vegetable round when my brothers all went away during the War. You didn't have to have a driving test in those days; you could just get in and drive. I picked it up going around with my Dad in his lorry, it just came natural to me… it was 'double-declutch' in them days, you had to sort of put the clutch in twice: bring him up out of gear, and then push him in again, put him in the next gear. I used to go delivering to Torcross and Beesands with Dad… you drove along the front of the houses in Torcross then, door to door.

My brothers Arthur and Lloyd joined the Air Force before the War, and when War broke out Henry volunteered to go as well, and he was a PT instructor. Lloyd was a Flying Officer, and he lost his life during the War.

Walter Hine

Born 23rd April 1911

Died 14th May 2007

Recorded on 26th February 2007

Walter. I was born in a little cottage called Woodleigh Mill, between Loddiswell and Woodleigh. My father and mother used to move around quite a lot as he was a gardener and he went near where his work was; and he moved several times in the village too. In them days there was a lot of TB, and my first sister died at three months. Then I had a brother who lived to sixteen and I can remember playing with him more than anybody else. He was fifteen when I was about five, and he had a trolley, a square box with a piece of wood fixed on the top at the back. He used to put me in the box, and then he would sit on sideways. We used to go up Town's Lane and to the top of the hill at Village Cross. We'd start up there and we'd shoot down that hill, round the corner. We were very, very lucky that we never met anything… 'course 'twas only horses and carts, or perhaps an odd cow in them days… but it's no odds to anybody, what would have happened if we'd met anything. You couldn't do it today! Well, my brother died of consumption in 1916, aged sixteen. You see, there was nine altogether of us, seven that lived.

We moved to Hazelwood in 1919 when I was eight years old. We had three miles to go to school, and because it was so far away Father's employers, called Peek of Hazelwood House, provided a donkey for us… see, I had twin brothers seven year old and Mother would get the children ready and go down and get the donkey… and sometimes he

would go along quite nicely, but other times he'd go as far as the gate, and wouldn't budge a bit… so I used to turn him round, smack him across the backside, and send the boys home; then I used to go on to school myself with me sister. We never went very far as children, because we had to walk.

Granny died in 1927 when there was a lot of snow around. I was sixteen then and I walked from Hazelwood to Loddiswell to be a bearer at the funeral. I walked on the top of the hedges, and down in the ditches to get there. I was leaking wet when I got there, but in them days it was a big privilege. I was still wearing short trousers then; yes, you never got in long trousers until you went out to work.

We had an earth closet… well, a bucket, and we used to take it down the garden every Saturday night. Father used to dig a trench out where we was going to have our runner beans, cover it up a bit, and then next week do the same.

Steve. What entertainment or music did you have?

Walter. We had a musical box. You'd wind 'en up with a handle and then he'd play one tune for each pull. Inside was a drum with about seven or eight different tunes that would play as it slowly went round: the little spikes would tingle with the arms as they went around.

When I left school I worked on a farm for three months; it was hard work, you was on the go all day long, and they had one nasty horse, he was a proper nuisance he was. Well, 'twas hard work for a youngster, so I went as a garden boy into 129 Fore Street, Kingsbridge: 'The Knowle'. That was a big private house and the owner had a studio out in the back yard and did a lot of painting. I used to cycle forward and back from Loddiswell to begin with, then I lodged in Kingsbridge. I had to turn ground, cut grass, any general gardening and general handywork. They used to supply a shop down the town with vegetables and very often I'd be up and down there, taking stuff down there in two trugs. I was there for about three and a half year, until I was old enough to drive. I was seventeen then and I went down to Dodbrooke Manor, for Major Stapleton-Cotton and his wife. He was an ambulance driver in the First World War and she was a nurse on his ambulance, that's how they got together. They taught me to drive in a thirty horse-powered Daimler, similar to what the Royalty use.

It had a crash gear-box, 'double-declutch', and there was no door on the driver's side: if anybody wanted to sit in the passenger's side they had to let me get in first, and then they shut the door.

It had a handbrake, something like a railway signal-box lever, or bigger than that. I had to keep the car clean, polish it up. There was gentry about in them days, they used to go around visiting each other; back in the twenties and thirties... Froudes out to Collapit, Robinsons at Fallapit House... an actor called Cyril Maude, and somebody at Redlap House at Dartmouth. I've been to Plymouth times for the old lady to buy a three and sixpenny hat!... and I've known her to take down an umbrella to be repaired and then go around to visit someone after. They supplied my uniform, the clothes, and I had to supply the boots and leggings. It wasn't very comfortable; it was very thick serge... baggy, you know, it didn't fit down like trousers. I was with them for ten years from 1927 until 1937, until I got married. They used to pay me thirty-six and sixpence a week.

I was called up in September 1940 and I left the boy, two year old and the girl a month old: you felt you had to go but you didn't want to. I went to Loddiswell Station, on to Brent and Newton Abbot. At Newton Abbot station a chap got in and from then on we were together nearly all through the War in the same Company; we went up on the same train, got de-mobbed together and came home on the same train; I left him at Newton Abbot station the same as when I joined up with him there..

Steve. I suppose it was a bit of adventure really?

Walter. Yes, definitely, it was all unknown you see; you didn't know where you were going. I did my basic training at Bulford Camp, Salisbury, then went over to Carter Barracks where they put me in the driving section and I was offered a job as a driving instructor. I was transferred to the RASC as a driving instructor, over at Tedworth until 1943 when we got moved 'lock, stock and barrel' up to Derbyshire. Later in 1943 they were looking for twenty 'volunteers' to do supply drops... air dispatch... "You, you and you will do"!... and muggins happened to be one of them.

Well, down in the south at 'De Havilland' airfield they were planning air dispatch. They had the fuselage of a C47 'Dakota' fixed in the field and we had to push panniers of sand up this ramp and along, on the rollers, to practice. These panniers were like big laundry baskets that would take three hundred and fifty pounds; there was a harness around each one, and we had to tie the top one to the bottom one on the four corners. Then on the front we had to fix up parachutes and there were like washing lines across the top of the fuselage, and from there you hooked up a lead going from the parachute, which would pull the ripcord when the pannier had gone out. There was sixteen panniers for one load, sixteen panniers on two banks, and they were put up and chained around. There were four of us and we each had our own job to do, and our own safety precautions. We had a big wide belt that went around your stomach and fastened at the back, and that could be hooked in anywhere on the plane to keep you from going too far, you see: that would allow you to go to the door and no further. On the dropping zone you've got a crowd of people down there that laid the ground out according to the wind. They put a big 'T' with white sheets, and the idea is that the pilot would fly up the 'T' and when he got to the top of the 'T' we had to start dropping. It was done on bells and lights; on the word 'go', a green light, one would give the stick a push and the other one would take the chuck out for the panniers to run down on the base boards. It was like railway lines, when one pannier went the other could go… and if everybody worked together it should go all right. I had a very good record for getting them out the fastest; they used to bet on it…'That was Wally's load!' As far as I know, by the time I came out of the Army, my crowd had got the record, sixteen panniers in six seconds! I was really proud of that… you'd see them all shooting down with their parachutes.

There were different stacks: ammunition, medical supplies, wireless parts, food… anything that was going. We flew over to Arnhem and then over to Nijmegen and the Falaise Gap dropping supplies, until the end of activities.

Ian Chart

Born 28th February 1920

Died 1st December 2008

Recorded on 27th February 2007

Ian. I was born in Hounslow, Middlesex, the third of four boys. I remember they used to have a lot of Fairs on Hounslow Heath and there was 'Peggy o' Death-Dive', and what used to happen was they had a huge tank of water and used to pour petrol on it and set it alight. Well, he only had one leg, and he used to go up this ladder, dive into the tank and directly he hit the flames they used to go out… but one day - I wasn't there at the time - he missed and hit his head on the edge of the tank and that killed

him! Yes, 'Peggy o'Death-Dive' they called him.

My father had a waxed 'handlebar' moustache, but if ever he ran out of wax he used to put soap on it! He was a disciplinarian; when I was a boy and it was meal-times we all had to sit up together, you know, and we weren't allowed to touch that food until my father had started first. We always used to have porridge for breakfast… and we had winkles every Sunday when the winkle man came round…. and the muffin man - he used to have a big board on his head with the muffins on, and used to ring a bell. We used to get the man with the barrel organ, which he'd wind up, and he came around on Sundays too.

My father used to ride a 'penny-farthing' and it used to make me laugh how he used to get up; he had a hell of job to get up there!

My mother's family was called May, and some of her relations were in Paignton, near the railway crossing. They had 'May's Confectionery', cake shop there.

When I was about sixteen I used to cycle down to Ashprington to stay with a cousin, Jack May. He was a Foreman at Tuckenhay Paper Mill where they used to produce the fine paper to make the five-pound notes for the Bank of England, and his wife was a schoolteacher in Ashprington school. It used to take me two days: I'd stop off for the night at a Bed and Breakfast in Dorset; I was fit then! I'd also cycle from Hounslow to Brighton, that was sixty miles, stop there for an hour and go back again.

I'd done five years out of seven of my apprenticeship as carpenter and joiner when I was called up. I was twenty then, in 1940. I did my training at Aldershot, which was only for about three weeks then. I think the money was fourteen and six a week, but I, like the thousands of others troops, sent money home to my mother, so therefore I was getting seven and sixpence a week. From Aldershot I went to Guildford, and then on to Granton-on-Spey, because then I was attached to the Fifty-first Highland Division.

One day they were looking for volunteers for Motor Boat companies, so me and another chap volunteered and we moved down to Teigngrace; that was still 1940. Then my proper posting came through, to go to Salcombe. We'd only been here about twenty minutes when I looked out of the window of the Salcombe Hotel and there was Dorothy and another girl, so I shouted to her, and then went down and started talking to her.

91

I started courting Dorothy then and we were married in 1943 - and were married for sixty years.

I was posted to several different Companies before I went across to D-Day. I went from the Isle of White on a harbour launch, an open boat... and it was bloody rough! I was never told what beach we were going to land on, but we landed at a place called 'Luc-sur-Mer', that's on the left side of Arromanches.

Later I was stationed in Antwerp in Belgium and we had to prepare four boats for the Rhine crossing, so we made the 'cradles' on tank transporters. The four boats were put on to the transporters and we went from there to the Rhine Crossing. We stopped overnight at a place called Vught, and there was a concentration camp there that had only been liberated three weeks before. It was ghastly, it smelt awful... and at Vught I took some photographs of some children, and several years ago one of them was traced. I had a two-and-sixpenny box camera... you weren't allowed to take anything like that, but I did and I took loads of photographs and never got caught.

Steve. *You are a Vice President of the Torquay Branch of the Normandy Veterans Association, and you go back to Holland every year!*

Ian. Yes, every year, and I make the plaques out of oak. I made seven about four or five months ago. Dorothy and I came up with the idea and I designed it. They go everywhere, and even Ex-President Clinton has one.

Peggy Whitehirst
Born 1st February 1934

Recorded on 5th March 2007

Peggy. I was born at Higher Soar, near Malborough, three and a half years before my Father died. It was very sad: as I understand it, he joined the Army, the Infantry, in the First World War, as a boy soldier and fought in France in the trenches. He came home at the end of the War suffering from gas exposure in his lungs and shell shock; he'd been through terrible times. I've got a vague memory of him: he used to keep chickens and ducks and I remember I stood on a baby duck and killed it, and he smacked my legs... but I didn't really know my dad. He was Herbert Alfred Pedrick because, of course, he was your great-grandfather's brother.

My mother was called Irene Marguerite, and she was very much like the Queen Mother who had the same name, Marguerite, too. My mother died when I was thirteen and a half so I was an orphan then, and my aunt took me in.

My mother had learnt millinery in Kingsbridge, and she used to make and sell all those beautiful hats that the ladies wore in those days; but it's a trade that's died out, because ladies don't wear big hats any more.

My mother's brother and sister farmed Lower Soar where the thatched farmhouse was a thousand years old. It was a Manor House in the fifteenth century, and in the seventeenth century it became a farmhouse.

I was five years old when war broke out and there was an announcement that there was a big aerodrome to be built at Soar. Of course my aunt was terribly alarmed because she knew that they'd be coming over

and dropping bombs, and we'd be a target.

However, they never dropped any bombs on the aerodrome because there was a big squadron of Spitfires and Lancaster bombers, and as soon as the Luftwaffe came in over the sea the Spitfires would go out, intercept them, drive them away or shoot them down… but of course, a lot of our Spitfires were shot down as well. I can remember the first lot of Spitfires that arrived, and the first lot of Lancaster bombers.

Well, as the war progressed some official people came to the farm to say that my aunt had to billet evacuees. They also went to Higher Soar and East Soar, and everywhere else in Malborough, Salcombe and Kingsbridge. They all had to take in evacuees; but my Aunt refused, because she said she hadn't got a hot water system or electricity and she wouldn't have coped with bathing and delousing children… you see they were full of nits, and they used to wet the beds because they'd been in the shelters in London with the bombs dropping; the poor little things were very nervous. So she had to take in the WAAFs and the Airmen; but the girls were a nuisance. We had a WAAF who used to curl her hair with curling tongs, on a primus stove, and she caught the thatched roof on fire! but the Airmen were good, they were easy to deal with. They used to go straight to the Camp in their little jeeps and have their showers and breakfast and everything up there, we didn't see them again until early evening. So the WAAFs were chucked out and we had four Airmen there then instead.

One of the Airmen used to bring his wife down and she used to stay with us, and then we had this famous cartoonist from New Zealand, Felix Kelly he was called, and he used to take me down to Soar Mill Cove on his shoulders… we used to paddle in the sea, and catch shrimps.

When the War was over all the land was handed back to the farmers and they were compensated. They then built a radar station up there.

When I first left school I went to work in a wool shop in Kingsbridge, but I had no interest in knitting, so my uncle got me a job in the Food Office, and I loved it. I used to issue the emergency and identity cards, register the deaths, take all the ration books and emergency cards to the Police station to lock them in the cells at night; because it was always feared that people would break in and steal them, to get extra food. I'd been there about twelve months when the Food Office closed down, because food came off ration. Well, then I got a job in the Gas showrooms in Kingsbridge… I used to sell gas appliances, cookers… and there was a lot of gas lights in Kingsbridge in those days, even Kingsbridge railway station was lit by gas.

Gilbert Ewings

Born 12th December 1914

Died 11th July 2007

Recorded on 15th March 2007

Gilbert. I was born at 'Southwood', Strete, near Dartmouth. Mother was a Bowden and her family lived at Manor Farm, Frogmore, opposite the pub.

I remember in about 1918 or 1919, hearing the planes come in over the sea; the very old-fashioned ones with two wings on 'em. We were all in the playground and could hear the noise before we could see the planes. Mother used to put up 'black-out' curtains, because the house used to face the sea - we were just up over from Blackpool Sands.

I remember Father sending us off when we were quite young… there was a linhay up on the Totnes road from Strete, and he used to keep the cattle there. We had to go up and tend to them, give 'em their hay and straw, bed 'em up and that in wintertime.

I remember me and me brother when us was youngsters, used to drive the cattle down to Grandfather's farm at Frogmore, stop the night, then drive them into Kingsbridge, and they used to sell the cattle at the market in Church Street. You was always busy from when you was very young… you had to go out and help clean out the cattle houses… in the Spring draw all the manure out, take it out in the carts, put it in heaps in the field and then cast it with a 'eavel, cast it evenly. I used to have my own little 'eavel, and when I was no more'n four or five my brother was using it and I didn't approve, so he let it go and it stuck right in my ankle. Within a quarter of an hour, after I'd done it, I couldn't walk. Do you know, for six weeks I was in bed, and you see they didn't have any antibiotics or anything. I had to have a kaolin poultice put on every day… they had to put it on as hot as they could, and it used to make me shout!

I can tell you that the horses used to go to Salisbury, for manoeuvres… about once a year the Army commandeered the horses from the farms, and I used to have to take 'em to Dartmouth, go across the ferry and put 'em in a truck the other side. They'd go away for two or three weeks and then you could go in and pick 'em up.

We come from Southwood to Woolston Court, near Kingsbridge when I was twelve. I had two years going 'school in Kingsbridge then, I used to drive the pony and trap into school and kept it in the 'Seven Stars', leave it there and pick it up four o'clock when I came out of school.

I left school at fourteen and went into a garage in Kingsbridge, I was going to have a ten-year apprenticeship… ten years… mind you, it's a long time.

I was going to do salesmanship and all the lot, but Father's health broke down and I had to come home to help out. I'd done two and a half years then: the first year you didn't get nothing, second year you got five shillings, third year you got ten shillings, that was the wages. My first car was when I was going in the garage to work, I had a little Morgan three-wheeler, 'AF1006' was the registration; it was air-cooled with two holes in the little bonnet for the air to get into the cylinders, to keep them cool. It had direct steering, just the shaft going down to a crown-wheel down below, between the seats, and just a little arm going out connected to the track rods. It had two gears, bottom and second… no reverse… driven by two chains going back to the back wheel, one each side. He was built in the early 1920's, because I had 'en in 1930, and he was seven or eight years old when I had 'en. He was blue and red and I think originally it may have had a little perspex windscreen.

Later I had an Austin 7 'Tourer' with a hood, and a little

Gilbert (above) and left, aged around 10 with a 'backpedaler' bicycle, outside Woolston Court

Morris Minor… fabric body, and just before the Second War I bought a big Riley, about two thousand cc., I reckon. I bought it because, when war broke out, they couldn't get petrol to run it; and I had a Triumph Gloria, it was a beautiful silver-blue car and he used to sparkle in the sun… everybody would turn their heads when they saw the car coming.

I was an Agricultural Contractor and Farmer, I had to farm right through the Second War. I had about ninety acres of 'off ground' and we let the other half and the house to a tenant. I bought my first tractor in 1936, a rubber-tyred tractor, and it cost £195.00. A few tractors were about in the First World War, they were worm-drive axles on the old Fordsons, and they had tremor coils, coils that used to buzz, you could see 'em moving up and down. They didn't have a magneto or anything, they were fed with a battery.

Steve. You told me you once went up in an aeroplane.

Gilbert. Yes, that was about 1937, before the War anyway. There was a couple of level fields out Soar, and Sir Alan Cobham had an air circus there; lovely coloured 'planes they were, all painted up bright colours, and we used to see 'em coming over Woolston, right down the estuary there… he'd take people out on trips.

Well Father said we were all going to have an afternoon off and go to this air display. They gave out on the 'mike' that they was going to do some stunting, they'd got one passenger and wanted another. Father said, "Would you like to go up, boy?" so up I goes, and this plane done 'loop-the-loop', nosedives, spins, upside-down… everything you could think of.

We were up there stunting about half an hour. It was an experience: it would take pilots years 'til they was able to do that sort of thing. It was out of the blue I went up… but I stuck it all right, I wasn't sick or anything!

Well, I've seen all machinery evolve; when I was a boy they didn't have much machinery then, all the hay turning was done by hand, you had to go along with forks, two or three of you, and turn all the field by hand. Since then there've been all types of hay turners, some of them had round pieces of iron with spikes on it that used to go round, they were gradually getting better and better.

In later years there've been more sprays about, but before you had to go out in the fields pulling up charlock… you'd plough a little bit deeper in the field one year and up would come all these seeds and you'd be out there for days pulling it in the corn and carrying it to the hedge; a lot of work 'twas!

You see, seeds lie dormant for years under the ground and the deeper you go the more seeds you bring up. Now they spray the fields, you don't see much weed. Perry and Spear used to hire out a sprayer, one fellow had to sit in the cart with a barrel filled with water and spray, and he had to pump it… there was a bar and it used to spray out on the ground behind the cart. Well, they gradually brought it in use on the tractors and that's how it developed.

Cecil Herd

Born 6th June 1921

Recorded on 20th March 2007

Cecil. I was born in Harberton, but where I was born up in Fore Street they knocked it all down to widen it 'cause the road was very narrow there, and they put some more houses further back. There were two shops in the village, one that was knocked down and the other was up the top of the village.

There used to be six farms then, now there's only one. All the cow houses and stables are made into living quarters and all the orchards be done away with and they've built there; it's quite different now. In Harberton then there was cow dung all over the roads, all over the place when they come in to be milked. I used to go over to the farm with a quart jug for a quart of buttermilk, two pence it was and very rich, it used to be lovely … used to get two pound loaves then, they were four- pence for a loaf, and used to get beef dripping. I used to like that, put on the bread, and a bit of salt on it.

Most of the houses up Harberton then belonged to Sir Samuel Harvey; they sold off a lot, a lot of people up Harberton bought their houses for about thirty pound.

There used to be a cattle market in Totnes opposite the 'Bay Horse Inn'; they've turned it into a car park now, and then they had one down the bottom on the racecourse years after; that's where the Industrial Estate is now.

They used to hold Totnes races there years ago, horse racing… oh yes, I've been in there when I was a youngster, 'used to have bookies in there, and us used to bet on the horses.

There used to be 'train' lines on the Plains, where a fellow called Blight used to have two horses and pull the trucks along the lines. Timber would come in be train further up, then he'd pull the wagons down with the horses to 'Reeves' timber merchants.

When I was a boy up Harberton there was no such thing as hearses then. There used to be a chap called Barnes who lived in Leechwell Street in Totnes, he had a biggish horse and a flat-bottom wagon, and he used to bring the coffins out and take 'em to wherever they was going to be buried. They wad'n covered in or nothing; just put the coffin on the wagon. There was no funeral parlours, people used to be 'laid out' in the front room and he used to charge seven and sixpence.

When I left school first I went down to Blakemore Farm for five shilling a week. Then I left there and went into Totnes to work delivering bread, then I went up and worked in the bakehouse for two year.

One of my uncles, Richard Parker was a rabbit trapper, so I took up rabbit trapping and I did that for twenty-odd year, until the myxomatosis came in.

I used to use the spring traps, 'gins', but they was banned in the end. I had a safe I used to keep in the field, locked up, to put the rabbits in and then a chap from Plymouth would come up; he had a key, and he'd take the rabbits and leave the money.

You had to buy the rabbits from the farmer… I gived thirty pounds for Blackmore Farm, that was three hundred and nine acres. That was a lot of money in those days: rabbits was only making sixpence each then, but when the War came they went up to two and sixpence; half a crown. Well, a lot of people lived on rabbits during the War, with rationing and that.

I used to have a cycle with a box on the front, and it had a carbide bicycle lamp. It had white liquid stuff in the bottom and you used to put a match to it and it made a gas which made it glow - but you could hardly see where you was going, you could hardly see your front wheel in front of 'e … and the wind would come and out he'd go and that would be the end of it.

I saved some money and then I bought a van. I had any amount of farms where I trapped rabbits, used to go to Diptford and different places. I had to pay each farmer; used to pay on Lady Day, that's March the twenty-fifth.

I was in the Home Guard in the Second World War, and we used to have to do practices. We even won a cup: we were in Totnes castle, and the regular Army was invading the castle, we managed to keep 'em out. They used to drop flour bombs on us… well, there was two planes and they collided, one Lysander and another fighter plane, they met in mid-air and both came down on Totnes Racecourse and they were both killed.

Alice Mason

Born 12th November 1915

Recorded on 11th June 2007

Alice. I was born at Well Cottage, here in Ringmore. My Father was a carpenter and undertaker here in the village and he would make coffins in his workshop. Sometimes I had to help him to 'line' them, in between my work on the farm…and you couldn't say, 'I can't do it!'.

My Mum wouldn't call people by their christian names…they had to be 'Sir' or 'Mister'; the Rector was always 'Sir'.

The ladies had to work very hard back in those days, picking up potatoes in the fields, and fruit picking. They had big families, you see, and no washing machines… just a tray and you scrubbed! My granny had twelve children, but the biggest family here was fifteen, and they were called Miller - but, you see the older ones looked after the younger ones.

There was a shop here in the village, first of all at the 'Journey's End', then it was moved to 'Challaborough Cottage', and then to 'Ivy Cottage'.

When you went for say, cocoa, they would weigh it out for you in a paper bag, there was no pre-packed things then.

We had to go and fetch our water in buckets, Dad had a proper 'yoke' and I would go with him with a little bucket.

I went to school here in Ringmore until the school was closed, and when I left I went to Modbury. When I left school at first I worked for some people that had come home from India and wanted somebody to look after their two little children. I did that for about six months, and then I went to work on a farm. I did the hand-milking and dairy work… I loved the cows, they were lovely, and I used to get tearful when they went 'off milk' and had to be sold.

When I was fourteen, in 1929, I joined the W.I. We used to do a lot of drama and social evenings… oh, and I played in a band; I was the pianist and there was a saxophone, the drums, the clarinet and a guitar. We called ourselves the 'The Avon Star', we travelled all around and played jazz mostly, then they brought in veletas and barn dances.

Well, my main job, I should tell you, was teaching music… you see, I had a master at Modbury who trained me. He was a Doctor of Music and he got me through my grades. I was still doing it up to about six or seven years ago… I've always loved music.

I tell you what I did too, I did 'Devonshire Dialect', you know, 'Mother and Me joined in' and all that… and I do monologues all in Devonshire, based on Jan Stewer. I was going to act the 'Mother and Me' with Tony Beard at Loddiswell, but then I wasn't well.

Stanley Efford

Born 27th July 1922

Died 25th November 2007

Recorded on 10th July 2007

Stanley. I was born over at Moreleigh Green in a little farm there. My Efford grandparents lived over at Moreleigh Cross where Granny kept a shop. It was the house on the corner and, years ago, was the 'London Inn'.

Grandfather and Father were road contractors and coal merchants. They delivered coal around the area with horses and carts, and they used to wash the coal bags and hang 'em on the wall to dry. Then Father went on to do cattle haulage, transporting the cattle from farms to market and from one farm to another; before that the farmers used to have to drive 'em on the road.

My mother's family were called Baker, and they lived down at Gripstone. Here in Moreleigh there was Mugridge the blacksmith, and Hallets, builders and wheelwrights, and Norman Clements was a taxi man and boot repairer.

We boys used to play football and when I left school I played for Halwell and Moreleigh; we won the league. The vicar, Rev. Green, played in the team, and there was Harry Treeby and Ron Lethbridge.

We went to Halwell school; Mrs. Bartlett was our infant teacher, and then she went out to East Allington.

Then I went to Totnes Grammar School; I was Grammar School Champion in 1939. I did very well and won a lot of cups for running… and the long jump.

Halwell has changed completely; there was a shop and bakery then, run by Miss Nicholls. I lived there when I was first married, on the left opposite the pub. There were cottages all the way along there then, and they were all pulled down to widen the road.

Hylda Thorns

Born 17th November 1923

Recorded on 17th September 2007

Hylda. I was born in Plymouth and came to Modbury when I was about seven. I remember being brought here in a motorcar, a very early model with an open top... I was enchanted by the primroses in the hedges towards Modbury, but particularly coming up Edmeston hill, 'cause, see, we'd never been out of Plymouth before that.

My mother was the eldest of ten children and they were very poor. Her father was a farm labourer and Grandma, dear soul, worked her fingers to the bone and died at an early age. My mother was a thrifty woman...well they had to be!

We lived above the shop in Church Street. We had to fetch water from the other side of the road and then carry it up two flights of stairs...we had no sink upstairs, so it all had to be carried down again to put it in the drain outside. It was difficult sometimes to make a cup of tea or do the cooking without sufficient water, and so Mother either had to go out to fetch it herself, or wait for us to come home.

My father started an electrical business, wiring houses and the appliances, because the electricity was just coming in then. He was a very clever man in every respect: he was a good sportsman, he was an artist, and he was a very good gardener. He could dress-make and used to make his own suits - yes, and he used to make dresses for Mother to wear. He taught himself wireless repairs, although they call it radio now. He had a shop that sold appliances as they came on the market; lamps and irons, and vacuum cleaners - but it was nothing like it is today. He charged up the accumulators for

peoples' wireless sets, and then there was his 'accumulator round': Father's first vehicle was a motorbike and sidecar, and he used to deliver them in that. Then later he had a car, a Riley, I think.

We used to make our own fun. I've got a wooden hoop hanging on the wall outside that I used to run up and down Church Street with... yeah. It's still there - see, you couldn't do that today.

We'd make a soapbox on wheels; we could play for hours in the streets, nothing came past, there was no traffic... well you might have a horse pass you.

I remember at about that time the whole village did a pageant and we performed it in the White Hart Assembly Rooms...nearly every family was involved in some shape or form.

When I was sixteen I used to do the ration coupons; all the customers' books had to be checked to see they got the right amount of rations each week. When they had their rations the coupon was clipped off so they only got it once.

I joined the WAAF when I was eighteen and aspired to be a driver. I went through the course but they decided I was not suitable temperamentally: see, I was a bundle of nerves. So I re-mustered and re-grouped as a wireless operator. It was a six months training and I was told I made a good job of it. I did the rest of the War as a wireless operator, and I enjoyed it.

Modbury is a very ancient town and there are some lovely buildings; they took trouble with everything and embellished things, and they are still standing; but it breaks my heart because, now today we've got all these great juggernauts coming down and you can see them literally shaking the properties as they go by. I think it's awful that properties that have stood for three hundred-odd years are being undermined, it's wrong... and it isn't only that, it's all the pollution off the exhausts, it's really dreadful.

The pavements, and a large part of Church Street were cobbled all the way down. They had the animal market there every fourth week, the sheep and pigs penned at the side of the road, and the cattle in the bottom of Galpin Street and Broad Street. The auctioneer would stand outside the White Hart.... "Three and six a live hundredweight", something like that... well, you couldn't do that today!

There were five butchers in the town.... a baker and a general store, a tailor, a cooper, a saddler, a thatcher and a wheelwright! You could get everything done in Modbury, 'trouble was everybody was a Rogers.... you had to distinguish between 'Daitcher Rogers', 'Butcher Rogers', 'Builder Rogers'.. and so on.

Margaret Lock

Born 30th June 1923

Recorded on 17th Sept 2007

Margaret. I was born in Ringmore, in a thatched cottage on the way down to Ayrmer Cove, and then when I was four *this* was for sale, and Mum was keen to get somewhere to take in visitors and 'earn a bob or two'. Mum was fortunately a very good cook so I was the parlour maid! We didn't have a bathroom or indoor toilet, so even the visitors had to go down to the bottom of the garden. My dad was a gardener and worked very hard, but money was poor.

Grandma Triggs had thirteen children and she was a dear old soul; I don't know how she managed, well, I suppose they didn't have any birth control in those days like they have now…. and Grandad was a very aristocratic old gentleman!

Grandad Rogers could turn his hand to anything, but he couldn't read or write… a lot of them couldn't in those days you know; he was, though, a nice old gentleman too! When there was a party or a celebration coming up Grandma Rogers always used to say, "Us be goin' to have a frawzey": Grandma always called it a 'frawzey'!

In Ringmore we had to carry our water from over by Rock Cottage, there was a well there; but when it was very hot weather it used to dry up and so we had to fetch our water from 'Town's Well' down by the Journey's End… and bring it all up that hill.

I remember dear old Bessie Ryder, she was a character. She used to go along in her pony and trap, and she'd have her fowls on the floor, and she'd be picking them and throwing the feathers out as she was going along!

Steve. I guess there's quite a history of smuggling around here?

Margaret. Oh yes, there is: out to sea from Challaborough, on a clear day, you can see the Eddystone, and of course there was a lot of smuggling around here.

When I left school I did the post round for a while; the old postman had died and they needed somebody badly, so I thought, 'This is the job'… I'm not going to say I didn't read some of the mail! There was a lot of postcards then 'cause postage was a lot cheaper on a postcard - I think a letter was three ha'pence and a postcard was a ha'penny…. and in spite of education not being very good in those days, people wrote quite well.

I was sixteen when the Second War started and when I was twenty, in 1943, I got me calling-up papers. I didn't want to join the Forces but I had to, I was conscripted! My dad nearly had a fit 'cause he'd been in the First War, you see. He said, "Bad enough for men, let alone a woman!"… oh, he carried on! Well it was a worrying time, but it wasn't so bad. I enjoyed it really… it was an experience I wouldn't have had else, and I met several nice girls.

I did my training at Blackpool and then I was stationed at Mountbatten for a while… it was an Australian Squadron there because, by that time, the Australians had come in to help.

Marjorie Hallworth
Born 2nd November 1921

Doris Wood
Born 2nd April 1912

Pauline Battin
Born 14th January 1930
Recorded on 24th September 2007

Doris. I was born at Silverhill, on the outskirts of Malborough. My mother was an invalid - very, very crippled with rheumatoid arthritis, and my sister and I used to take her out in a 'Bath' chair; it was a wheel-chair made of wicker and canvas, with a bit of lace at the sides.

We lived in Malborough and my dad used to get a pony and trap from the farm where he had worked once, and bring it home on Sundays to take Mum, Edna and I for a ride in the afternoon. We used to go and visit Thirza down Collaton, but I don't think we ever met anyone else on the way in a pony and trap of a Sunday afternoon, 'twas just us; though I do remember seeing people walking.

In Malborough there was a blacksmith, and George Cole was the cobbler. There was a little shop down in Lower Town and

Doris

another general store in Higher Town, and they used to weigh everything up; cut off the margarine and wrap it in greaseproof paper, and weigh the sugar from out of a barrel into blue paper bags.

I remember when we went off to school one day Mum said, "When you come home, we're having roast duck for dinner today", and when we came home 'twas a blinkin' marrow that they'd scraped all the seed out of and stuffed it with sausage meat! - 'Mock Duck' they called that... and sometimes we'd have a pudding made in a cloth, 'babby's head' they used to call it.

It's some different today; we had a 'bungalow' bath, a long galvanised bath, and used to put it in front of the open coal fire.

I went on the last train from Kingsbridge to Brent, that was in 1963. It was a lovely ride...they should never have closed that line, never!

Marjorie. My father's name was John Owler Luckham: he was called that after his aunt who married a man called 'Owler' from Cornwall, and of course 'Owler' means smuggler, doesn't it!: they were 'night owlers'... so perhaps he came from a family of owlers!

There's Luckham's Lane here in Malborough, and that name came from my family. The Baptist Church was started in the home of one Thomas Luckham, and we've still got his bible in the Church, dated 1792.

There was a 'Dame' school here, many years ago, long before our time - before the National school was built, in 1873.

My father was an invalid pretty well all his life, as a result of the First World War. I was eight months old when my father was diagnosed as having TB and he went away to a Sanatorium at Lustleigh on Dartmoor. I think I'm right in saying that he went there three times in our childhood 'cause he used to get better and then get ill again. There wasn't much you could do in those days except fresh air, rest and good food. He had both lungs affected, you see, as a result of being gassed.

Marjorie

Then the Second War came and I had to go in the Army when I was eighteen; it was conscription you see, I had no choice...so off I went, to be a soldier!

My brother was killed in the Second World War. He was in the submarines and he died in 1941. Several years ago they located his submarine in the Aegean Sea... it was on the news. There was talk of it being raised but they kept it as a War grave... it was heart-rending really.

There was always a policeman up 'Turnpike'...he lived in Alma Terrace but he would stand there at Turnpike, you know. I don't know why they changed that name to 'Townsend Cross', 'cause 'twas always 'Turn-pike', and it tells you just what it used to be doesn't it.

You never locked your door in those days; Mother would leave the coal money on the table, for the coal man to come in and get it... and he'd leave the change.

Where the new village hall was built there used to be allotments there ... wonderful allotments, and a reservoir at the end where all the fresh water was kept for the village; it came up from Yarde and it was beautiful water. I remember when Mrs. Widger turned the water on, 'cause it came from her farm, and she wore a blue dress, and a fox stole around her neck.

Pauline. My family was called Moore and my mother was a Wood before she married. Both my mother and my father were one of twelve... and they only had two bedrooms.

Steve. You always had open fires and candles; did any of the thatched cottages catch fire?

Pauline. No, 'cause quite frequently they'd pull a holly bush down through, to sweep the chimney... it was done quite regularly... a filthy job, soot everywhere! But that was what was done, because we were constantly burning wood and coal for cooking with the Lidstone stove, you see.

I remember that if you had a bad eye you'd bathe it with cold tea...and I've heard 'em say that years ago they used to prepare for winter by rubbing their chests with goose-grease; put it on and keep it there.

I never went to any other school but Malborough. I had three teachers: Miss Lethbridge was one, and she rode her cycle out from Kingsbridge each day. Then there was Miss Weymouth, who is now Mrs. Dickson, and she still lives down at Galmpton now.

Steve. She was my Primary School teacher at West Alvington!

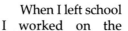

Pauline. Yes, she went to West Alvington after, and then the War came and we had a variety of teachers then.

Pauline

When I left school I worked on the bread round for Ellis's of Kingsbridge, and I was on the Hope Cove new road when all the boats were going for D-Day... you couldn't see any sea, it was all boats... and barrage balloons, I shall never forget that.

Then there's the 'pound' up there by the church - they used to put stray animals in it years ago, but during the War the Home Guard used to go up there and there are gaps now in the wall, where stones were taken out to make gun emplacements.

Terry Stone

Born 25th July 1919
Died 16th January 2008

Recorded on 27th September 2007

Terry. I was born here in Rose Cottage, East Portlemouth. I've moved around a bit and then came back because my sister was living here on her own after my parents died, so my wife and I came up to live with her.

My father was in the Royal Marines until about 1890 when he was invalided out and then he went fishing with Grandfather, that's my mother's father, in a rowing and sailing boat. After they'd done their crab pots out here, sometimes they used to row and sail to Plymouth to get bait for the following day. Occasionally they were lucky and they'd pick up with a trawler out in the Channel, and they'd get bait from them. They were the first ones in the harbour to have a boat with an engine.

My mother was called Pope, and they go back generations here. Her family lived in a cottage right down by the water at Waterhead, and my grandfather fished from there. One of my mother's sisters married Sir Harold Hewitt; he had a house down by the ferry, and she had been working there as a servant. They were married at the Church here and they had two children, but, twelve months after the second one was born, she died.

My Grandmother Stone was a Powseland before she married, and in that family there were several cousins who married each other. One ran the Post Office up here and I believe she married her cousin,

and then her daughter, Emily Powseland married her cousin, Bill Powseland who lived out Rickham. Well, that's what happened, they used to marry like that, close to each other.

Steve. Were there any pubs in East Portlemouth?

Terry. There were four pubs in the village but I can't remember them all. There was the London Inn, just before you get to the shop, that was done away with about 1907, I reckon. There were two pubs down here at the end of the grounds, and one down in the brake. Well, they used to say that it was fishermen and smugglers that used these pubs, and Father told me there was a pub out the back of this house - that was many, many years ago.

Then there was another one at 'Newhouse', as you go to Prawle, and my father and his brother lived there in the end cottage. They used to go down to the malt house at South Pool on ponies and get malt, and they also used to get barley down at the mill at Waterhead and bring it up for the pub. Then they used to brew their own, what they called 'White Ale'. I've never had it, but Father said it was very good; pretty potent stuff, but they used to drink in those days!

Abraham Yabsley used to live down at the Mill at Waterhead, and he had machinery down there for cutting up trees into coffin boards. The machinery was made by his brother William, who lived in the little cottage as you go up round the corner. It was driven by water coming down from the top; they had a big mill-wheel there. They used to get big trees come in and roll them up on planks and put 'em in position in front of this machine. The saw blade was horizontal, he'd set the machine going and the

tree was self-feeding. He'd have a look at his pocket watch to see what time it was, then he'd leave it and go back to his workshop and come back when it was near the end. Then he'd roll the tree back and start again.

I remember when my poor mother used to do her washing on a Monday with a tub and a plunger thing: all I do is open up a machine, stick it in with some soap powder and switch on, and that's it. It was hard work for 'em, but they didn't seem to think anything of it. We used to go down across the road to get buckets of water to fill up the copper. There was a man down the end house who was in charge of the pump, and, if water was getting short, he used to take the handle off, so nobody could go there pumping water.

I've heard my mother say that years ago they used to use a goose wing, like a brush: to brush around the hearth and that.

Nearly all the cottages in Portlemouth were occupied by farm workers, and all the land and farms, from the Rectory, on either side of the road, were owned by the Duchy of Cleveland. There was a lot of children here then, about forty going to the school up here, and right up through the village was all grass, no road like there is now… right up to the Church, and that was all village green. They used to have maypole dances and all that sort of thing there.

There used to be a lot of houses in the village then that were thatched, but the only two that are thatched now are those two in front here. They knocked the old thatched Chapel down in 1931 and built the one there now in the same place.

Before the Thorntons, I think there were people called Hannaford who ran the shop here. We used to go over to Salcombe a lot before the days of cars: there was only one car here that I can remember, belonging to the Rector, and then when these big houses got built, 'course they used to come with their Rolls Royces and chauffeurs. All these big houses all the way along to Millbay had their Rolls Royces, and chauffeurs in uniform.

In 1940 I was over in France with the B.E.F, building an airfield. We had the runway finished and some of the taxi tracks, then the Germans broke through and we gradually made our way back to Dunkirk. We then came back to England and got sent up to Aberdeen doing defences there, 'cause there was an invasion scare on. Then when they started bombing London they shifted the Company down there and I was there for eight

months, right through the whole of the blitz. We were all sleeping in a five-storeyed house on the top floor! And the blimmin' building was rocking all night. None of the other floors were occupied, so we got on the ground floor. I tell you what, after a fortnight you get used to it, and we used to go to pictures in Edgware Road, go to the pub playing darts. We used to go to dances twice a week, as if nothing was happening! I was on a messing committee and one Sunday morning we had to organise the food and everything in the Company office. I'd just walked back to my billet and some bombs dropped. Ben Lyon and Bebe Daniels - well-know actor and actress - were leaning out of the window next to the house that had been bombed, and we asked if anyone was living there. They said there was about five, and we said we'd have to go and see if we could get anybody out. Well, we got to one lady, she had a piece of wood through her side so we couldn't move her, you had to have a doctor there; and there was another woman who was on a raft of concrete that was a toilet and washbasin and she was stuck there, absolutely dazed, so we got a ladder and got her down out of it. Then the ARP people came and said, "You lads must go, this is our job", and so we left.

Wendell Burden

Born 5th March 1931

Recorded on 1st October 2007

Wendell. I was born at Lifton, North Devon, but my father moved from there to Sherford, down Kingsbridge where he rented Newhouse Farm from about 1934 until 1938… I was only knee-high to a cock sparrow then.

We moved to Townstal Farm, Dartmouth in 1938 - where the new road goes down through, past the Royal Naval College, with the farmhouse on the right and the farm buildings on the left.

We had to cross the main road, but there wasn't much traffic then; you couldn't do it today. It ceased to be a farm when they sold the land off for development after the War.

My mother was the youngest of thirteen… I don't remember my mother's father and mother because they were older, see, but, on Father's side, I do remember my great-granny; she was ninety-nine when she died, and I was old enough to drive a car then. She died somewhere about 1948, but her husband had died when he was fifty-two; she lived virtually twice as long as him.

She didn't have a lot of money but I remember on my birthday, it must have been about 1935, she gave me a sixpence and my grandfather said, 'That's too much for that boy, you know there's no money about'… and, do you know, I treasured that sixpence for a long time!

I remember seeing the raids on Dartmouth, 'course we were in a first-class position where we were. We had one or two hilltop gunnery positions on our place. They bombed Noss shipyard and killed twenty-three people there, and they bombed 'D' Block in the College in one hit. Then, of course, they bombed Dartmouth down near the Butterwalk and seven or eight people were killed there.

They tried to bomb the water tower up 'Jawbones', at the top of the hill there; if they'd blown it up the town would have been out of water. We had one aeroplane crash in a field down beside us… and the poor chap… there was his feet in his boots, and he was burnt to a cinder, he never knew what hit him!

Another pilot came down in a tree, he was soaked in petrol, but us got 'en down and got 'en out of the way, so he didn't catch fire, he was lucky!

We had to give up farming for twelve months when the Yanks were here. The cadets were cleared out of the College and sent to a big place up in Chester, so the College was empty ready for the Yanks. Churchill came down here and toured the training area; he went in around Dartmouth College and I saw him in his Rolls Royce, I think it was, when I was bringing our cows across the driveway and into the yard at the back. They wanted our farmhouse for a mortuary, and gave us a week's notice to get out. Then at the end of the week they came and said they didn't want it, but the Government paid us to stay there to look after the livestock and that.

We used to see the Motor Torpedo vessels go out, 'cause they had a Squadron of sixteen boats up the Dart, and they'd sail out quietly just before dusk and harass the French coastline - sinking coastal shipping… next morning they'd be back again.

When D-Day came everybody had to stay off the roads for a couple of days to let the tanks and trucks down through 'cause they came down both ways from the training area, down from Warfleet end, down Weeke Hill, and from the Sportsmans Arms, down that way too. The Landing Craft were built at Coronation Park and assembled over Noss shipyard; the shipyards were going twenty-four hours a day. They had hundreds of these LCT's and LCI's: that's Landing Craft for Tanks and Landing Craft for Infantry.

It was not good remembering having had bananas and oranges, and then all of a sudden the fruit was gone… and we didn't see them again until after the War was over by about five years… goods, food and petrol was all scarce for a long time, right through to the 1950s.

–❖–

John Hannaford

Born 1st June 1927
Died 23rd January 2009

Recorded on 3rd October 2007

John. I was born in Torcross, in this cottage. My father was John Hannaford too, and there have been four generations of butchers here: Grandfather, Father, myself and my brother Reg, and now John and Richard. It was a butchery business before my grandfather came here in 1892, there was a family called Lidstone then, apparently. Butchering then was a bit different from what it is today; a bit more raw, and people weren't so fussy in those days. We had our own slaughterhouse here, and we always bought locally, from the farms round about. The bullock was brought in and tied up and in Father's time they were shot with a humane killer, but probably back in Grandfather's time they were just pole-axed, and then it was all hands to skin and dress it.

It *was* the Village Farm, the farmhouse is where the butcher's shop is now, and the buildings were around the back, a six-stall cowshed with a loose box on the end and a barn above, and on the end of that was the root-house. Along the side were three or four pigs' houses, the calves' houses and a washhouse, but, during the Evacuation, all the farm buildings were flattened, the Yanks just put their bulldozers through them and knocked them down.

Slapton Ley has frozen over two or three times in my memory, the hardest one was in the early part of the War, it froze over then good and solid.

Mr. Garrett, who owned the garage over there at the time, was in two minds whether to drive his car across or not. He took me across on his shoulders one night... he put me on his shoulders and skated across on the ice!

I was only a boy when the War started, and yeah, it was great fun; we never saw the dangers, it was all an adventure... we never thought of the implications of War. My brother Reg and others used to go out on the farms picking up potatoes or something of that nature, and they were up at Coleridge and got shot at by a plane coming back from Kingsbridge or Salcombe.

We were lucky because the first bombs were dropped along the front of the village, then one up on the hill behind us, and another in the road on the Ley side... so it was all around us, it was a bit dodgy!

There were troops here, soldiers at Greyholmes Hotel and Stokeley Manor House, and there was a unit of Bren Gun Carriers in there. Well that was fine 'cause they used to come out here and wash them down and tidy them up, and of course, as kids that was just what we wanted, clambering all over them. For some time there was a roadblock right outside the front of the shop there, with a sentry posted there at night.

Well we went to Chivelstone to live during the Evacuation, because we had the biggest part of the business left: Beeson, Beesands, Hallsands, Kellaton, East Prawle and Frogmore, that wasn't evacuated. In the August Father and myself walked up and over the top, and looked over the wall, and realized that all the buildings had gone and the house was stood on it's own.

Gwen Foster

Born 4th August 1916

Recorded on 5th October 2007

Gwen. I was born and brought up on a farm called Lower Newton, between Liskeard and Bodmin, and we lived there until I was thirteen, when we moved to another farm called Penkestle. I was the eldest of twelve, I had two lots of twin brothers, and we had a wonderful life, we were extremely lucky. My brother Jack and I did everything together, we used to go in for milking competitions and all that sort of thing, we were a very close family.

Our farm went right up to Bodmin Moor where we could cut turf, so sometimes my dad would cut turf and we'd burn it in the fire. It would stay in all night … and we used to bake in what we called a 'baker', in the open fire. It was like a huge frying pan, and you'd have a good fire to make the iron ring in the bottom really hot. You'd make your pasties and put them in there, cover with what we called the 'baker' and light the sticks to get a really good fire going to get 'em browned. Then you closed down the fire with turf - and those pasties would taste absolutely beautiful.

My mother had been a Lady's Maid to the Carews before she was married, and she had been used to quite grand things really. In those days she used to have her hair 'marcel-waved'; real ridged, up and down. She used to play the piano very well, and used to do a lot of crocheting and I remember she often used to crochet our school dresses. My little brothers used to wear 'tussore' suits which were made of pure silk. We had about four cats on the farm and they were not allowed indoors… and we drowned the kittens, because you didn't need

all those cats. You had a bucket of water and drowned 'em… simple as that!

Well, I killed my first chicken when I was about thirteen…just chopped his head off! They jumped around a bit afterwards, but if you're used to seeing things killed you don't take any notice of it. You'd always see the pig killed and hung up… it was part of everyday life.

Our dairy had slate all around it and in one corner there was what they called a 'trundle' made of granite, rough like stone with a wood top, for the salted meat. First of all you had to make a salted brine, and then rub salt into the meat and put it into the brine. You had to turn it each day and then after three days you would take it out and boil the brine to bring any waste to the top, and skim it off. When the brine had cooled you put the pork back, and left it for about a month, then you'd take it out and dry it off on the bacon rack in the kitchen. I'll tell you what I miss more than anything…I'm always trying to find some…you can't even buy 'chittlins', they were the smallest intestines in the pig…they've got a taste all of their own; I love 'em.

After I left school at fourteen I went to Truro Dairy School, because I'd always wanted to be a dairy instructress; you never hear of it now, but in those days the dairy instructresses went around to the different villages and showed people how to make butter and cheese, and truss poultry. When I was seventeen I left and managed a dairy between Exeter and Crediton…and cried every night when I went to sleep because I missed those other children so much.

I pretended to be happy and I stayed there for just over twelve months, but in the end I confessed I wasn't, so I left there and came home again.

We came to Kingsbridge in 1948. George, my husband was a blacksmith at Otterton and then we had the chance to take over the blacksmiths down near to my home; but George landed up three times in hospital with a bad back, because in those days there were so many 'entire' horses, and he would be always shoeing heavy horses.

The doctor said, "You can't do it, you'll have to give it up" so we went to Kingsbridge in 1948 and there we were working for 'Steer's Implements' in Church Street, and we lived in a flat up over the shop there.

I remember Joe Brockenden, he was a character, a part of Kingsbridge...he used to be the road-sweeper, and his daughter Daisy Brockenden went away to be a 'Bluebell Girl', a dancer in London... that was quite something in those days.

– ❖ –

Jack Tanner

Born 21st September 1918

Recorded on 9th October 2007

Jack. The Tanner family goes back to 1685 when our family had cloth mills at Crockerton, near Warminster. We sold the Mill in 1701 and we did not weave cloth any more, we became wholesalers and retailers of clothing in Burford and Cirencester.

My Grandfather, Joseph Tanner, was in partnership with his family and he broke away from the family business and moved to Brixham in 1878. Then he moved from one watering-place to another, and he moved with his family to Kingsbridge. He bought numbers 95 and 97, Fore Street, Kingsbridge; adjacent to the Kings Arms Hotel. So Joseph was running his business in 1882 with his daughter Jessie Tanner, and his son, Edward John Elsworth Tanner. My grandfather sold top hats... silk hats... opera hats that collapsed: you see, if you went to the opera you would wear your white tie and top hat, and a cloak probably, and when you got to the reception they couldn't deal with three or four hundred top hats, so they would collapse! The top hats were made from the coney, American rabbit.

My father wore a boater sometimes... butchers and fishmongers wore boaters too...and sometimes he used to wear a trilby.

When my grandfather died in 1910 Jessie and John ran the business and called it 'J and J Tanners'. In 1924 they purchased the adjoining property, 99, Fore Street, which was owned by Balley and Flower, photographers, and Miss Tanner opened a ladies department, because previously they were only men's outfitters.

You always had a 'Sunday best;' whatever you

wore to school in the week you had to have something different for Sunday... usually a black jacket and striped trousers... the girls were the same: before the Second World War it was remarkable to see children on the beach all dressed up. In 1934 / 35 going to the beach... oh yes, "You'd better put on a nice little dress, dear, with a red sash on it"... to go and sit on the pebbles!

At 'Tanners' we did a lot of business with the farming community, but the farmers and their families couldn't get into Kingsbridge, so in my Grandfather Joseph's time, he used to tour the countryside with a pony and trap, and he would take the orders.

In 1910 my father bought a 'Phoenix' car, and in 1922 he purchased a Fiat 12. He would drop Miss Tanner at a village and she would take the orders. The first Thursday of every month she would do Slapton village on foot. She would be taken and dropped off at the beginning of the village by her brother at about nine o'clock in the morning, and she would walk all around the village taking orders. You see, Miss Tanner's visit on a Thursday was very much looked forward to; it was someone from outside coming in.

She would go from house to house taking orders from the families and take them back to the shop on the Friday. As many as thirty or forty parcels had to be done up, in those days with paper and string... our assistants apparently loathed Fridays!

Our porter would take them down Fore Street in a wheelbarrow to the carrier who was parked, along with other carriers, on the Quay where the Tourist Information Centre is now. Then they would be delivered on the Saturday, and on Wednesday he would bring back what they didn't keep and deliver that to the shop. The wonderful thing about this is that all the parcels that were left on the wagons and vans on the Quay were not controlled in any way, they were just left in the wagon, or on the seat of the wagon... pounds and pounds worth of clothing just left open on the Quay and no one would steal it at all... and that's how it worked until the beginning of the Second World War.

Steve. Can you tell me about those rubber collars?

Jack. ... xylonite collars; you washed them... you'd spit on them and clean them!...and the deeper the collar the smarter! ... you would ask for, say, size 16, and we would ask, "What depth do you want? One and a half, one and three quarters, two inch?" You had a back stud and a front stud to fasten them. We used to sell a lot of breeches and leggings; the farmers would wear breeches made from Derby tweed, or Cavalry twill, and here again, the thigh, the balloon... the more balloon the smarter they were! And with the breeches they wore leggings made of leather, and hob-nailed boots; now today it's all jeans and wellies.

We did trunks and tuck boxes for children to go away to school, you could get a very good cabin trunk for six and sixpence; hatboxes; when ladies went away they would take two or three hats in hat boxes... now, of course, they don't wear hats.

As the motorcars came in and it was wet and cold the men would wear peccary overcoats - peccary was from the pig - to keep them warm... and in the summer the jackets would be made from alpaca ; it's a very, very light material indeed. We had a large Artisans Department in those days; carpenters worn brown bib and brace overalls, painters wore white, engineers wore blue... chef's uniforms were blue check trousers and big hats.

In many cases, in the Thirties, a lot of farmers would have an account and they would only pay once a year, on Kingsbridge Fair day. They would bring the wife and children in to the fair, and they would pay their accounts to the grain merchants, and the same applied to Tanners... they'd say, "Fix the kids up while we're here, Jack!" The children would be fixed up and they wouldn't pay until the next Fair Day! - twelve months credit!

Actually we weren't tailors, we didn't tailor on the premises, we took the measurements and they were tailored in Leeds. If there was a funeral we gave a twenty-four hour service. It would be wired through to the Midlands, and it would be done in twenty-four hours, 'made-to-measure'... it would be transported by GWR train to Kingsbridge Station: 'Red Star', that was a goods wagon attached to an Express train.

– ❖ –

Minnie Noyce

Born 30th November 1913

Died 9th December 2008

Recorded on 11th October 2007

Minnie. I was born in Frogmore, in a little thatched cottage called 'Riverview'; but it was burnt down, and then about six months after they re-built it; then several years after that again they knocked it down to widen the road. I was twenty on the same day that it was burnt. Well, Jerwoods had a new lorry that was driven by coal, and they put some fresh coal in the fire and poked it, and as they passed the cottage sparks came out and got on the thatch.

When we used to go down Frogmore Hill we couldn't go straight on then, we used to have to go across the bridge, around by the malt house, up the hill and around Frogmore corner where Vine House is, and you'd be on the Dartmouth road… and our cottage was just there, on the brow of that hill. At the bottom of South Pool hill there was the chapel and the Police house. I used to go to Sunday school in that chapel, now it's a private house. If you walked around the corner where the little bridge is, you can walk around to go to Winslade and the Mill, and go up Mill hill to Ford.

Of course there've been a lot of houses built since I lived there, the Council have built little bungalows over the Moor. Behind the big house by the bridge there used to be what they called 'willow plat', it was just marshy ground. They used to grow willows there and the Beesands fishermen used to come and cut them to make crab pots.

We used to get all our shoes and boots at Whites in Chillington; yes, there used to be a shoe shop in Chillington. My mother used to have our clothes made, my sister's and mine, by Lily and Ethel Codd; they were dress-makers in Frogmore. They worked from home and they used to make my brother's as well, make his little trousers and jackets. I used to have a little brown velvet dress… oh it was lovely… we used to get so excited when we was going to have something made new.

Steve. What do you remember about Christmases ?

Minnie. My father would bring home a holly bush, and when we were gone to bed they would hang it up on a big nail from the beam in the ceiling. Then they used to put oranges and apples and some sweets and biscuits for you… it was really lovely! Sometimes there wasn't many berries on the holly and another year it would be pickled with them; this was all done on Christmas Eve.

I left Sherford School when I was fourteen and went into Bonds on the Quay, and was there for years. I used to clean the stove and clean the bedrooms and everything. I used to do the ironing and help to do the cooking. They used to advise you to go 'into service' and 'do', it was a good grounding for married life.

Earle Warth

Born 3rd June 1929

Recorded on 18th October 2007

Earle. I was born at number 5, Beesands. Mother was a 'Beesander', Sarah Jane Steer, and Father's mother was called Emma Steer… 'zanderlins', that's what they called Beesanders!

We're all related really, round here: the Steers married Stones, and Lynns…. they're all my lot! My grandfather and my great-grandfather were fishermen, and my old uncle, Alfie Steer, and he was a bit of a character - he used to drink about eight pints of scrumpy a day until he was quite old.

The crabs were put in barrels and kits; a kit was like a small barrel.

When Granny was young she went off to London to work 'in service', and Mother worked 'in service' over Charleton, at Croft, where the Mayes were murdered.

Mother's father's older brother drowned in Slapton Ley in January 1880; his wife had already died of puerperal fever, and she'd had four children. The youngest was only a baby and died soon after her mother, but Miss Oldrieve from Landscove, at Strete heard about the plight of these girls and she got them in a Muller's Orphanage up in Bristol.

My father was killed in the bombing down here at Beesands, and my sister Phyllis, and she was only nineteen. I was thirteen then, in 1942 and I was stood beside them, by the front door, and I finished up at the foot of the stairs… I never got a scratch but they were both killed. It was twenty to six, and it must have rained sometime during the day, but at that time, evening time, it was sunny. The bomb was dropped down near the beach at the end of the village, and it bounced down through and veered inward, 'cause it touched the corner of number six and then exploded. The pair of cottages next to that was destroyed; and then, next to that, was the pub. My sister had joined the WAAF in April 1942; she was a cook and she had been stationed at Torquay for three weeks; she should have been back, but, because she hadn't had any weekend pass before, they gave her an extra twenty-four hours, otherwise she'd have gone back. Mother was upstairs getting ready for church and must have been looking out of the window… and when she came down the stairs that's what she saw!

Steve. *That must have been a terrible experience for you!*

Earle. Eddie Hatherley was a coastguard, and he was on lookout- duty that night, he was looking out of the bay window of the pub, upstairs, 'cause the Government had taken that over. I went along just after it had happened and saw the poor chap trying to climb down over all the rubble… he said, "I can't see" … when they got him down his eyes were all cut up, he was blinded… and he had other injuries as well.

The village was completely different years ago; there was a big fowls house out on the front there, and a hut, where the fishermen would sit outside on the bench making their crab pots. There was a big furnace, like an old copper, with a chimney at the back of it, where they used to 'bark' their nets once a year. I think it was birch bark they used to put in the water, boil it up, and then put their nets in. It was supposed to help prevent the nets from rotting; see, the nets used to be made of hemp, but as soon as nylon ropes came in there was no need to do it.

I knew Jack Lynn, 'Curly' they called him. He was the last to be born down at the old Hallsands; thirteenth of January 1917, and the storm was on the twenty-seventh, so he was only a fortnight old when it was washed away.

111

Hubert Snowdon

Born 11th April 1918

Died 9th September 2008

Recorded on 6th November 2007

Hubert. I was born at Lipton Farm, East Allington, just at the end of the First World War. I was just eighteen months old when we left there and I grew up at Langman's Farm, Buckland, near Thurlestone. Mother's father was Roger Moore; I remember him as a tall thin man, and Granny was a nice old soul. They lived in a house called Rose Cottage, next door to us, and my Snowdon grandparents lived the other side of Langmans, so we had grandparents either side of us. The Snowdons were Thurlestone people and can be traced back to about 1600.

We lived in the lovely Buckland Valley and as a boy I was so happy, I never wanted to go out of it.

There is a stream there that ran from the edge of our farm right down to the sea, and as a boy I used to go off on my own quite a lot. I had absolute freedom and I loved that valley, I had everything I wanted there.

There was a lot of fishing going on down at Bantham, they used to go out and later come in with their catch and walk around the village, the fish still alive and kicking! That's the way to have fresh fish.

Paddle steamers used to come up to Bantham from Plymouth, but the tide had to be right because it's a bit narrow and shallow down in what they call the 'salmon pool'. They'd turn around at high tide,

yes, that was quite a sight and the band would be playing. It was an outing, a day trip from Plymouth… and Aveton Gifford people used to come down on a barge and have picnics down at the salmon quay.

There was a lot of ship-wrecks around Thurlestone, but I was in Salcombe staying with my sister when the 'Louis Sheid' came in… it got in the bay there and got in on the 'book' rocks and broke in half.

My grandfather and they used to go 'wrecking', going around the beach, to see what had washed in. We had a lot of timber one time, beautiful planks. Another time there were boxes of soap and tins of meat washed in. I went down to Bantham and saw the boxes had broken open and there were cakes of soap all the way out, nearly to Burgh Island; you could hardly walk between them.

Farm labourers didn't have much education; at one time it was reckoned they only had three hundred words. They spoke the broad Devon, but they used the same word, and if they put an emphasis on it, it could have a different meaning. Of course, they didn't travel much, there was no motorcars, so these old folks almost had a language of their own. You didn't have to go far to find another dialect. The market towns were the centres for people in that area, that's as far as they travelled; they either walked or travelled with horses.

There was no such thing as the 'dole' back in those days, and if you couldn't work there was only one place to go, you went to the Workhouse. I can just remember several old widows in our village, looking out of their little old thatched cottages, with little dark small windows, and they used to stand out to the doors and gossip; they looked donkeys' years old!

You see, most of these people were farm workers, and their husbands had died in their fifties or sixties; with the physical work the men were worked to death… and the cottages in Buckland were filled with widows.

My father only knew one word, and that was 'work' - and he expected it! He was an early morning man, anytime from four o' clock in the morning he was awake… and he wanted me to milk the cows before I went to school. Apparently, before they altered the clocks, that was the thing to do…go to bed by eight o'clock so you could get your eight hours sleep by four o'clock in the morning.

It was all horses and hand tools… I was brought up to help as a boy… used the Devon shovel to repair and re-turf the hedges. That was a big job, because the fields were a lot smaller then and there were a lot of smallholdings. Our farm had a lot of small fields until eventually we bulldozed down a lot of hedges to make bigger fields.

Seaweed was regularly collected from the beach at Thurlestone; the men watched the tides and my great-uncle and another man who lived opposite him in Thurlestone, would get up at four o' clock in the morning and walk around the beach to see what was washing in. They'd come back to the farmers and say, "There's seaweed washing in down Yarmer" or whichever beach, and down they'd go with their horses and carts to draw up the seaweed. I've done it down Bantham, as it's very good for potatoes… and it's better when it's got a shine on it.

We had a completely mixed farm; we kept all the different animals, a few pigs and a flock of sheep. We started with eight dairy cows and at the end of the farmhouse we had a dairy. People would pull the bell when they brought their jugs and cans to fetch their milk.

In the end we were asked to deliver the milk, so we took on a dairy round. I remember the cowsheds had cobbled floors and there were hollows and pits, and a lot of them were broke, so when the 'Clean Milk Regulations' came in the premises were not good enough and we had it all concreted out… it was much easier to clean down.

Jean Parnell

Born 11th June 1932

Recorded on 14th November 2007

Jean. I was born in Strete, just down the road from where I live now. I've always lived in Strete, apart from a year during the Evacuation, and my family have been here for generations. I can trace four or five generations on my mother's side - she was a Bridgeman before she married, and there were Bullens and Ferrises going back on her side: Ferris is a Devon name and the family goes back a long way… it is good to have roots. On my father's side, his mother's name was Baskerville, which is also a Devon name; so we're Devon born and bred, all of us really.

Grandmother Bridgeman used to wash the choir's white surplices; they were starched and she used to put them on the lawn to dry on a Monday. She could remember the Great Blizzard of 1891, 'cause whenever we had snow she'd say, "Snow, you don't know what you're talking about"!

Steve. There are some quite extensive properties down over the hill towards the beach!

Jean. There was a lot of gentry in the village; there was Lady Lawson, she lived at Asherne, and the Tolls, who were landowners here for hundreds of years and were know as the Lord and Lady of the Manor. They lived at Seacliff, right on the edge of the cliff, and then they lived in the Manor House down at Strete Gate, which later became the Manor Hotel. It is now a picnic area, and the house there now, opposite what was the Manor, then was gardeners' cottages, and stables.

When Mum was about six the girls used to dress in their best clothes and they had to stand outside the gates and curtsey when the gentry came out of church.

When my mum left school at the age of thirteen she went to Asherne to work and worked her way up to be cook for Lady Lawson.

The National School was opened in 1839. It was built for ninety children and my mum started school there in 1905, and there were eighty-eight children there then. I remember an open fire in the infants room, with a very flimsy fireguard, and a 'tortoise' stove at the back of the big room… but it used to get so cold that the ink in our little inkwells would freeze over, and you had to push the pen through the ice to get the ink!

In 1941 the evacuees came from Bristol, and they came with two teachers, so that swelled the numbers in the school. Mum and Dad took two evacuees, but after about a fortnight one of them was very homesick so she had to go back. The other one stayed for about eighteen months, and we still heard from her until she died about six years ago.

I went on then to the Grammar school at Dartmouth, and half way through my first term I came home to be told that we were to be evacuated. I couldn't understand it because we had evacuees from the city, so why would we have to go?

We left on about the twentieth of December, 1943 and we went to Brooking, Dartington. So I had to transfer to what was then Totnes High School for Girls.

When we were evacuated out of the area no-one was allowed back inside, so we didn't know what was happening, but I had an aunt and uncle who were living at Stoke Fleming and we used to come

and see them, and they'd seen rocket ships firing, and different things. When we were at Brooking there were hundreds and thousands of Americans, and it was said that from Plymouth through to Torbay was an unending line of every type of vehicle you could imagine. There were tanks, there were DUKW's, that's amphibious craft, there were lorries, there were jeeps, there were motorcycles… they had all been collecting there for weeks, all under camouflage. Then on the first or second of June we went up to catch the bus to school and everything had gone… no rubbish, not a thing left, only the tracks in the fields! They'd gone over to Dartmouth or Torbay for embarkation to go over to Normandy.

We came back in January 1945, to a different house, and my grandparents came back to another house; a lot of people didn't come back, because they'd settled where they'd been moved. Everybody had to go to the school and collect things that were given to each household: there was a doormat, a kettle, a large brown teapot, two plates, a galvanised bucket, a scrubbing brush and a sweeping brush, a quilt for every bed or a pram cover… and a photograph of the King and Queen!

– ❖ –

Mary Dickson

Born 14th December 1914

Recorded on 28th November & 4th December 2007
Mary. I was born at Motherhill Farm, Salcombe, and I was the eldest of four girls and two boys. My

maiden name was Weymouth: Grandad Weymouth farmed at Motherhill, where my dad was born and took over. My mother's family was called Hannaford and were a very old Salcombe family; most of them were butchers down there, and that's my mother's cousins.

We all had a job to do on the farm: if my dad said, "Mary, I want you to help drive the bullocks" you had to do it. In those days we had to drive the bullocks on the road and stand in the gateways to prevent them going the wrong way; there was no question whether we wanted to do it. Sometimes we had to jump on the old cart horse and ride it up to the blacksmith's shop, bareback, to be shod. Then perhaps Mother wanted a chicken plucked... or a duck or goose. At harvest time it was my job up on the rick, to pass the sheaves over to Bill, to make the rick. I used to help down in the yard to clean the cows out and feed them; we didn't query it, 'cause my dad was the Boss!

There was a butcher down at Hope Cove called Butcher Adams who would buy local cattle and slaughter them down there. They had to be brought from the farms, driven along the road to Hope Cove...I've helped so many times, to drive cattle from Salcombe to Hope Cove. Well, this old butcher had a little pony called Trixie, and he used to take meat around to his customers, riding this little pony and carrying the meat on his arm in a big wicker basket. When eventually he died my dad bought this little pony for me.

I went to Salcombe Infants' school, which was in Courtenay Street, then Salcombe Girls school. We used to walk from Salcombe up to Galmpton to run in the sports, I think it was sixpence if you won a race. From there I went to a boarding school in Plymouth, and at the school a friend of mine and myself decided we would be schoolteachers, 'cause they had a month's holiday in August!

Steve. You were my very first teacher when I started school at West Alvington in 1966.

Mary. I went to West Alvington School in 1958. I started off first at Malborough school... you see, in those days you could be an uncertificated teacher, after you'd done six months pupil teaching. Then during the War an inspector came around and said, "You know, after the War you girls won't be wanted unless you get certificated".

So Audrey and myself then went to Teacher Training College together at Stockwell College, that had been evacuated to Torquay. We went there for twelve months and then went to Maidstone in Kent for the second year. We got our Teacher's certificate, and it was the best thing I could have done. I taught at Slapton after I came out of college. I lodged there with a friend and then a vacancy occurred at West Alvington, and of course it was nearer home because I lived at Salcombe with my parents.

I was forty years teaching kids until I retired in 1974.

Steve. I remember having a third of a pint of milk, when I was in your class!

Mary. Oh yes, the little bottles of milk. Did you think I was bossy, strict?... give them a clip under the ear... or the ruler? I know at dinner times one or two of them would be flipping the mashed potato about, they'd be trying it on, and I wanted them to behave themselves when they had their dinner, so I had this ruler and I used to call it my 'stinger'. I only had to mention 'stinger' and they knew what it was. It was on the palm of the hand but it didn't hurt them really! - and they daren't cheek you, 'cause they'd get a clip under the ear. If you did it now you'd be put in prison!

We had an old barn outside here which in the old days was a cider pub called 'The Fountain'. Years ago an old man in the village said that the fishermen used to come up to the 'Fountain' which had benches all the way around. They would bring their nets up to dry, up in under the roof, while they all sat around drinking cider. The fishermen had a right of way to come up through here to the willow plot, where the willows are growing in a very swampy enclosure, to cut the willows to make their crab pots.

Mary with her Grandfather Weymouth

Ken Parnell

Born 7th July 1927

Recorded on 18th December 2007

Ken. I was born at Slapton, my Parnell grandparents lived there at Town's End, and then later on they bought Brooklea, which was the old workhouse, down at Brook Street. It's a three-storey building and the rooms were all large, the bedrooms would have had six or eight beds probably. Downstairs was the big kitchen, scullery and the front room… and also there was an icehouse, you had to go down steps to get to it; that's where they used to store their ice. A lot of big houses had ice rooms, but, being the workhouse, with a lot of old people, it was probably used as a morgue as well.

We lived at Strete and when I came out of school I used to deliver bread from Trowt's shop, which is the Post Office now, in a 'kit': like a wheelbarrow, with three baskets on it. It was beautiful bread, you can't buy bread like it now. I used to go down to the Lawsons at Asherne first, with a basket of bread for them. Then I came back, loaded up the 'kit' and then delivered out to Fuge, down Snail's Castle, down around Burlestone and Blackwell, and then home.

As a boy going to school, when there was a service at the church, a burial or anything like that, I used to have to go up and blow the organ with built-in bellows; I did that for several years.

On Empire Day, May 24th, we had to go out in the playground and salute the flag, and Major Chandler used to pay for us to have a chelsea bun, a great big 'un, with icing and a cherry on the top…and lemonade.

I left school when I was fourteen and went to work down at Blackpool gardens for Ralph

Newman, who later became Sir Ralph Newman. Then I joined the Navy in 1943 when I was sixteen, it was what I was always going to do.

I was away from Strete for four years; I left before the Evacuation in 1943 and didn't come back to Strete until 1947 'cause my parents were evacuated to Hazel-wood at Loddiswell, and when I came home on leave I spent all night trying to find the place! I came out of the Navy in 1957.

Strete used to have two seine boats and a lot of people in the village had shares in them. In the summer the bay used to get full of mackerel, and old Bert Foale used to sit up Old Hill, in the field, watching for 'macker' playing. He had a seashell, and he used to blow this shell and come up the village shouting, "Seine boat, seine boat", and the men would go down to catch the mackerel.

Pamela Pascoe

Born 13th December 1926

Recorded on 9th January 2008

Pamela. I was born at my Grandparents' house in Stokenham, but we lived in Totnes until I was eleven. We lived in a flat above a shop, just below the Arch; it was a pram shop, the old-fashioned 'Swan' prams. My Grandfather Williams was a tailor in a bespoke tailoring business further up the street and he used to sit cross-legged on the table and stitch the trousers, and Grandma Williams always used to be knitting socks. My aunt's mother-in-law used to do 'tatting', that's like crochet but in little circles all around the pillow cases, and I used to embroider… that's something else that isn't done much nowadays. I used to darn socks until there was nothing but darns! …now people don't darn and sew, they just throw it away and buy new.

Father was a clerk in the cider-works in South Street, which is now a block of flats.

My mother's father was William Mabin, and he had a smallholding in Stokenham, but the land and buildings were away from the house. They lived in a thatched cottage, which was originally called Hall House.

Granny was Augusta Caroline Putt, but she was known as Kitty. She had a sister who had five little girls, but four of them died of diphtheria. Her father was Gabriel Putt and he was head quarryman at Torcross or Beesands.

In the summer holidays Mother would put me on the bus at Totnes and Granny would meet me at Stokenham. I'd stay there all the summer and Granny used to talk to me all the time about her life before she married Grandfer. My granny said that when she was a girl her mother was pregnant with triplets. She was a fisherwoman at Torcross, and when she came back from fishing one day she jumped out of the boat and had a miscarriage - she lost three little boys.

Granny also told me that Grandfer had been up in the orchard one day and he came down, he'd cut his knee with a hook, so Granny put cobwebs all over it to stop the bleeding.

Steve. *Where did she get the cobwebs from?*

Pamela. Oh she had plenty of them … and Mother would put a bread poultice on a boil or anything like that … tear up a sheet and fold it in … it kept the heat in, you see … and another thing, up in the orchard Grandfer would hang rabbits up in the trees, and then the flies would blow in them and the poultry would eat the maggots as they dropped out.

When Granny was young she was a Ladies Companion for a Miss Rivington, her brother was the Reverend Rivington. They went to Switzerland and used to sit up in the mountains, and Granny would read while Miss Rivington would paint. They went to Italy and Mount Vesuvius erupted while they were there. Then she came back and married my grandfather, and after she was thirty-two she had five children.

When my mother was a girl she said that there was a whale washed in on Torcross beach, and somebody put a tent over it and charged a penny for people to go in and look.

My Mother 'mangled' my fingers when I was only two and a half. When you used to mangle the clothes you pushed them between the two wooden rollers. My brother was eighteen months younger than me and Mother was folding the nappies; she looked down to turn the handle and didn't see I was pushing in the clothes, so I got three splits in my fingers. I can remember my father going up under the Arch to see the district nurse, with me screaming, and I can remember a kettle of steaming water, probably to sterilise something.

I was thirteen when War broke out and we were living in Paignton then; Father had bought a milk round in Torquay and we rented a seven bed-roomed house in Kirkham Street, a wonderful house with pillars outside. It had seven flights of stairs as well… and underneath there was a cellar with a domed roof and places all around to store wine. We could have bought that house for £500!

We had lots of evacuees from London while we were there because we had all those bedrooms, and we used to go in the cellar when the sirens went off - but they didn't actually bomb Paignton.

Alfred Cleave

Born 25th July 1926

Recorded on 23rd January 2008

Alfred. I was born at Home Farm, Slapton, right in the village there; 'twas only a small farm, about twenty-five acres. See, Father was a butcher not a farmer, and the land was more to run the bullocks and sheep on, 'cause he wouldn't want to kill 'em all at once. He had his butcher's shop there on the corner, as you go down Brook Street, and the slaughterhouse was down in the courtyard behind the house. He used to buy his bullocks and sheep in Kingsbridge and Dartmouth markets, walk 'em back from town and they were all slaughtered on the premises. Father never had a motor vehicle at all; he had a pony and trap and went round with the meat to all the farms. Saturday's round was always to East Allington, and Tuesday's round was out to Slapton Start and out to Vegeford, that old path there where you can get over to Harleston; you can only walk out there now, I reck'n. Then he would make away for Sherford, and all down around Frogmore and back. He used to drive the horse and four-wheel wagon then, 'cause that was the bigger round and he had to take more meat.

Steve. *'Course there were no health and hygiene rules then!*

Alfred. Oh no, none whatsoever, there was flies on the horses, and on the meat as well! ... bound to be!

There were no fridges then, people used to keep their meat in these gauze 'safes' outside the back door, facing east as a rule, 'cause you didn't get so much sun that side.

When Father used to kill pigs, the head, tongue, heart and the 'enge'- that's his lungs - and his tail - well all the oddments like, would be boiled up to go in the hog's pudd'n. The meat would be took off the bones, like his head and that, and that would be put through a mincer: a hand mincer in they days, no 'lectric, touch a button!

Then it would be all put in a big bath and all mixed up with groats, to fill the intestines.... 'andsome! They used to boil the trotters and use them... everything was used of the pig, everything except his squeal!

My father was the first one in Slapton that had a wireless, and 'twas a lot of old coils and valves and all o't! Only one person could listen to it and that was with earphones; and ol' Ned Thorning come up, "Yer butcher, how be you getting on with that there 'arkenin' 'een set?"

Steve. *Tell me how you used to cook the fish down on the beach.*

Alfred. Well, back in they days there was two wooden houses out there where the fishermen used to keep their ropes and oars, and general fishing gear. Well us boys would go out there and give a hand pulling in the net... and anyrate, if they had a good catch all they that had helped would have two or three mackerel... 'macker'! They would fix up three flat stones, like a box, and they had saved all the driftwood and made a fire. They'd cut the head off the old fish and scrape 'en a bit. Take out his innards, wash 'en off in the salt water and do 'en in the frying pan... right out of the water and in the frying pan! They would give us boys a bit of fish on a flat stone and that would be our plate! ... 'tis 'andsome too! They always say if you want to eat a 'macker' right, you've got to take 'en out of the water and put 'en right in the frying pan.

– ❖ –

Jim & Marina Trout

Jim born 26th August 1931
Marina born 29th October 1934

Recorded on 23rd January 2008

Jim. I was born at number 10 Fordsworth Cottages, North Hallsands. It was number 10 then but in 1930 or 1931 they built two more, and then they changed the numbers around, and number 10 became number 1… then we moved to number 11!

My Grandmother Trout lived in number 6, and when we got married in 1956 we went to live in number 2: well, the whole row was nearly all relatives, 'cause there were also Trouts in numbers 11, 7 and 3, and in numbers 1 and 5 were great-aunts of mine who were Trouts before they were married. The rent then was twenty-six shillings a month.

Patience and Ella Trout were my grandfather's cousins. I can tell you about Patience; she was the eldest, and there wasn't a thing she couldn't do. She could take a motorboat engine to pieces and put 'en back together… she could build concrete block walls, and she used to do all the gardening. My father was ten years old when he was in the boat with Ella, when she rescued that chap, and he was awarded a medal when Ella got the OBE. Patience and Ella both died in their early fifties… well, they worked too hard, they was the first to have a big boat in the area. They had a thirty-footer and used to moor 'en off the old village, and use a smaller boat to get out to 'en.

It was good growing up in Hallsands, there was all the crab and lobster fishing, and in the Spring we used to catch the grey mullet and the bass with the seine nets. We used to go down the old village waiting for the grey mullet: there would be a chap up on the cliff-top looking out, and he'd have an old cap … we'd be down there with a boat and he'd guide you by waving his cap: straight out, turn… and then, when he thought the fish was up in the net he'd make a sign and you'd have to row like anything back to the shore.

Marina. The women had to go down as well to pull the nets in. We used to get a third share.

Jim. They were still doing it in the fifties; well, I packed in fishing in 1959 but me uncles were still catching the grey mullet after that. We used to catch them down by the old village, and then we'd have to carry them from down there, right up to the top where Trouts Hotel is. We carried them in 'mauns', that's big baskets… and in them days we used to wash 'em all in big tubs before we packed 'em in seven pound boxes to be sent away to Billingsgate.

When I was going to school during the War, you was allowed so many days or half days off, to help the farmers; you had a card to take with 'e, for them to mark off that you'd been there. So us was out Down Farm, near the BBC Station, down in the steep fields, putting in cauliflower plants. In them days they used to mark out squares in the field, and us youngsters had to drop the plants where the squares met. Then the farm labourer would come along with his digger and put the plant in and tread 'en in with his heel. Well, me and this evacuee boy, and Den Steer from Beesands, made some pipes out of elder wood, had a bit of reed with a stem, and used to smoke dock leaves and dock seed!… so us sat down having our lunch and me cousin, Stan Crispin, let us smoke some 'digger plug' in our pipes… I was bent down dropping the plants, and all of a sudden the ground was coming up and hitting me… and the sky was going round… cor, wad'n I sick! So I had to go home early and I told me granny it must have been the solution you dip the cauliflower plants in, to stop 'em getting club root… and she never knew. Well, I don't think I've smoked since… that put me off.

Marina. I was born at Frittiscombe Farm, up the road there, and I was nine when the Evacuation came and we went to Loddiswell to stay with my Uncle Lethbridge at Coombe Farm. Then after the Evacuation we came over to Stancombe and lived there, until I was  fifteen. We never came back as a family again, because some got married, and two of my brothers were out working on other farms and living in… and, of course, my youngest brother had been killed by an hand grenade… he was eight years old. That was the worse ten months of my life, and my Father was so upset.

Steve. Can you imagine what it was like down in the old village of Hallsands during the storms?

Marina… and not having any back entrances to get away, 'cause it was cliff, wasn't it, they had to come out their doors towards the sea, it must have been frightening for them.

Jim. My Granny Trout was there with six children and Grandfer was in the Army. They got washed out twice, and they ended up for a while living in part of the old chapel, between Trouts Hotel and Hallsands Hotel.

Marina. She used to sit and tell me about when she was washed out. She said they had to sit the chidren up on the table, and the water was coming in under the table… and the cupboards fell over and broke the crockery! How they stuck it I don't know, 'cause sometimes it used to go up over the roof and come in the bedroom windows… when you think, they could have been taken out to sea.

Jack Rhymes

Born 28th December 1927

Recorded on 24th January 2008

Jack. I've lived here in West Alvington all my life - in the same house as I was born, eighty years; I was born in 1927 in the blizzard. There have been five generations of builders going back, yes, Grandfather was Tom Rhymes and he built these two houses next to this one, in the late 1800's. There's a photo of them in their white corduroys and bowler hats, and they had a pony and trap, for work. They had wooden scaffolding then and I've heard Grandfather tell about how they used to make cob. He said they used to mix chaff, that's straw cut up with a chaff-cutter, and put it in the pond where it was clay, and they'd turn the bullocks in there to tread it up… there'd be bullocks' dung in it too! Cob will last forever if it's kept dry.

There'd be cow hair in the mortar: when I was at school I helped to make it. You'd beat it up with a fan of three laths and work it up like a fox's tail, then throw it in your heap of mortar, and turn it with a 'mortar pug'. Everything was hard work… and I've only ever once done a complete house with lath and plaster, and lime and sand. That was one in Kingsley Road, next to the ones that were bombed ; the ceilings had all rattled down and had to be put back. We had a big lime pit, 'puddy pit', with stone lime; boil it and sift it out, and it was lovely to use.

My father was George Rhymes and he had five sons. Mother's maiden name was Hill and her brother drove the old fire engine. Their father used to drive the old stagecoach from Kingsbridge to Dartmouth, for the King's Arms.

I never liked school and we didn't like Sundays either. It was a busy day for kids; we had Sunday School and we had to go Church twice a day and sit still… we daren't move 'cause there was about sixteen boys in the choir… we'd be a bit hungry and somebody's belly would start rattling and we'd start giggling… then we'd get a clip up under the ear from the men behind. We had choir practice Tuesdays and Fridays, then we had Bible classes… and you had to go, and sit still.

West Alvington was some different to what 'tis now; there was only about five or six cars in the village then, if there was that. The noises was so different, I mean, all day long there was horses and wagons going about, and bullocks shouting, and sheep. There was always cattle up and down the road, always - well Wednesdays was market days, and it may sound extraordinary but butchers in Modbury would buy sheep and bullocks and drive them all the way back to Modbury… as kids we'd help them, run up the road and keep them from going down the wrong roads; we got to know the names of the drovers.

There was a 'pound', down near the fork in Lower Street, a big, stone-built pound with high walls. It was built for stray cattle… they used to put 'em in there until they were reclaimed. It was about two foot six off the house, and there was a passage between, 'course that was a rare place for kids to play, but the thrashing-machine and lorries had a job to get down to 'Woodhouse'. I think that was the reason they took it down, and it made more room for parking cars there. There used to be a blacksmith's shop where the school playground is now… and there was a Post Office there too, years ago… but that was all pulled down.

During the War everybody was asked to keep poultry and rabbits, and we had a pig that we fed on waste. We'd go round the village collecting scraps… and it's strange how the health of the country was better during the War than it had ever been.

We had troops down here in the woods and that was another extraordinary thing; they just appeared from nowhere and there was hundreds and hundreds of them, not just here but everywhere… and, then one morning they were all gone, there was none left! That's when they went off for D-Day.

Looking back it is so different today; everybody knew everybody along here, and everybody helped each other, but now there are people here I don't even know; it's a different way of life altogether. There used to be a blacksmith's shop, two bakers' shops, butcher's shop and slaughter-house and there was a rabbit trapper. There was two dairies, and Saunders the thatcher, lived at Piers Cottages. We had a village 'bobby', he lived in the Constabulary, just next to the old Ring o' Bells, that's opposite the telephone box, and there was a big iron plate over the door - 'Constabulary'.

Marjorie Buckpitt

Born 20th November 1924

Recorded on 26th February 2008

Marjorie. I was born at Little Cotton Farm, Dartmouth; in the parish of Stoke Fleming. It was a very small farm and we made our living with our cows. We never went very far, sought to go any-where; we were very contented at home.

My dear father was in the First World War, for more than four years. He was in India and he had malaria while he was there. He talked about the monsoons... and he was caught in a sand-storm; it was dreadful, you see you can't breathe. He wasn't injured at all but the effects of War left a lifetime problem. There were times when he would wake up and he'd be in a dreadful state, streaming wet with perspiration.

An uncle of mine was in the Yeomanry, and it's so sad: he used to take the horses and the guns up to the lines during the night. You see, they had to look after these horses, they had to feed them and keep them clean... and it was so cold that winter. He told me that he slept with his horses one night, and then another night there was a lot of gunfire and a shell hit the horses and.... that was the end of them.

After the Great War there were a lot of spinsters - women who had lost their fiancés...and women that had lost their husbands, and many of them never remarried.

The ladies years ago did everything for their men: the chair was put there, the dinner was always put out on time, the clothes were always aired and put out for them... the boots were always cleaned. The housewives, they did so much indoors, and so much out... the men weren't domesticated at all. I mean, every week I used to scrub all the milking stools; used the hot water from the copper, it had soda in it you see, and to remove the grease from the candlesticks.

There was a boot and shoemaker in Stoke Fleming called Mr. Bowden, and we would take Father's boots to be repaired. Well, we were only little, so we'd carry one, and next day we'd carry the other, so he had the pair... and then we'd bring them home one at a time... well, they were hob-nailed boots and they were heavy 'cause Father was a big man... I should think he took elevens or twelves.

Everything in farming was on a smaller scale than it is today... all the milking was done by hand, and unless you were near a town you wouldn't have much dairy, because you couldn't get rid of the milk in the early thirties, prior to the Milk Board coming in. We were near enough to town to be able to take our milk in churns to the dairies, in Dartmouth.

We didn't have mains water laid on; I remember pumping water from the hand pump and taking it out to the cows evenings so they could have a drink.

They were all in stalls, tied up individually... the cow-house joined the back of the dwelling house. Then in about 1936 my father took on a milk round, and so we used to bottle our milk then, in bottles with wide tops, and you had cardboard discs you pushed into them. We used to bottle our milk in pints, pint and a halfs, and quarts, and when I used to wash the bottles when I was young I used to think the big fat quart one was the 'Daddy', and then Mum was a pint and a half, which was slim, and then you'd get all the little pints after that!

We used to deliver twice a day, right up until the War. You'd go in the afternoon... somebody would say, "I'll have a pint in the morning and a pint in the afternoon"; you see, there were no refrigerators then! When the Second War started there was only once a day delivery then.

Steve. *Do you remember any extreme weather conditions?*

Marjorie. I remember, I think it was January 1941, when we had that terrible freezing fog... They called it 'ammel'; they get it out on the Moors now sometimes. It was a fog, but it froze, and all the telephone wires were like hosepipes, they had ice around the wires and it brought them down. I remember the cows had icicles hanging down over their faces, and their horns had ice all around them. Well, everything froze 'cause fog was all around everything and it froze, like all the gates and the wire netting was all one sheet, and the trees looked absolutely beautiful 'cause all the little twigs had ice all over them; it was phenomenal!

Barbara Wotton

Born 27th February 1915

Recorded on 7th March 2008

Barbara. I was born at Peverell, Plymouth, and came to Dartmouth in 1919, so I don't remember much about Plymouth. When we came to Dartmouth first we lived at Sandquay, near the Higher Ferry. My father was a shipwright in Philips' Yard, he learnt his trade there and then went to Plymouth and then came back. Mother used to walk everywhere; even in her old age, at ninety-four, she'd walk from Townstal to the town every day.

I liked going to school, which began with a hymn and prayers, and then we'd file out and go to our class. We had the same teacher for every lesson and in the summer we used to walk single-file to the Castle in Dartmouth to swim… that was our summer treat. We had to behave ourselves at school - there was no nonsense.

We used to walk a long way to school, all around the Higher Ferry and over to Newcomen Road. There was a yard there, 'Lavers Building Yard' by the water, and we used to go down and paddle and play there. The area was filled in and a new road built to celebrate the Coronation of King George VI. It was opened in 1937, and well, made a big improvement to the town. There is a lot of old scrap in under there! We used to play in the old submarine as kids; go down one end, run through, and come up the other.

I learnt to swim in the river, off the Higher Ferry slipway… we all did, all the boys and girls did, and we were very good - we'd get back if the ferry was coming or starting up… that was the very old, original ferry, run by steam. I had a bathing costume with sleeves, and a skirt out over, so you kept yourself decent… and a mobcap!

We didn't have the amenities they've got today, well there wasn't the money about… people were very poor when I went to school. We had a big soup kitchen in the old Market and that fed half the children in the town. We had gas lighting and we used to have to put a penny in the slot, in the evening, for gas. Then the lamplighter man used to come around and light the lamps in the streets, and turn them out again, with his pole.

We had dolls and spinning tops… and we used to play out in the road, play 'Lizzie Pottie', you know, where you jump the squares; 'hop-scotch', drawn in the road… there were no cars then you see.

We used to walk to Blackpool sands occasionally, that was a treat, but it was a long walk. Lady Freake lived at Warfleet; I never saw her… but I knew girls that worked out there… and out to Norton Park we had Madam Sullivan, she was a big opera singer, and I knew the girl that was lady's maid out there.

When I left school I was a waitress for seven years in a big restaurant in the town. I had to wear a black dress, black stockings and black shoes… and that was lovely, I enjoyed it. We worked from eight 'til six for twelve and six a week… give your mother five shillings and you'd be left with seven and six… put it away for a day or two until you wanted a coat or a hat, or a pair of shoes.

Steve. *When did you have your first telephone?*

Barbara. They had one in the shop where I was a waitress, you had to lift the receiver and wind a handle to call the operator in the telephone exchange. You dialled 'O' and the operator would ask what number you wanted then connect you.

Son Arthur. *We were one of the first to have a telephone in Dittisham and our number was 30... but you couldn't phone out of the area anyway - one exchange served an area and that was all you could telephone. The only way of going outside was sending a telegram.*

Steve. *I've been told that big stores years ago had a cash system operated with wires or cups!*

Barbara. Yes, you'd sit at the counter with your feet on a board, pay your money, and then they'd put the money in a cup, screw it into a holder on the wire and give it a push. It would go to the girl in the cash desk, and she'd send it back with your receipt and any change. In those days there was always chairs in the shops so you could put your feet up or lean on the counter and talk; no need to stand up, there was always chairs to sit on.

Things are different today; you could cross the road then and not bother to look. I wonder how we lived really, looking back, but we didn't know any different... you walked everywhere, you didn't have much money... everybody was the same.

Joy Heath

Born 30th August 1920

Recorded on 7th March 2008

Joy. I was born in Paignton, that was my home, and that's changed so much now, really you can't believe it. I remember the trams, well I used to go to school on a tram... tuppence I think it was! ... and I always say my one claim to fame is that I was one of the last people to use a bathing-machine!

I can only have been about four or five, and it was horrible. It was dark, with a tiny little ventilator at the top... it was claustrophobic and you undressed and left your clothes there, then you had a key that you hung around your neck, and you went down the steps and into the sea. There were three of them on the main Paignton beach, but they soon discontinued them after that.

My maiden name was Deller, 'Deller's Café' was owned by my cousins, and it was a very favourite place to go, as it was very upmarket. It was just down the street past the railway station and the old picture-house, but just after the War they razed it to the ground; it broke everybody's heart because it was such a lovely place. There were marble steps up to the foyer, and marble pillars. Inside it was all wood, beautifully done, and downstairs the head waiter was always dressed in his dress suit with a stiff collar, and he bowed you in. There was another one in Exeter too, but the Paignton one had a domed roof and they had imported all the green slates from Italy.

Grandma Deller was very stately; she thought she was like Queen Mary, very upright and she had

the same hair-do, little 'sausages' across there, and up there… and a choker… and when she came out to our house for dinner everyone had to go out to meet her, and more or less line up… "Grandma's arrived", sort of thing.

Steve. You used to work at the old telephone exchange. Can you tell me how they worked?

Joy. Yes, I used to man the telephone when I worked for the Paignton Council, and there were about twenty different holes. You had two plugs and you had to plug one in where you wanted the message to go, and one where the message came from… if you weren't careful and you touched the wrong one you got an electric shock!

They had a telephone exchange like that in Frogmore and the lady used to sit there plugging in. You know, you had to 'phone her up; "I'd like to get number so-and-so, please, Miss Lakeman"… then you had to wait while she searched around and did it; and they always said that she listened in if she thought it was interesting! … you wouldn't dare do a secret deal or anything!

I was a typist at the start of the War and that wasn't a reserved occupation you see, so you had to go either into munitions or the Services. Well, I wanted to join the WRNS because they wore black stockings and a nice little hat, and I rather fancied that! but everyone else fancied it too, and it was full when I tried to join up. I didn't fancy the Army because they wore khaki, and khaki didn't suit my complexion, so I joined the Land Army and within two months I was accredited, I was just twenty-one.

My family were quite amused that I'd joined the Land Army, but they were very pleased that I didn't have to go too far; although in those days nobody had ever been to Frogmore or anywhere around here. My father drove me mad 'cause every

morning before I left home he'd come into my room with a cup of tea and he'd cluck or moo!, or did some other animal noise!

Steve. Do you remember the first time you came to Keynedon?

Joy. I thought it was marvellous 'cause I came down by the little train that came into Kingsbridge. I had to go from Paignton to Newton Abbot and change, Newton Abbot to Brent and change, and then into Kingsbridge. I came down with a family so that was very nice, they were very like my own family, but a lot of the girls had to go out with gangs. I came down to Keynedon Barton, and I've been there ever since. Well, I was engaged to this other fellow, but being apart for so long we decided to call it off, then I married the farmer's son.

I went to the Seale-Hayne Agricultural College first, for five weeks - in January… it was a terribly bleak place and so cold. There was no heating 'cause it was wartime, so we slept with all our clothes on the bed, and the mat on top of that! We were allowed a hot water bottle at night, so we used to make cocoa in the morning with the water out of the hot water bottle; that kept us going 'til breakfast time.

I came down in 1942 and I'd only been here less than twelve months when the Evacuation started, and we had to deal with all that… it was so unexpected, and such a job. The old boys would call us the 'Land Maids' then, not Land Girls, but I loved it. I took to it like a duck takes to water 'cause I loved being outdoors and with the animals.

I was in the Women's Land Army for just over four years until I was going to get married… then they gave us a month's 'housewives training'; they taught us basic cookery and how to iron a man's shirt and that sort of thing, that was our reward! … but the good Queen Elizabeth wrote a letter to all of us thanking us very much for our help during the War.

Steve. Nowadays we just flick a switch, don't we, for entertainment and household chores! It was hard work years ago!

Joy. Yes, I wouldn't be without my dishwasher! Well, when I first went to Keynedon to work they didn't have electricity there, but after a while they had a battery set-up - but it was only 120 instead of 240 volts, so you were limited as to how much you could have on. As soon as the cows came in and they wanted the milking-machine on, everything went down in the house! You had to wait until the cows had gone! We could have an iron on, but only just for a little while, 'cause it drained the battery and annoyed everybody else.

Later on, when we moved in we had to wait for the electricity company to come in, and my youngest son was born one evening and the Doctor fell down the front steps as he left!

Tom Smaridge

Born 24th November 1927

Recorded on 11th March 2008

Tom. I was born at Blackawton at my mother's aunt's, but I was brought back here to Borough and I've spent all my life here. This was a very primitive place; even to this day behind the Aga is a Lidstone stove, it was never took out; and where those two cupboards are was an open chimney... but Mum would only light the Lidstone about twice a week, that would be, say, Wednesdays and Sundays, to cook the dinner, otherwise she did it on the open fire. We used to pull that settle across the back door in winter-time, and you'd sit by a lovely roaring fire, but there was no draught-proofing; the sash windows would be rattling with the wind, and there was a rat's hole in the corner of the door... eaten away... oh yes, the rats used to come in the farmhouse.

Steve. *What do you remember of the War years?*

Tom. I remember the gas masks; they were like the pig's snout really; and as children we used to say, "There's the pig"! They were issued with a filter, but later on there was another piece, about an inch long, to put in, for if there was another kind of poisoned gas. We had to carry it to school in a heavy cardboard box.

This farm was right on the edge of the evacuation area and we had to give up seventy-two acres of our land, on one side of the farm. We had about six and a half acres of swedes, which was food, and we 'tapped' 'em off and put 'em in caves to store 'em for the winter. They were alright, but I remember a lot of farmers took up some, but some they had to leave behind; and over the hill there was a nine acre field of swedes that went to seed, all yellow, and of course the seed dropped out, and for years and years, when they ploughed the ground, they were ploughing up swedes.

They say that a lot of the motorbikes and stuff like that was put in quarries and buried in by the Americans... and all the lorries and jeeps and tanks and that must have been cut up for scrap, I suppose.

Children, years ago, didn't know their parent's business; I mean, you didn't ask, but I don't think you'd be told anyway; it was totally different. I remember my grandfather saying that people of 'the old school', didn't trust the Banks and used to keep their savings in a bag under the bed. I think that money didn't come into it very much, years ago;

they worked hard and didn't get much. When a farm worker was being interviewed for a job and there was a cottage with the job, he'd say, "Has it got a garden to grow vegetables?" and, "Is there a pig's house?"… and they'd have milk from the farm; but the money part of it came as the last thing.

Doctor Billy Stear was the vet, years ago, from Aveton Gifford, and they've told me that when he cut the 'stones' out of lambs he'd put 'em in a bucket and take them home and cook 'em; yeah, years ago they used to eat lambs' testicles… but I've never tried 'em… and another thing, when my Father cut lambs' tails he saved back all the biggest ones, and put them in boiling water, and then just pulled all the skin and hair off. Then Mother would make lambs' tail pie! … well, there was a fair bit of meat on them really, the big lambs, not like the baby ones today!

A lot of old farms had huge buildings, built with local stone, and some had a square slate on them with the initials of who built them and the date, but now so many farms have been converted. You take East Allington… Fallapit is all gone, all developed… Flear… Pitt… all these old farms have disappeared.

Out here in our court there was a corn-granary on stilts; nine pillars of stone with a big round slab on top. There was a wooden building built on top with corn hutches inside. They were built like that so that the rats couldn't climb up. You used to have to tar the building with thick tar.

Archie Saffin

Born 4th March 1925

Recorded on 17th March 2008

Archie. I was born at Drewsteignton, near Fingle Bridge, up on the Moor, and I moved down here to Holbeton when I was four years old. I was an only child, but Mother brought up her sister's children: her sister had died of consumption (T.B) and left two girls, and they would have been put in a home if Mother didn't take 'em. They were older than me, one was six and the other was twelve when she had them. So Mother had three to look after, 'cause I was born on the fourth of March and her sister died on the sixteenth.

Father was a farm labourer for most of his life, his wages were only thirty-two and sixpence, so Mum had to go out to work, scrubbing, to make ends meet.

There are some nice old Almshouses in Holbeton, just before you get down to the School; it

used to be six, but there's only three there now - they've made two into one. I can remember when I was a boy an old lady there caught the place on fire, 'cause it was candles then, and our schoolmaster pushed the door down to save her. They were built for the poor, but today they are nice houses.

We had to make our own amusement. We had a bat made out of a bit of board, and three sticks for stumps, to play cricket. I went to Holbeton school until I was thirteen, and then we were the first senior ones to go to Modbury school - that was in 1936.

I had a bicycle and we'd ride down to Holbeton Point, down amongst the marshes… and we used to walk down to Mothecombe Beach… but we didn't go out of the village very much. Sometimes us boys used to walk through Flete drives to walk from Holbeton to Ermington, and if Lord Mildmay was there he'd shout and wave his old walking stick… "You boys"… and us used to run like anything then.

We had three shops in the village then, but years ago they delivered everything to your door: you had the butchers, the bakers, and the candlestick makers!

We went to Modbury for the Doctor or anything like that, as Modbury was the nearest town.

Lord Mildmay used to come in from Flete, in a carriage, to go to Church on Sundays. I went to Sunday school and one day we had an outing to Stoke beach in a carrier's van, we thought we were going out of this world!

Steve. *Did you ever go on a train?*

Archie. The railway used to come into Yealmpton and I've cycled down there to catch the train into Plymouth. Well they used to bring the coal up to Yealmpton. I worked for the council and we had steam engines then, and we had to unload the coal from the trucks, put it on to a lorry to take it back to the depot at Yealm Bridge. They always said they were going to extend the railway into Modbury but they never did.

I left school in March and the War started in September, 1939. I was working at Manor Garage and, of course, a lot of the smaller garages had to close down, so I went tractor driving then and when I was eighteen I wasn't called up because I was in a reserved occupation. I was on the Flete Estate and during the War the house was turned into a maternity home. There were several bombs dropped around Holbeton, incendiary bombs, 'cause we were near Plymouth. We could see when it was blitzed, the sky was all lit up red. I was

coming home from work one night and I could hear them firing at 'em, and the shrapnel was dropping down in the woods beside me.

Things have changed since I was a boy. I remember I cycled into Plymouth and stood the bicycle up against the rails there; he'd still be there when I come back, pump and lights still on 'en; but it id'n safe to leave anything today.

The world's too fast now. The technology has got tremendous: they've all got computers now… but it was good in the old days. Well, we never used to lock the doors and windows and I can remember my wife used to go to work and she'd just pull the door shut, she'd never bother to lock 'en. The Insurance man used to come on Monday mornings and she'd leave the insurance money just inside the window. He'd pick up the money, sign the book, and it was all done by the time she got back home again.

Chris Wills

Born 7th October 1939

Recorded on 1st April 2008

Chris. My earliest memory is of when us lived out Strete in a little old thatched cottage where the thatch at the back of the house went down nearly to the level of the grass field behind. I remember as kids we had an old wheelbarra' and one day we scralled up over the thatch and stood beside the chimney… and then us scrambled across to the other chimney at the other end. When Father came home we knew all about it! He taught us a lesson; us didn't go up there again. That cottage was burnt down during the War; it was where 'Kings Arms' car park is now.

Us used to walk on stilts made from old two-pound treacle tins. We put a hole in each side of the tin and threaded a bit of cord through and tied it. Then as you lifted your foot up you lifted the tin up; you'd walk for miles on them. You couldn't do it on the tins today, they'd just collapse.

We had our own baker in the village, Cousins he was called, and then Edmonds later; and at Christmas - time he used to cook a lot of peoples' turkeys and geese in the oven down there, 'cause they couldn't get 'em in their little ovens. We didn't have no electric here until fifty-two or fifty-dree, before that us had oil lamps. Sometimes he'd run out of oil and burn the wick and then he'd 'smok'… and then us had an Aladdin lamp, a wonderful light then, something out of this world; you had to sit back and put your dark glasses on almost, it was so bright! Then it was the Tilley lamp, you used to pump 'en up and hang 'en up to the ceiling. You could see all over the place then, a wonderful idea that was.

There used to be ol' 'oss' troughs, but they used to be higher than they are now, 'cause gradually, over the years, the tarmac has built up on the road surface. They were always called the 'oss' trough, but the cattle used to drink there as well. There were about five farmers who used to drive their cows through the village for milking, and occasionally, if you got your timing wrong, you'd get 'em mixed up… and all hell would be let loose then!

Grandfer Jerwood used to work fer the Council, used to do road cleaning: keep the buddle-holes clear and sweep the village up. Each 'road-man' in they days had his own area… and in the summertime he used to go around and paint the signposts. He had

his pushbike with a little basket on the front, then he'd have a bag with all the letters, and a little bag of screws, and if some of the writing was gone he'd screw on new letters or numbers… and then paint 'em in place.

Granny was a biggish lady and she didn't stand no crams from us little kids, us had to behave ourselves, but I remember, at the age of seventy, she could skip with a double skipping rope, 'er'd just keep going! I used to get hanged up and fall down, but Granny never gave up, 'er'd go on swinging the rope!

She used to do a lot of rug making; draw the design on the canvas, and then push the little bits of wool through and twist 'em… 'er made hundreds of 'em.

Father's father, Grandfer Wills, was a shoemaker out Strete. He had a cobbler's shop down the bottom of Church Hill… and I'd go in and speak to him and he'd go, "Uh-uh-uh"… his mouth would be full of nails. He'd just go 'tap tap': he was so quick with his hammer, he'd grab one out of his mouth and in the shoe, 'bat' and then another one, and another… but that was his trade, see.

Steve. Do you remember motorbikes and sidecars?

Chris. Yes, I used to hate riding in the sidecar, it was horrible, you felt like your backside was going to drag on the ground… and most of the sidecars were built on the right-hand side of the bike, so when you go round a corner to the left, you go up and think you're going to tip over, but when you go right the sidecar is down and he'd stay down. They had springs on 'em but you'd always be bobbing about, as soon as you got on a bumpy road.

I was only a small boy during the War, and we were evacuated just before Christmas. It was a big concern because, as a little kid we thought, 'Will Father Christmas find us?' - but anyrate, he arrived, so it was alright!

What I remember mostly was the big lorries going by, and tanks going by with sparks coming out from the sides of the tracks; as a boy I thought that was wonderful! Then all the soldiers would chuck out chocolate… cor, that was lovely chocolate, that was.

– ❖ –

129

Viv Freeman

Born 29th December 1937

Recorded on 1st July 2008

Viv. I was born in Britannia Cottage, here in Kingston, but I was brought up in Chapel Row. The water tap was just outside and on Sundays they would fill up the baths for washday on Monday. Well, there were steps going up and I remember one Sunday, Father and Mother had been to church and were all dressed up, and they were carrying this water up the steps: Father was in front and Mother was coming up behind and he slipped… the water went all over Mother and she was soaking wet!

My father was Wallace Freeman and he worked as a roller-man on the roads for the Kingsbridge Rural District Council. He had joined the Council just before the War, about 1937 and after the War he came back to it. They used to do all the tarmac and chippings by hand, and he was one of those who spread the tarmac, which by then was in general use. I can remember 'em tar-spraying with just a tar barrel, one man tipped up the barrel and they brushed it along, and then threw the chippings on… and the roller would roll it in. The lorries that delivered the chippings were Burgoyne's and Jerwood's from Kingsbridge, and Guest's from Loddiswell. My dad drove the last steamroller, and he would cook his egg and bacon on the fire, on his shovel!

They had one gang, but every village had its own lengthsman, who did his own area and kept the buddle-holes clear. There were boundary stones between each parish, but a lot of them are grown in now. They had an initial or name on them, of the next village.

I was only two when Father went to the War in 1940, and I didn't see him until 1944. You see, I was only about two when he went and he was away five years. In them days you used to get a telegram from the Post Office to say what was happening, and everybody hated the telegrams because a lot of times it was notifying of people missing or dead.

When I was growing up the village was self-supporting. We had carpenters who doubled up as wheelwrights and undertakers; they were Bob and Bill Fox, and Alf Fox used to tap shoes and were where the Fire Station is now.

There were a lot of small farms in the village and when it was harvest-time all the farmers would pitch in and help each other; there was always a community spirit in them times. The big farm in the area was Scobbiscombe, Co-op farm; they employed about eighteen men out there.

Steve.Who was Martha Jane Freeman?

Viv. Martha Jane Freeman married Bert 'Sharky' Triggs; she was known as 'Jinny' Triggs, and she was an amazing lady. She only had one arm; she was working as a housemaid on a farm and somebody had left a shotgun lying about… she picked it up to move it and it went off. Yes, she lost her arm; she was only twelve, 'cause they left school and went to work younger then. Yet she managed - she took in washing, did a paper round and cleaned the chapel… and she served teas down on the beach. She lived in Kings Cottage, down at Wonwell, and used to charge a penny a teapot for the picnic people who came down on to the beach.

On Christmas Eve she used to go to Plymouth to buy her turkey cheap: she'd go by bus and go round the markets to get the best value for money, then go back to Goutsford Cross by bus, and walk from there to Kingston with the turkey and a parcel of dried fish hanging over her shoulder.

Steve. *I'm interested in the old remedies that people used for illnesses.*

Viv. Yes, bread poultice, for tooth-ache… but the only cure really was to get the tooth out, wad'n it, the old people used to do it theirself. If Bob and Bill Fox down here had toothache, they'd work it out with a pocket knife… it may take 'em all day, but they'd loosen 'en off until he came out; they never went dentist much.

When I left school I went farming, There wasn't the opportunities to do much else unless you travelled out of the village. I did three years National Service; I was deferred for twelve months 'cause I was on the farm, but I got called up and I had to join the Army. It was a good thing, I wouldn't have gone to Germany if it wasn't for National Service. After that I did some timberwork, and then went to work at Torr Quarry for E.C.C.

Bridget Eccles M.B.E

Born 2nd June 1919

Recorded on 25th July 2008

Bridget. I was born in Plymouth and moved to Whitehall, Churchstow in 1923; and I left there in 1956. One end of the house was supposed to be Tudor but I don't know whether it was. We had fourteen bedrooms when we were there, but then we had a cook, housekeeper and two maids, living in. There was the drawing room and dining room, and the big Hall with the lovely log fire, and a staircase going up to the bedrooms. Then there was the 'snuggery', which was a sitting room for when we didn't use the drawing room. The drawing room was quite large and we had a piano there. My mother was a good pianist, and I had piano lessons. I had to get up at seven o'clock to practice for half an hour. I saw that as a penalty so I gave it up, but I used to do stamp collecting, and press flowers… and we had a tennis court of course, yes I loved my tennis. There was a lovely long conservatory, which ran along the front of the house, where my father grew geraniums, roses and plumbago…it was really gorgeous. It's all been converted into apartments now.

My father was kept busy doing all the garden: it was quite a large garden, and of course, every autumn we had the job of sweeping up the leaves, because there were a lot of lovely trees; oaks, beeches, sycamore, horse chestnuts and eating chestnuts, all down the drive; but I adored it.

We had our own well and we had a paraffin pump, which let us down sometimes, and when that didn't work we had a hand pump. I remember the villagers getting water from the well next to the pub, but when that went dry they had to come down to us to get their water. Our telephone number was Kingsbridge 107, so it shows that few people had phones then. In the Hall there was a lovely bell system, little bells in a box on the wall, from each room - to call the servants. Those were the days weren't they! The maids did the cleaning and laid the tables, then we had a 'char' lady who lived in the village who came down to do the scrubbing.

Mother and Father did a lot of entertaining to afternoon tea, because they played a lot of bridge. My mother would always wear a dress and a hat, and she always wore a fur coat in the winter... and I've still got her fur stole in my drawer here.

I used to come here to Kahala Court as it is now, when I was a girl; it was then called Windsor Lodge and it belonged to the Harrisons...Harold Harrison was a solicitor.

Each year a circus came to Kingsbridge on the recreation ground, and sometimes in Archery field, in front of Stentiford Hill, before the houses were built there. There would be Wall's 'Stop-me-and-buy-one' ice- cream sellers on the Promenade - a tricycle with a big box on it... oh, those lovely choc-bars!

My father was injured in the First World War, he was gassed, and that had really awful effects on him. His father was a G.P and surgeon in Plymouth, and he built Sherwell House opposite the reservoir on North Hill... and all the stables. It's still called Sherwell House but it's all been converted into offices now.

My mother's brother was a poet and critic, and he was knighted, Sir John Squire: that was in the days when they knighted people for their work. Mother's father was a vet in Okehampton, but all his work was done on horseback then. My mother was a swimmer and, before she was married, before the First War, she swam from the Breakwater into the Hoe, and also up the Tamar from Cargreen to somewhere... I had the two cups that she had won.

My mother had a box camera, which is now in the Cookworthy museum, and my brother used it in India when he was out there in the Second War. Photography has developed more than anything I think...

Steve. *... to cine film, to video, and now you can take photographs on mobile phones!*

Bridget. I went to Twyford school for a short time before going to boarding school at Tiverton. I was there for seven terms, until it closed down. I was twelve and went by train from Kingsbridge station, all by myself. I was a bit frightened at first but, once I was settled, I was terribly happy there. After that I went to Malvern, Worcestershire.

While I was at school I did a secretarial training course, and when I left school at eighteen the headmistress asked me to come back and work in her office, which I loved. I learnt shorthand and typing... it was difficult at first, but I adored it. They covered your hands with a shoebox, when you were learning typing, so you got to know the positions of the keys.

Later I went to work in the Kingsbridge Rural District Council office, and during the Second World War I was in charge of getting the people out of the evacuation area.... all the people and animals! I was responsible for making sure that they'd found somewhere to go, in six weeks.... some of those people had never been outside their own little patch.

At Whitehall we had American soldiers camping out in the garden; we had a kitchen and so we did quite well with some of their lovely meat! We had two evacuees, a brother and sister, and they had a jolly nice time actually. I used to take them down to Bantham. Then their mother came all the way from Dartford to fetch them, because she couldn't stand it without them. After the War I stayed on with the council as Deputy Clerk, and finished up being made Acting Clerk.

Steve. *Can you tell me about your M.B.E.?*

Bridget. Since I retired I've done an awful lot of money-raising, selling raffle tickets... and I love it! I'm still doing it now. I support the National Trust, Cancer Research and the Cookworthy museum, because I was a founder member of the museum. Well, it was three years ago now that I went to Buckingham Palace to receive it.

Win Brooking

Born 22nd January 1917

Recorded on 1st August 2008

Win. I was born at Buckland Park, near Bantham, and I was one of a twin; there was a little boy but unfortunately we both had the 'flu in the First World War. They thought I wouldn't live, and the little boy died: we were twelve months old, and he could walk but I couldn't; I was lucky to survive that.

Then we went from Bantham to Topsham Bridge at Loddiswell, with me sitting on the furniture on a horse and wagon. There were three cottages there near the railway line and, oh we used to have a lovely time, standing on the wire fence watching the trains... wonderful... 'used to see the trains going by, and the cows heads looking out as they went by to market in Kingsbridge. We used to play, and catch minnows down in the water there, and pick wild strawberries on the side - but we had to be careful, we weren't to go too far down. Once I did go up the line and there were about two or three other children with me. I had a muff over my ears and didn't hear the train, and they didn't pull me off the line. The train blew it's whistle and they were all shouting! ... I could have been killed... so that's two lucky escapes I've had. Anyrate I got a hiding from Mum for that.

Oh, I tell you what...we were sitting in the sitting room one night there at Topsham Bridge about nine o'clock, well it was dark, and there was one hell of a noise... Dad went down where the railway lines cross the road and there were great big gates they used to pull across; well, the man in

charge of the gates hadn't pulled them back so 'course the train went into the barrier and broke it...the whistle was blowing, and it's a good job nobody was hurt.

Steve. *Did you used to go on the train?*

Win. We could go up to Gara Bridge to catch the train; sometimes we went to Kingsbridge, or to Paignton. The last train was nine o'clock at night and of course, there wad'n any trains on a Sunday.

I got the stick in Loddiswell school once, and that was because my brother and his friend put me up to get some sweets in Elliott's shop, and then in school they were making signs for me to throw a sweet to them... I got the stick on my hand, but my brother got the hiding from Dad when he got home.

We'd go pinching apples from up in the orchard, and then we'd get a hiding for that too!... but 'twas lovely times really, we was always happy.

My dad died young; I was only about eleven and the last thing he did was plaited my hair to go to school, and oh I did love my dad. Do you know, they carried him all the way from Topsham Bridge to Woodleigh to be buried; no car, no horse, no nothing. My mum was in a state really, see there wad'n the help there is today. She used to have to go and get a tiny bit of money to keep us going... I remember Mum standing by the table crying, and Mr. Elliott, the baker, used to come around with a horse and wagon, and I remember him saying, "You shall never go without bread for your dear kids Mrs Stone"... 'twas sad, when I think of it, 'cause Mum had to come out then see, 'cause the farmer wanted the cottage for another labourer. So we went then to my uncle and aunt at Clyng Mill, Kingston.

Mum was clever, she'd done millinery in Kingsbridge, 'used to make hats, and she always had nice hats to go to church. I used to look and say, "What have you done, it's all different, you've put something all around and changed it"? She had hatpins, and a little stand to put them in; but who wears a hat today?

Anyrate, Clyng Mill belonged to Lord and Lady Mildmay of Flete, and they were lovely. It was a working mill when my uncle was there, and I still remember the wheels turning... and they had a farm there as well. I helped on the farm when I left school, milking and making butter and cream; and once cream went all the way over to America, taken

by people who were flying home in the morning. I was working there when the Second World War began, and I wanted to go, 'cause everybody else was going, but I was working on the farm so I didn't have to go. I played up merry hell 'cause I wanted to go; they all had their uniforms and I wanted to go too.

Ed Dornom

Born 20th April 1916

Recorded on 2nd August 2008

Ed. I was born in Buckley Street, Salcombe. My father was called Aaron Dornom, and he was a boat builder with his two brothers Sid and Wilfred, and cousins of mine carried on after them. Father's father

was also called Aaron and he'd been a boat builder before them, so the skills were passed down the generations. Their workshop was at Whitestrand and they built mostly fishing boats, pleasure craft, rowing, motor or sailing boats, up to about thirty feet long. They used to put the wood in a big kiln where they would steam it, and I used to hear them talk about 'anti-fouling', they'd paint something on it, to stop seaweed growing on it. Everything was done by hand of course; I've seen them use an 'adze', a tool with a long handle, that they'd use to chop away the wood, but of course I wasn't in the trade so I only knew what I'd seen others do.

Steve. Did they ever get commissioned to build a special boat for anybody?

Ed. Yes, a number of cruisers for different people.... the 'Careta' for Sir James Owen, he was the editor of the Express and Echo in Exeter, I remember that one.

Father's mother lived in Salcombe and she died when she was ninety-six, and Father lived to ninety-five... but I shall beat both of them! I vaguely remember my grandmother, typical of that age, dressed all in black with a big brooch on her throat.

Steve. What did you do for entertainment when you were a boy?

Ed. We'd play football in the streets and go to the local cinema... that was tuppence ha'penny! Later I played rugby, started in Salcombe and then in Exeter. We had the Regatta, like they do now, and I've still got two or three cups I won for rowing.

We had a radio and a gramophone: Henry Hall and his Dance Band, and Larry Adler... and dance bands used to come to Cliff House on Saturday nights. A lot of people made their own fun at home, playing a harmonica or an accordion.

We'd go out scalloping, then Mother would fry 'em or boil 'em... and cockles - go out on the mud between Salcombe and Snape's Point to get them; well, it was free food and I suppose Mother was glad to see us bring something in.

Steve. What do you remember about Salcombe years ago?

Ed. I remember Fairweather's photography shop: Len Fairweather and his Father, about four doors along from Hannaford's the butchers... Alf Cook the fishmonger, and Ernie Cranch, bakers; that's Fore Street. There was a 'Salcombe Times' once, independent of the Kingsbridge Gazette, and that finished sometime about the 1920's. Then there was Central Garage, right opposite the King's Arms pub.

Years ago the paths and roads were dirty all the

time, and by everyone's doors there used to be a mud-scraper, like an iron bar and you'd drag your foot over it. There's no need to use them now because everywhere is tarmac and concrete, but life was different back in those days, it was a much more simple life.

We didn't travel very far out of Salcombe, only locally in our boat, but I had a motorbike as soon as I was eighteen. Well, I went to Exeter to work then. I had worked in the Council offices in Salcombe, but there was a job going in Exeter in the Surveyor's office. I was away from this area for a long time then. I worked in Exeter, Torrington, Barnstaple and back to Honiton; I had an opportunity to do something different to boat building.

When I learnt to drive a car I had a Morris 8 at first, but cars were different back then, they were small and didn't have the power like today's cars. It would take a couple of hours to get to Exeter 'cause, of course, the roads weren't made up like they are now and a lot of people carried their own bag of tools and did their own repairs where they could.

I had to dress in collar and tie, and I always wear a tie every day, even now. You could get a suit from a 'Fifty-shilling' tailors; you'd go to be measured, and the suit would be made to measure… not bad for fifty bob!

I volunteered at the start of the Second World War and joined the Navy, thinking I was going to do something wonderful: I was twenty-two and I thought I was going to win the War, like a lot of other people! I went on Motor Torpedo Boats, based at Dover, for the first couple of years. We used to go patrolling on the French coast, looking for their convoys that were nipping through the Channel. There was a lot of shelling going on across the Channel of course. I went across to Dieppe and one or two raids, and after that we went out to the Far East. It was an experience; I saw things I didn't really want to see, but you had no choice. It was a big relief when the War was over because you never knew what was going to happen next, or where you were going, or why. I was in the Navy for six years, all the time of the War.

I got married in 1940, just after the start of the War. Of course, before the War young married women were expected to stay at home weren't they! have a meal on the table ready for when you got home, and look after the house, warm your slippers: put them in front of the fire for half an hour. All the clothes would be put out ready for you for the morning. The War changed things; it's a different way of life now, men do a lot more in the house.

– ❖ –

Mike Pedrick

Born 10th November 1936

Recorded on 6th October 2008

Steve. Today I am at my old home in Belle Cross Road, Kingsbridge, to speak to my father and record his experiences. I have recorded ninety-nine other local people over the last five and a half years and I wanted to make my father the hundredth and final one.

Mike. I was born at number 52 Church Street, in Kingsbridge. My earliest memory is of going out to Slapton to see my grandparents. We used to go by bus out to the Ley, and then walk into the village, because in they days the bus didn't go into Slapton... that was quite a walk for a little tacker!

Living in Church Street then was absolutely brilliant because there was a good relationship with all the neighbours. We used to get together in the back yard, and put the dartboard up against the toilet door, to play darts; that used to be great! When I was a young boy my job was to clean out all the weeds from between the stones up on the bank, but nowadays people don't bother about things like that. Our neighbours were Mr. and Mrs. Clark... the Harrises, Mr. and Mrs. Moore... the Frasers were there for a while.

Opposite where I lived was a little shop, 'Legg's' grocery shop, and further down was Moysey's, and I used to go around with them when I could, delivering oil and that. An old lady, a neighbour in the street, used to boil up eggs and give me a couple for my lunch all wrapped up in a hessian cloth, and I remember they were all black and dirty when I came to eat them. There was a sweet shop way up Dodbrooke, right opposite the Junior school which was known as 'Greenhill' then. There was another shop near what they called 'the Dump' - Duncombe Park now - and they used to collect jam jars. They used to pay a ha'penny for a half-pound jar, and a penny for a pound jam jar, so me and a mate called Mike Gosling would go round peoples houses and ask if they had any jam jars they could give us.

There used to be a milking-parlour where 'Codds', the plumbing business was later, and when I lived there on the bank four or five cows would go from there down past home, behind the Cinema and along Ebrington Street to the fields. On Wednesdays, market day, Bob Kerswell out at Bearscombe would drive his cattle down through Church Street to the market, until it was closed a few years ago now. There was always horses up and down Church Street too, back then, so I'd be out with a bucket and shovel picking up what they left behind, for Father, for the garden.

We didn't have electric, we had gas with a little gauze mantle; they'd burn out sometimes, or they'd break up, so you had to be careful or you'd catch the house on fire. You only had coal and wood for heating; go up in the woods to get firewood with a trolley, cut it and drag it back; youngsters don't do anything like that now... but the only heating you had was in the sitting room, and when you went to bed it was like a fridge!

We had to share a toilet with three other houses, and I can't remember having a bath... we must have stood up in a bucket!

A chap called Wonnacott used to be the Town Crier, and when the water was going to be turned off he'd go out shouting, "The water...will be turned...offff "! Then there'd be a standpipe down in Windsor Road, and I'd go down there with a bucket getting water for everybody... I'd be up and down like a yo-yo!

My father was a builder by trade and he always did masonry work. At one time he was helping to build the stone wall around Kitley, on the main roadside there, and he push-biked there, it was the only way they could get around then. He was a bit of a character in his own right, and well-liked by everybody. My mother was a bit of a one for cleaning... her scrubbing brush was her best pal, I think.... she always used to be out scrubbing the front step. She was one of eleven that lived, and they were all girls except one boy who was a twin to one of the girls, but he died when he was two. She was a good mother, she worked hard... she used to go picking up spuds in the fields in her younger days.

In they days you had to eat the food that was put in front of you; if you didn't have it for dinner you'd have it put in front of you for tea, and if you didn't eat it then it would be put up again for breakfast! Kids today they choose... if they don't like it they have something different. To have chicken at Christmas was really something 'cause you never used to eat chicken back then, they were too expensive - 'cause there wad'n many chickens about then.

We never went on holidays and I never got in a car until one of my aunts and her husband, down in Plymouth, had a little Austin 7, and I went for a ride in that one... and when I started work first I went in a lorry, went to Hallsands to do a little job. I came home and said to my parents, "Guess what

I've been in today?". Other than that we'd go by bus or on the train - but not very often, 'cause we couldn't afford it. We never went to Plymouth, just went to Loddiswell or somewhere like that, to get out and go for a walk. I don't think I ever got as far as Totnes in they days.

I used to go ferreting for rabbits with Bill Blank and Leonard Tucker; we used to go on Sundays, and we'd march down through Dodbrooke when they were coming out of church. We'd have wellington boots, and rabbits and ferrets... yet nobody took any notice.

Ray Bartlett, my best mate, was a good boxer, and boxing was a big thing back then. We had a boxing ring in Burgoyne's garage and used to all box there. My mates were Ray 'Goosey' Gosling, 'Brassy' Pearse, Dave Steer; they all had nick names, see... Tony Maunder was 'Monty'... and the Perrett boys, Frank and Jim. The Hockin boys, Terry and Roy, lived here in Belle Cross Road and we used to play football and cricket in the street. We would put stumps up and practise cricket all evening, there wouldn't be any cars coming along. I played football for the 'Minors' and our pitch was over by the hospital, you had to go over the railway line to get to the field.

Barry Rowe was a big mate of mine, and still is; they were a family of twelve children and if you went there on a Sunday his mother would have two great big tables covered with food, you never seen nothing like it... and they didn't have a very big house. Every Monday morning Mrs. Rowe would start washing at four o'clock.

Me and Tony Maunder, a cousin of mine went out to Thurlestone when this ship went down, and all this soap had come in, and we filled up these sacks with soap and brought it home. We must have walked out there, but then there was a lot more freedom for youngsters. My mother didn't know where I was from the time I got up in the morning until I came home in the evening, and she didn't have to worry.

I remember me and Mike Gosling went up to the Market one day: they used to have boards between the pig stalls, where the auctioneer used to stand. Well, we went along the plank one day and opened the doors so the pigs were coming out and running all over the market... nobody knew who did it!

During the War we didn't have an Air Raid shelter but we had a big flat-topped steel cage, with wire around the sides and me and my sister had a bed made up in there where we used to sleep... Mother used it for a table.

Me and a boy called Ernie Steer were playing football in Church Street when they dropped a bomb up in Fore Street, where Woolworth's is now. Some Council workmen were working near us and they dragged me down the lane and held me against the wall. When I came out the road was littered with rubbish and our front door was half blown off. I was six or seven then, but as kids we didn't know what it was all about.

Steve. *Tell me about when General Montgomery came to Kingsbridge.*

Mike. Me and Tony Maunder and Mike Gosling caught up with him marching along the road by Ryeford Garage. We didn't know who he was no more than the man in the moon, but being cheeky we started marching along beside him.

When we got a bit older we used to go to dances, riding the pushbike; I'd ride and Roy Bartlett would run and try to hitch a lift, but if he didn't get one he'd jump on my crossbar. We went down to Salcombe once and decided it wad'n any good down there, so we went back to Stokenham... him running or jumping on the crossbar! You couldn't do that today; those were the good old times.

I can remember my great-grandfather Pedrick who was a carpenter and coffin maker. He died in December 1943 at Slapton, just at the time of the Evacuation. My grandfather was also a carpenter and coffin maker... he was a wonderful fella, and he meant everything to me. He had been in the Navy and I've still got his trunk upstairs that he made from wood from a boat. I had his Navy coat too, a 'monchus' great thing it was... the wind and the snow wouldn't get through that one! Both my grandfathers were in the Navy, but Grandfer Foale had done a long service.

My Father got me an apprenticeship with Perrotts in Duncombe Street; you had a six months trial period and then you got your indentures. It was a five-year apprenticeship, and you had to go to Plymouth Technical college once a week, and evening classes in Kingsbridge. I learnt me trade there and we were all good friends: Russell

Hender, John Andrews, Wilf Maunder, 'Doey' Luscombe, Brian Stone, Horace Stone... and Wallace Jeffery who worked for me later on. I did the undertaking side as well; we'd work together, probably John Andrews would be making the box and I'd be making the lid.

In the time of my grandfather and great-grandfather everything was done by hand, but now of course, everything's done by machine... we don't use a brace much now and I've got a spoke-shave in me tool-bag now, but I don't use it. It's easy to drill a plastic gutter now, but you imagine trying to drill through a cast iron one.

When you go around to the Cathedrals and the big National Trust houses, and see the standard of the work they used to do, you look in amazement at how it was done, but people specialised in just one area of the job, and they had as many men there as was needed. You see, carpentry and joinery are different trades, you can have joiners making up joinery, and carpenters are site workers, putting on roofs and that sort of thing; then cabinet-making is a different trade again.

— ❖ —